Preface

O N LOOKING THROUGH MY late husband's collection of facts and legends of Lewis, I felt that this was much too valuable a source of information to be lost to all but the few to whom it might be lent from time to time.

Accordingly, with the substantial help of Mr Alex Urquhart, retired deputy rector of the Nicolson Institute, Stornoway, I have arranged these collections in chronological order as far as possible and decided to have them published in book form. I wish to thank him very much for his assistance and also my brother-in-law, Mr Albert Nicoll, present deputy rector of the Nicolson Institute, for his help, Mr Grayson, for his beautifully done genealogical tables, and Mr Longbotham of the *Stornoway Gazette* for his very useful advice.

The reader will realise that many tales are old ones re-told, and that a number could even be found in various other books, but that requires specialised knowledge of which books, and the expense of buying them or the trouble of borrowing them from a library.

In this volume the reader will find a collection of articles which can be read straight through or dipped into as interest or fancy dictates.

If the matter is sometimes rather brief and more in the nature of notes, that is because my husband did not live to amplify it for publication and I feel myself insufficiently knowledgeable to undertake this task. However, I hope that these random writings may give as much pleasure to Lewis men and women at home and abroad as they have given to me, and that they may also serve as a memorial to my husband and his love of Lewis and his great knowledge of his fellow islanders both past and present.

Emily Lever Macdonald

Tales and Traditions of the Lews

Tales and Traditions of the Lews

collected by
Dr Macdonald
of GISLA

Birlinn

This edition published by
Birlinn Limited
West Newington House
10 Newington Road
Edinburgh
EH9 1QS

Reprinted 2004, 2009

ISBN 978 1 84158 055 5

British Library Cataloguing-in-Publication Data
A catalogue record for this book is available from the
British Library

Typeset in New Baskerville by Brinnoven, Livingston
Printed and bound by CPI Cox & Wyman, Reading

Contents

Contents

Introduction

DONALD MACDONALD WAS BORN at Stornoway on 14th September, 1891. He was the eldest son of John Macdonald of Carishader and Annie Gillies, daughter of William and Marian Gillies of Shawbost and Stornoway. He attended school at the Nicolson Institute, Stornoway, and in due course graduated Master of Arts at Aberdeen University. After teaching for a time he decided to enter medicine and took the diploma of L.R.C.P. and L.R.C.S. at Glasgow and graduated MB ChB at Edinburgh. He distinguished himself by obtaining the medal in medicine and being third in his class of surgery. In 1923 he married Emily, daughter of an Edinburgh-born journalist Alexander Paul and his wife Lucy Anne Lever, youngest sister of Viscount Leverhulme, then proprietor of the Island of Lewis. Dr and Mrs Macdonald made their home in London where at first he carried on general practice and later practised as a West End specialist. On retiral to Gisla he combined for a time his interests of farming, fishing, and the Gaelic language and culture. As the crippling osteoarthritis from which he suffered got a firmer hold of him it so reduced his activities that latterly his interests were more and more directed towards less physically though not less mentally exacting research into the history, traditions and archaeology of his native island. Dr Macdonald also set on foot the project for the Lewis and Harris Folk Museum in which to preserve the many and varied objects associated with the ancient and more recent Hebridean way of life. Through his energies considerable sums were collected towards this end and though by his death in September, 1961, he was prevented from seeing its completion, the committee are hopeful that the museum for which he worked so hard will become in the near future a reality. Incidentally, a very substantial nucleus of exhibits has already been made available. An additional activity which was very near his heart was the Stornoway Old Folks Welfare Association of which he was president. For his happy conducting of the Wednesday parties for the Old Folks he will perhaps be particularly remembered. In aid of charitable causes he gave many interesting lectures locally and on the mainland illustrated by his extensive collection of unique slides of Lewis views. He contributed numerous articles to the *Stornoway Gazette*, many of which are to be found incorporated in this volume. The local and national Mods and Gaelic culture in general had no more enthusiastic supporter than the late Dr Macdonald. His active brain had ample opportunity during his retirement for extensive study of the folklore and legends associated with his native island, and his profound knowledge of the Gaelic language, and a lifelong interest in these subjects fitted him admirably for the task of collecting and making accessible in book form these interesting stories of bygone days. The Scottish Society of Antiquaries, in recognition of his researches, conferred on Dr Macdonald their Fellowship.

Striking a personal note, I may add that Dr Macdonald was a companion of my early youth before the breaking of this century and I am convinced that it would have pleased him greatly could he have but known that some day his collected notes would be made available to the general public and he would have understood that it is not outwith the bounds of possibility that with this volume as an introduction, a reader may well be attracted to a more serious and intensive study of matters Celtic. The present collection which just touches the fringe, contains much material never before, so far as I know, brought together in book form. True it may be that many of the tales and excerpts are familiar to Celtic savants, but although much material is collected by academic bodies, relatively little is published or made available to the general public in Gaeldom, and many will therefore appreciate Mrs Macdonald's action in sorting out the rough unedited notes, arranging them for publication and eventually seeing the book through the printing press.

C. Scott Mackenzie
Stornoway

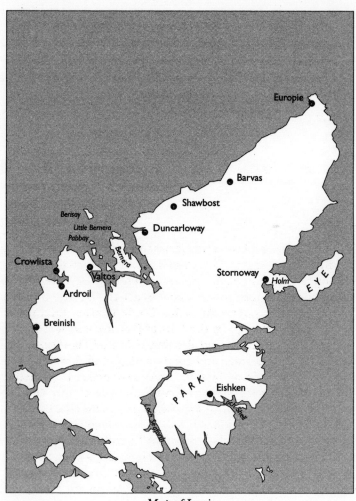

Map of Lewis

1

The Macleods of Lewis

THE ISLAND OF LEWIS and Harris together formed the Ljod-hus of the sagas. The chief's residence was the Castle of Stornoway. One of the earliest references we have to the Macleods is that they got the island by a marriage with the heiress of Macnicol, but we know that Gunni Olafson (Macaulay) was banished in 1154 by the Earl of Orkney, and sent to the care of Liotolf in Lewis, and also that Thormod Thorkelson was in Lewis with wife, men and goods in 1231, and that the name Leod is probably from 'Liotulfi', who was a chief in Lewis in the middle of the twelfth century. Lewis was held by crown charter by the earls of Ross until 1335, when it passed into the hands of the Lords of the Isles. The first of the Macleod chieftains was Torquil the son of Leod – hence Siol Torcuil (Lewis).

1344 – John (Lord of the Isles) retained Lewis when he made peace with David II: Torquil Macleod held Lewis as a vassal of the House of Islay, and a royal grant of Assynt was also given to him.

1494 – Roderick Og Macleod made submission to James IV. He died in 1498.

In 1480 Roderick his son was killed* at the Battle of Bloody Bay, fighting against Angus Og of the Isles on the side of John, his father. Torquil Macleod, his brother, married Catherine

---

*According to W.C. Mackenzie mortally wounded and died later at Dunvegan.

of Argyle. He was distinguished in his day and succeeded and supported Donald Dubh, son of Angus, last heir of the Lord of the Isles. He was forfeited in 1502 and the Earl of Huntly besieged Stornoway Castle in 1506. This is the first mention we have of a castle at Stornoway. The whole island was reduced to obedience, and Torquil disappears from history.

1511 – *Malcolm*, Torquil's brother, was made chief by the Government and died in 1515.

1515 – *John MacThorcuil* was made chief by the Macleods as the more direct heir. He led them against the MacIains and was present at Creag an Airgid 1518, in which MacIain of Ardnamurchan was killed. John MacThorcuil died in 1538 and was succeeded by Rorie Mór his cousin, Rorie MacChaluim, notorious for the slaughter of his kinsfolk and who lived till 1595.

He married:

(1st) Janet MacKenzie – widow of Lord Reay and daughter of John McKenzie. Son Torquil Cononach.

(2nd) Barbara Stewart – daughter of Lord Avondale had Torquil Oighre, drowned in 1566.

(3rd) Jenette Maclean, Duart – had sons, Torquil Dubh, decapitated at Ullapool 1597 by the MacKenzies. Norman, died in Holland.

Old Rorie disowned Torquil Cononach and said he was the son of Hugh Morrison the Brieve. The MacKenzies backed up his claim and were supported by the Morrisons of Ness, hence the MacKenzies were pulled into the strife over the succession, and finally got Lewis by guile and payment. Donald Cam and the Macaulays backed up the Macleod heirs of Rorie Mór.

1610 – The deeds of Lewis given to the Fifers by James VI, and sold to MacKenzie of Kintail for the woods of Letterewe.

Summons Against Torquil Macleod VIII of Lewis

The 24th day of the month of December, in the year of God 1505, I, John Ogilby, Sheriff-depute of Inverness, passed with these our sovereign Lord's letters, and sought Torcuil Macleod of the Lewis, and because I could not apprehend him personally, nor was there a sure passage for me to his dwelling house, I passed to the Market Cross of the Burgh of Inverness at 11th hour before noon, and there by open proclamation, made at the Market Cross, I summoned, warned, and charged the said Torcuil Macleod of the Lewis, to compere before our sovereign lord the King or his Justice in the Tolbooth, the 3rd day of February next to come in the hour of cause, with continuation of days, to answer to our sovereign Lord or his Justice for the treasonable act, part and assistance taken and done with Donald Isla (Dubh), bastard son to Angus of the Isles, taking part with him, and invaded our sovereign Lord's lieges of the Isles and destroyed, to the effect that the said Donald should be Lord of the Isles and upon all points and articles in this our sovereign Lord's letters, and after the form of the same, and this I did before these witnesses.

Sentence of Forfeiture

This Court of Parliament shows for law, and I give for sentence, that Torcuil Macleod of the Lewis has committed and done treason against our Sovereign Lord and his realm in the special points of treason and crimes aforesaid contained in the summons, for the which he has forfeit his life to our sovereign Lord, also his lands, his goods, offices and all his other possessions, whatsoever held within the Realm of Scotland or Isles, evermore to remain with our sovereign Lord, his heirs and successors for his treasonable offence. And that I give for doom.

2

A Macleod Vengeance

JOHN THE BRIEVE OF LEWIS entered into a compact with Torquil Conanach, and the Mackenzies of Kintail to capture Torquil Dubh, the then chief of the Macleods of Lewis, and do away with him.

The Brieve waited his opportunity, and when he captured a Dutch ship, which was well supplied with wine, he sent word to Torquil Dubh, who was then over at Uig paying a visit to his friend Donald Cam Macaulay, to come and enjoy the good things, and that he was making a present of the captured ship to him.*

They went aboard not suspecting any treachery and that the Morrisons had picked men concealed in the ship. When the wine and the feasting was at its height the Brieve got someone to cut the ship's ropes, and allow her to drift out to sea, and then the Morrisons appeared from their hiding places, fully armed, and overcame Torquil Dubh and Donald Cam with their followers who had left their arms in another part of the ship and so were helpless.

Donald Cam escaped along with Alasdair na Sàile Bige, his brother-in-law, while the Macleods, including the chief, Torquil Dubh, were cruelly murdered at Ullapool.

The news of Torquil Dubh's death caused great consterna-

---

* Fuller account appears in Chapter 25.

tion among the other island clans, and the very name of Mackenzie stank in their nostrils. It was a black day for Lewis for Torquil was reckoned a very good chief and on the morning of his decapitation, July, 1597, it is said that the sun was darkened and there was an earthquake in Lewis and that the dairy maids could get nothing from their cows but squirts of pure red blood.

The Macleods gathered in force to seek vengeance, but the Morrisons had taken the alarm and cleared out of Ness and made for the wilds of Edderachyllis and Durness, along with their kin there; but there was a special hunt for Ian Dubh the Brieve, who could not be located anywhere.

At this time there lived on Eilean Handa one of the family of the Assynt Macleods, Little John mac Dhòmhnuill mhic Uisdein, a man of low stature, but of matchless strength and skill in arms who determined to get him dead or alive.

He and the Brieve John Morrison met accidentally in a house at Inverkirkaig in Assynt, and they set to fighting, and although the brieve had six men, and John of Handa but four, the brieve and five of the Morrisons were killed without any loss on the side of the Macleods. It is suggested that God deprived the Brieve and his men of the courage or ability to resist. Thus was the treacherous death of Torquil Dubh of Lewis amply revenged.

After John Morrison had been slain his friends came in a galley to bring home his corpse for burial in the family ground at Ness, but, contrary winds arising, they were driven on to one of the islands of coast of Edderachyllis, where they were forced to disembowel the body and bury the innards, and on the wind changing, they arrived in safety at Ness. This island is called to this day Eilean a' Bhritheimh.

Malcolm Mór mac Iain, who succeeded, was some time later surprised by the same John Macleod of Handa at Coigeach and was taken to Stornoway and handed over to Norman the brother of Torquil Dubh, who caused him to be beheaded. This was stated to be about 1601.

3

The Early History of the Macleods

THE ORKNEY SAGA GIVES the earliest information – The island of Lewis and Harris formed the 'Ljodhus' of the sagas, the residence of whose lords was at the Castle of Stornoway, and we are told in 'Origines Parochiales Scotiae' that Haco of Norway came into Stornoway Bay to keep a tryst with Earl Birger at the castle of that name, and that he came again with his fleet in 1263 on his way to help the offspring of Somerled, the Sudoreys' lords, against Alexander III and his Scottish fleet and army. We have no record that he called at Stornoway on his way back after his defeat at Largs.

Earlier we read from another source that the Macleods got Lewis through a marriage with the heiress of the Macnicols, the premier family in Lewis, and as the tradition has it 'Torquile the first of that name did violently espouse the only daughter of MacNeacail and cut off immediately the whole race of Mac-Neacail (Nicolasen) and did possess himself of the whole of the Lews and continueth in his posterity during thirteen or fourteen generations.'

We can go back to the sagas again where it is stated that 'Gunni Olafson [i.e. Gunni Macaulay] was banished by the Earl of Orkney in 1154 and took refuge with Ljotulfr who was chief in Lewis at that date.'

Is this 'Leod' the progenitor of the Macleods? We also read that 'Tormod Thorkelson was in the Ljodhus with his wife and goods in 1231'. Was this Tormod the son of Torcuil the son of Leod?

Old Rory Macleod gets the blame for the slaughter of any of the Macleods of Raasay who had the taint of the MacKenzie blood. This massacre was really carried out by Roderick (Nimhneach) MacAilein of Gairloch in the island of Isay. There, after a warm welcome and a sumptuous meal, he had his guests assassinated without mercy. A contemporary Macdonald poet and warrior, Domhnull MacIain MhicSheumais says:

> 'N tulgadh so gu Eilean Isaidh
> Far an d'rinn Macleòid an dìneir,
> Par an d'rinn MacAilein dìobart,
> Dhòirt e fuil 'sgun chaisg e iotadh [thirst]

Rhyme sung by girls at Valtos school while playing:

> An robh thu an Gil a Braunda
> Na Sgorr 'iain 'ille Tharmoid?
> An robh, thu Lag-na-clibhe muigh
> Na Giosladh bho dh'fhalbh thu?

4

The Indictment of Neil Macleod, Lewis

Indicted for Fire-Raising – Burning – Murder – Theft – Piracy, 1613

NEIL MAKLAUD, SON NATURAL, to Rorie McClaud, sometime of Lewis – Ye are indicted and accused that from your very youth, you being trained up in all manner of barbarous cruelty and wickedness, and following the pernicious example of your godless parents, kinsfolk and country people, having committed innumerable oppressions, heirschipes and violent deeds against such persons as you disliked, dwelling within the country of the Lewis and other Highland Isles thereabout, to the high offence of Almighty God, displeasure of the King's Majesty, contempt of his royal authority and violation of his Highness' laws; for further manifestation of your extreme and unnatural wickedness, understanding that the King's most excellent Majesty, for repressing of the abominable villainies, cruelties and oppressions committed by you and your associates dwelling within the Island of Lewis, out of his princely wisdom, had directed a great number of his Highness' peaceable and good subjects from out the Lowlands, provided with all manner of furniture, and necessary provision for their sustenance, towards the said Isle of the Lewis, there to have planted and set down towns and villages, and to have established all good order and civility, of purpose, thereby to have extirpated and routed out the name of barbarity from out of these parts: Ye, accompanied by Norman McClaud, your brother, and with two hundred barbarous, bloody, and wicked Hielandmen, sorners and avowed malefactors, ancient inhabitants and lawless persons within the Lewis, whom ye convened to yourself to resist and withstand the purpose and godly intention resolved upon by his Majesty, concerning the pacifying of that country, came, all in warlike array, with bows, darlochs, two-

8

handed swords, hag-butts, pistols and other weapons invasive, in open and hostile manner about fourteen years ago or thereby, to the said Island of Lewis where umwhile William Lord Pittenweem, the Laird of Wormeston, the Laird of Fingask, the Laird of Balcomy, the Laird of Airdrie accompanied by diverse inland gentlemen his Majesty's peaceable and obedient subjects were landed, and in planting of diverse houses, partly of timber and partly of stone and thickcut turf, for the time, trusting for nothing less than to have been invaded and withstood in these honourable proceedings; and there most fiercely invaded and pursued the said Lowland Gentlemen and their companies, most cruelly murdered and slew the umwhile Robert Traquar the erstwhile James Young, erstwhile . . . Wedderburn and divers others to the number of twenty-two persons, most treasonably put hands on the person of the said Laird of Balcomy by taking him as captive and prisoner. As also, most treasonably, raised fire, burnt and destroyed to the ground all the houses erected by them, with the provisions and containers of meal, malt and other food stuffs to the value of 20,000 merks: and thereafter by way of masterful theft and stoutriff, stole and took away all the horses, cattle, oxen, sheep and other beasts pertaining to the said Lowland Gentlemen, to the value of £10,000. And, you, the said Neil, are art and part of the said treasonal and barbarous crimes, and was the special ringleader and chieftain, with the said Tormod, your brother, in putting of the same to such merciless execution which you can not deny. Also, you are indicted and accused for as much as John Pullet and Robert Blair, Burgesses of Perth, having passed with a ship belonging to them to Loch Broom, to the fishing, ye having got information thereof, came with a number of thieves and limmers, your associates, to the number of fourteen men, or so, in battle array; and having divided your company in two separate squads and went aboard two separate boats, you thereafter rowed from the land towards the said ship, and there as pirates, thieves and sea robbers, after discharging of divers muskets, hagbutts, and other engines of firearms at the said ship and company thereof ye boarded the same, took possession of the whole furnishing, merchandise, wines, cloth and other provisions there aboard, disarmed the merchants, skipper and crew, and took from them all their clothing and apparel, put two of the company of the ship on land, and in most piteous manner murdered and slew the rest of the company, to the number of seven or eight men, and thereafter disposed of upon the said ship, merchandise and goods that were therein at their pleasour; And the said Neil was and is airt and pairt of the thefts and cruel murders above written. Also, you are indicted and accused for as much as

9

you persevering in your former develish and abominable way of life, you, accompanied by divers thieves, sorners and broken men, your accomplices, to the number of three hundred persons or thereby, all armed for war, with swords, dirks, bows, darlochs, hagbutts, muskets and pistols, resolving with yourself to put all and whole the Lowland Gentlemen being then within the said Island of Lewis to the sword, whereby they nor any others should have any power or command in the Island to withstand your wicked attempts, in the month of April, the year of God, 1607 years, you again came to that part of the said Island where the said Lowland Gentlemen had built various towns and villages and erected diverse houses. And the better to bring your wicked resolutions to pass, you, in friendly manner, humbled and offered yourselves to be willing to do all manner of good and serviceable duties, as you should be employed upon, in regard ye found cas declarit their coming to that land to be for no evil intent but for good. And the said Gentlemen believing your fair promises and expecting that at least no treason should have been practised by you upon them, having granted you some oversight duty, you with your associates, most treasonably, under trust and friendship, and in the dark and most quiet time of the night, entered within the Camp belonging to the said Lowland Gentlemen, raised fire, and burnt and destroyed with fire a house erected and belonging to Sir George Hay of Nether Liff, one other house belonging to the Laird of Airdrie, one other house belonging to John Dalgleish, with divers other houses, newly built within the said Island, and along the sea coast thereof, burnt and destroyed the food supply and furnishings and plenishings within the said houses to the value as estimated of £10,000. And at the same time, most cruelly murdered and slew the erstwhile Patrick Gifford, servant to the Laird of Airdrie, with divers other servants and office men within the said encampment, in their coming out of the said houses to save themselves from the rage and violence of the fire, being all his Majesty's faithful and good subjects. And ye, the said Neil, are and were art and part of the said treasonable and cruel facts. And finally, ye, the said Neil, in regard of your abominable life, fearing your own apprehension, and having for your greater security and relief fled from the mainland of Lewis to a crag called Beirghesaidh, one mile within a certain Loch, which you manned and fortified with men, munitions, and all manner of provisions for your sustenance, and having also two boats provided for you and your accomplices' passage and repassage from the land to the said Rock, you with your associates during your abiding within the said Rock and keeping thereof, came ashore and ran diverse forays through the country and in a most thievous manner stole, reft, and took away with you to the said crag, divers goods and cattle beasts from the inhabitants of the country about, namely from Gillechalum McAlastair Coule (Dhughaill) and Gillechalum McCòneill, from either of them, twelve kye and oxen, which with diverse raids of cornvictuals and other necessaries, stolen and reft by you, was transported by you to the said Rock, in most thievous manner; whereupon you shared out and lived upon and fully enjoyed yourselves at your pleasure. And ye, the said Neil, was art and part of the said crimes. To the taking, ye have confessed the whole premises to be true, during the time of your late examination in presence of the Lords of his Majesty's most honourable Privy Council.

Verdict

The Assise, all in one voice, by the mouth of David Wemyss, skipper in Leith, spokesman of jury, found, pronounced, and declared the said Neil, by reason of his own judicial confession, to be ffylet, culpable and convict of the whole treasonable crimes of fire-raising, burning, murder, and several robberies at length set down in his depositions and accusation founded thereon.

Sentence

To be taken to the Market Cross of Edinburgh, and there to be hanged upon one gibbet, until he be dead, and thereafter his head to be struck from his body, and affixed and set upon a spike, above the Netherbow Port of the said burgh: and all his lands, heritages, tacks, steadings, chambers, possessions, goods and gear, pertaining to him to be forfeit and escheat to his Majesty's use.

5

List of Some of Those Who Made the Stand with Neil Macleod on Berisay

Neil MacRuari mhic Chaluim, the leader of the band (illegitimate) sometimes called Niall Odhar.

Donald MacNeil Macleod
Ruari MacNeil Macleod
Calum MacNeil Macleod
William MacNeil Macleod
} his 4 sons.

Malcolm [Calum Mor] MacRuari Og
William MacRuari Og
Ruari MacRuari Og
} sons of Rory Og Macleod of Lewis (illegitimate half brother of Neil).

Torquil Blàr Macleod – Neil's uncle
Murdo MacTorquil Blàr
Torquil MacTorquil Blàr
Tormod MacTorquil Blàr
John Roy MacTorquil Blàr
} Neil's foster brothers.

Calum Caogach MacAngus mhic an t-Sagairt
Murdo MacAngus mhic an t-Sagairt
Donald MacAngus mhic an t-Sagairt
} grandsons of the Vicar of Eye.

Calum MacAilein mhic Fhionnlaidh
Donald MacNeil mhic Fhionnlaidh
Ian Dubh MacAngus mhic Gille Mhicheil

Donald MacAngus mhic Gille Chaluim
Donald MacDhomhnuill mhic Gille Chaluim
Calum Dubh MacAlasdair
Calum MacIain Riabhaich
Donald MacAngus
Donald MacIain Duibh (a Morrison – brother of Alan the
  Brieve who quarrelled with the Tutor of Kintail. He had
  been refused a quarter of Lewis area on the return of the
  Morrison from Durness, etc. Mother was an O'Beolan).

The Macleods around the Carloway area are descended from
Tarmod Uigeach (illegitimate) who had the farm of Dalmore.
He was given a tack there by Rory Mór his father. Murdo,
another bastard son of Rory by the sister of Uistean (brieve),
was given tack of Shawbost.

6

Massacre of the Macaulays by the Macleods of Pabbay

ABOUT THE YEAR 1480 there lived in Eilean Pabbay Norman Macleod and his family. He was married to a woman from Skye who was a virago but zealous for the good of her sons, who had a bad reputation, and this grieved old Norman. The sons of Dugald Macaulay at that time were in the holdings of Valtos, Kneep and Beirhe (Reef), and the Macleods could not but pass over these lands in coming or going to the island. On one of these days, when old Norman was ferrying some cattle to Pabbay, one of his servants allowed a stirk (heifer) belonging to the Macaulays to get in among the Macleod beasts. The Macaulays were very indignant and claimed the heifer as their own, but Macleod, who had the beast tied to the boat, refused to let it go, and gave orders to the servants to push off. The Macaulays rushed and grabbed the rope and pulled it so violently that the old man was jerked forward on his face and had his front teeth knocked out and there was much bleeding and the old man suffered a great shock. He was not going to say anything to his wife about the fracas over the heifer, but the wife, seeing the grey face of her man, and the bleeding gums, questioned a servant, and got the story of how roughly the Macaulays had treated old Norman. He was put to bed, and when the sons, who were fowling out at the Flannans, got back, their father's front teeth were put on a plate on the table before them and the story of the attack by the Macaulays told them with much embellishment.

They were furious, and made their preparations, and when everyone on the mainland was asleep in bed, they sneaked across the sound and attacked the Macaulays and massacred them. The wailing and the uproar could be heard at Pabbay, and when old Norman asked what was the meaning of the uproar, his wife told him that her whelps would now have plenty of blood on their teeth. He was angry and told her that she was a wicked woman to cause this bloodshed and that for this night's work her progeny would pay dearly some day.

The Macleods killed off all the family of Dugald Macaulay except one illegitimate boy, whom they threw over a wall, and who was crippled from it all his life.

One of the sons of Dugald Macaulay escaped the slaughter. This was John (Iain Ruadh), who was being fostered by Finlay Ciar Macritchie, at Mealista at the farther end of Uig. John Roy was now without family or friends – with no means of defending himself from the rapacious Macleods. While his desperate condition was being considered, a messenger came from the chief in Stornoway with a message to the effect that he was very angered by what his nephews had done and never wished to see their faces again, and that old Norman was to take John Roy into his own household, protect him, show him every kindness, and solemnly bind himself and his sons to keep him safe and teach him all the arts he should know. When John Roy was thirteen years of age, the Macleods, ever replete with malice, proposed a hunting party to the wild forest that borders upon Harris. It was the month of November, and much snow had fallen upon the hills. Towards evening these young men repaired to a deserted hut called Tota Choinnich, a mile to the south of Kinresort, and the Clàr Mhór. Here they were to pass the night; but, without pity or remorse, the Macleods seized John Roy and bound him hand and foot, then stripping him to his shirt, they tied him to a large stone, and left him upon the bare snow, exposed to all the horrors of a dark and bitter night.

In vain he entreated these merciless men to spare his life and he would engage to forgive and forget all that had passed before, but they left him there to perish, and turned a deaf ear to his cries and entreaties. While John Roy was thus exposed Finlay Ciar was suddenly warned in his sleep of the hapless situation of his foster son at Tota Choinnich. In great alarm he wakened up and told his wife what he had dreamed, but she said anxiety had wrought upon his imagination. He fell asleep again and again a spirit came to him and repeated with earnestness his previous warning. His wife bade him go to sleep again and said he had imagined it all. He had hardly closed his eyes when the spirit again appeared and with great vehemence directed him to rise and save his foster son ere it was too late. Finlay Ciar then got up and made his wife milk the cows into a *cragan** and boil it on the fire. When it was boiling hot he wrapped the cragan in a skin, and on this frosty moonlight night set off for Tota Choinnich. There he found John Roy bound hand and foot, and almost dead from cold and hunger; but he soon revived the boy by a great draught of the warm milk, and wrapping him in his coat, he took him on his back and returned to Mealista before *daylight. Finlay* Ciar, dreading further attempts on John Roy's life, sent him with a faithful attendant to a cave on Teabhal in the Uig hills. Here they followed him, but he managed to defend himself with his bow and arrows. John Roy took leave of Finlay Ciar, and went to Harris, from whence he went across to his mother's people, the Macleans of Lochbuie and told them all the bad treatment his family had received. He was sheltered and taught all the arts of the day by the Macleans. When he arrived at manhood Maclean of Lochbuie wrote to the chief of Lewis desiring him to force his nephews to make restitution of the property belonging to the massacred Macaulays, or he would send John Roy himself to Lewis to demand his rights by force of arms. The chief of Lewis replied that he was highly incensed at the treachery of his nephews and that they were ruthless and incorrigible, and that he did not forbid him to seek revenge upon them. When Lochbuie received this reply from Macleod of Lewis, he called John Roy before him and tried him in the use of the broadsword and the other martial arts. Then with only one

---

*cragan: earthenware pot.

attendant Maclean landed him on the coast of Harris from where he found his way to Finlay Ciar who received him with much joy. After this he made for Penny Donald (Ardroil), which was only a mile from Balnacille where Norman Og Macleod had his tack.

Norman Macleod, Balnacille, was not at peace in his mind, and knowing that Ian (John) Roy was still alive, he kept watch by turns from a viewing point called Sgorr a' Choimper near the churchyard. One Sunday Ian Roy left Ardroil as the people were going to church, but he had arrived there the previous night and had caught two of Norman Macleod's bodyguard who were visiting and whom he terrified and made them promise to prevent their master from running away when he came to take vengeance upon him, for vengeance he was going to exact; and mingling with the churchgoers he made towards the ford. Norman Macleod, who was watching from the Sgorr, said, 'If Iain Ruadh were in this country I would say that is him coming.' His two followers said, 'Nonsense! that cannot be him,' but Macleod said, 'We shall know when he comes to the ford, for he has a habit of scrogging his bonnet down on his head with one hand before he enters the water.' Sure enough the approaching figure lifted up his kilt with one hand and jerked his cap down on his head with the other, so Norman Macleod said, 'That is indeed John Roy Macaulay so I must be off to the safety of St Christopher's,' but the two body servants hung on to his arms and said, 'No you are mistaken.' Meanwhile John Roy hastened his pace, yet Macleod dragged the young men along with him in his frenzy and was on the point of leaping the sanctuary wall when John Roy thrust him through with his blade, and putting it to his nose remarked, 'That will do for Norman Macleod.'

John Roy then made off for Valtos intending to get a ferry from there to the Isle of Pabbay, but he found that two of Macleod's sons were busy courting in the village and he stealthily came on each in turn before anyone could forewarn them of his arrival. He attacked each in turn, one was killed at Leòb Uilleim and the other at Tràigh Ailein. (Other names given, Lian Fhearchair, Buaile Tharmoid, Gleann Aonghais.) The only son left of Norman Macleod, Pabbay, was one who was fostered at Lochs and had not been concerned in the massacre of the Macaulays. John Roy then got a boat, went across to Pabbay, and there in scorn and contempt of the wicked woman who had been the cause of all these misfortunes, he ordered her clothes to be cut off from below her waist and made her fly the country back to her native Skye. John Roy ordered one third of the cattle and goods to be given to Old Norman and he kept the rest for himself. He then, accompanied by his illegitimate brother, Malcolm, set off for Stornoway Castle to see the chief. Malcolm was the child that was thrown over the wall on the night of the massacre and was left a cripple. When nearly at Gallows Hill they came upon the only son left of Macleod (Pabbay). He shouted out, 'Mercy, mercy, Macaulay,' but John Roy said, 'I will show you mercy if the young man Calum will do so.' On hearing this young Macleod ran down the hill followed by Malcolm Macaulay and he jumped into the sea and tried to swim over to Stornoway Castle, but he was shot in the head by an arrow. When he reached the castle rock, he was not allowed to land, and he had to return to Aird Chléirich where he was killed. This finished off the Macleods of Pabbay.

Old Norman was very ashamed of the way his family had treated the Macaulays and shared half his goods with Iain Ruadh and gave him Balnacille and Crowlista for his portion.

7

John Mor Mackay or Macphail

WHEN JOHN MACKAY HEARD that Donald Cam, son of Dugald Macaulay, had got back to Uig he was very frightened so he betook himself to the Dùn of Bragar along with his wife. She was a niece of Donald Cam and deeply resented the treachery towards him of her husband. John Mor was of such uncommon size and strength as to be reckoned one of the giants of the country, yet he knew Donald Cam would seek to avenge the dirty treachery.

Donald mustered all the Uig warriors and then picked out twelve of the strongest and best swordsmen and sent them away to take John Mor MacKay dead or alive. These twelve, fully equipped, set out for Bragar, and arrived by night at the shore of the loch. They got a boat, rowed to the Dùn, and without delay entered the hut in which MacKay was in bed. They attacked him furiously, yet he defended himself with advantage against the twelve. They then closed and grappled with him, but their combined strength could not bring him to the ground. His wife then called out, 'What poor fellows! Did you never see a boar libbed?' Acting on this treacherous hint they brought him down and bound him hand and foot. In the morning the Macaulays set off with their prisoner, with his hands tied behind him with a rope in a cruel manner whereby six Macaulays had a hold in front and six secured him behind. In spite of this, while the party were fording the Grimersta River, MacKay made a lunge in one direction by which he overthrew the six Macaulays in front, and by a lunge in the opposite direction he brought down those behind, but he was unable to make his escape.

Soon afterwards they arrived at Kirkibost in Great Bernera, and there rested while word was sent to Donald Cam that they had John Mor prisoner there. The next day the people of Uig repaired to Kirkibost and the last one to arrive was Donald Cam. When he came near, MacKay cried out, 'Mercy, mercy, O son of Dugald!' but he was coldly reminded that he had shown no mercy to him, but that he had treated him with great indignity when a prisoner on board the ship.

A court was held and it was decreed that John Mor MacKay should die that very day, and that every man should give him a cut with his sword. MacKay was brought forth and placed upon a hillock, which was named from a different circumstance the Hill of Evil Counsel (Cnoc na mi-Chomhairle). Then every man began to hew and thrust with the sword at John MacKay, but although they struck him with all their might they could make no impression on his body; he was invulnerable, and only a little smoke ascending as a consequence of each stroke. All were amazed, but a pedlar among the crowd cried out, 'Let the ground be cut from beneath his feet, and the charm which now renders him proof against every weapon will desert him.' This was done and he was instantly killed, and his body was minced by the swords of the Uigeachs,

8

The Gobha Bàn – The Smith of Kneep

ONE OF THE BEST warriors of the parish of Uig was the
Gobha Bàn, the fair smith, who lived at Kneep while
Donald Cam was settled at Valtos. The Gobha Bàn was stronger
than Donald Cam but was not as clever as Donald with the
sword. The smith had a cess of grain from the parish, and when
a cow was killed for domestic use the smith had a right to the
head; but Donald Cam had neglected to pay his dues for seven
years. It happened that a horse belonging to Donald Cam fell
over a cliff and was killed. Donald Cam had the head of the
horse skinned and sent to the Gobha Bàn. The smith saw that it
was the head of a horse and ordered it to be preserved and dried.
Not long after Donald Cam sent his servants to the smiddy to
get various iron tools mended, but the smith put all the irons
together into the fire and made them into one lump. He then
told the servants to take the mass of iron back to their master
and to tell him that he would not do a stroke of work for him
until the seven years' dues owing were paid.

The Gobha Bàn knew that Donald Cam would be angry
and as he was no match for him with the sword, he took the
precaution to heat red hot six feet of iron bar. As he expected
Donald Cam was soon seen coming fully armed and displeased,
on which the Gobha Bàn came out of the smiddy with the long
hot iron bar and drove Donald Cam back home in a great rage;

some say he attacked the smith, who blinded him in one eye, hence the nickname 'Cam'. The Gobha Bàn's smiddy was on the shore below where the Rev. Malcolm Maclennan built the house. The children used to dig up pieces of iron within the ruined tobht that used to be there.

Donald Cam came next day and promised to pay the dues outstanding so long and they became friends once again, and the Gobha Bàn invited Donald to dinner next day. He ordered beef and mutton to be cooked, but also the horse head in a separate pot. Donald Cam said he would like some of the cow's head and he was handed the dish and ate a big feed of it. When the Gobha asked Donald how he liked the head, he said it was extra good. The Gobha then told him that it was no cow's head but the horse head he himself had sent him. Donald Cam was very angry and got up, and it was a long time before they were friends again. For all that, when there was any emergency the Gobha Bàn was sent for by Donald to be near himself in a fray.

9

Donald Cam and Neil Macleod at Stornoway Castle, 1607

The Camp at Holm (Fifers) was captured in 1610

In 1607 Stornoway Castle was taken by Neil Macleod, assisted by Donald Cam, on which occasion Angus, a brother of Donald Cam, was killed by a shot from the castle. About this time the ship of Abel Dynes, a Bordeaux merchant, was piratically seized by the Macneills of Barra, in which transaction Donald Cam and other Lewismen were likewise engaged. Donald Cam and his brother Malcolm were wanted by the Privy Council for this and other wicked acts, 1610.

William of Islivig

William Macaulay, the youngest of Donald Cam's sons, had the tack of Islivig. He was so expert that he was able to fight with two swords at once, ie., with a sword in each hand. William, after all the Lewismen had been killed around him at Auldearn, with his back to a wooden paling in a gateway, defended himself with a sword in each hand against his enemies, but they climbed into a loft and got above his head, and so they killed him.

10

Stac' Dhòmhnuill Chaim

WHEN NEIL MACLEOD FORTIFIED himself at Beirisaigh, Donald Cam did the same on a rock to the westward of Uig near Mangursta, which has ever since been called 'Donald Cam's Stack'. He was there attended by his daughter, known as 'Big Anne', who used to carry to him milk and other provisions over the sharp and dangerous crag which connects the high rock with the mainland. Tradition says that after a time he embarked for Ireland. He was probably with Macleod of Harris who was fighting in Northern Ireland about that date, and having greatly distinguished himself there he received a pardon for all past offences, and settled down quietly at Valtos in Uig, where he devoted himself to farming and bringing up a family. In 1610, the year the Fifers sold the title deeds of Lewis to Kintail, he is on record as marrying a Miss Maclaren (Nic Illeadharain) of Galson. He died before he became an old man, and tradition says he is buried inside the old chapel of St Christopher, Balnacille.

There is no doubt that after Neil Macleod was driven west by the MacKenzies, Donald Cam must have been hard pressed to find a safe hiding place. There is an old sheiling on the Lochs moor called Airigh Dhòmhnuill Chaim, and he was probably hiding there during this period.

Donald Cam had to betake himself to places of retreat in the most sequestered parts of Uig, in dùns upon islands in the lakes, or in caves to which he and his friends could resort safe from their enemies, or when they did not think proper to engage them at a disadvantage. Donald Cam and John Dubh-Chròig took up their abode on an island dùn on Loch Barravat, at the back of the village of Crowlista. Stones led out to the dùn, but these stepping stones were never in a straight line and one of them Clach a' Ghlagain made a warning sound. Here they had a boat hidden near Gallon Head and they lived mostly on fish and venison.

Privy Council, July, 1610

Warrant to Rory Macleod of Harris to keep in his custody until the last day of May next – Donald Cam McCoul and Malcolm McCoul to the effect the Lords of the Council may at that time give such other directions anent them as shall seem most meet and expedient, for the quietness of the country.

11

The Drowning on Langavat

THE GAELIC LAMENT THAT was found by Calum J. Macleod of Nova Scotia in the Kintail area, and which appeared under the heading Iar Ogha Dhòmhnaill Chaim refers to the time of Zachary Macaulay in the first half of the eighteenth century, and the story goes as follows:

Murdo Macaulay, grandson of Donald Cam and the father of Zachary Macaulay, chamberlain of the Lewis, held the lands of Valtos, Reef and Kneep, and a vast extent of moor on both sides of Loch Roag. One summer Zachary went to visit his father's family, who at that season of the year were living on their summer grazings at Strome to which they had brought their milk cows and other stock.

Zachary, along with his brothers Donald and John, with their servants set off to fish the famous Loch Langavat (Langabhat), a distance of at least seven miles from Strome. The three young men began fishing opposite an island in the loch called the Eilean Dubh, when presently John saw a deer of a queer light colour grazing upon the island. John Macaulay made some contraption to keep his gun and powder dry and swam towards the islands but the deer saw him and disappeared in an instant. John searched for the deer throughout the island but nowhere could he find a trace of it, so he swam back to where his brothers were fishing. He told them that the deer had disappeared but on looking towards the island they all saw the deer grazing in the same place as before.

The brothers blamed John for being careless, and Donald said, 'I'll go along with you this time, and then the stag shall not escape us both.' They swam together to the island but the deer quickly disappeared, and although they hunted for it everywhere it could not be found.

These visions of animals appearing and disappearing are called seeing a tàbhoradh in the Gaelic language and usually they were the precursor of some awful catastrophe.

John Macaulay began to be very sick, and to shiver all over, so his brother gathered a heap of heather and soon had a grand fire blazing. John warmed himself at the fire and gradually the shivering ceased, but he said to Donald, 'Brother, this is the last time I shall warm myself.' 'Nonsense,' said Donald trying hard to hide what was in his mind, but it was of no use. After the lapse of some time when John seemed all right again they both took to the water, and made for the point where Zachary was fishing, but ere they had got half way, Donald in alarm called out to his brother that he was swimming too deep and too slow; but John feebly answered 'Dear brother save yourself for I am done for,' and quickly sank from sight.

Donald got ashore, and with Zachary and the servants got back to Strome. At first they told their mother that John had to try and find some horses, but after a time they told her the truth.

A boat was dragged from Loch Roag across the moor to Langavat, and the body of John Macaulay was soon recovered from the loch and the seanachie relates that on the abdomen the outline of a flounder was imprinted.

The mother was a Skye-woman, and was very stricken with grief at the loss of her promising son, and being gifted with the poetic temperament, she composed an elegy to him on every Wednesday for a whole year, for that was the day on which he was lost.

It must be one of these laments that Calum Iain has retrieved from Kintail. Zachary Macaulay himself was an excellent Gaelic poet. Yet though they were copied at the time into song books, sung and greatly admired, one does not come across them easily at this date.

12

Did the Macaulays Turn Their Coats?

I HAVE BEEN READING the rent roll of the Seaforth Estate as given on oath to the commissioners who came up to Lewis to collect the rents after William Dubh had been attainted for his share in the '15' and '19' Risings.

In the Stornoway and Lochs areas the MacKenzies had rewarded those who had come across to help them, i.e., their own Kintail folk, MacKenzies and MacIvers, with large portions or tacks of land. One is struck with the fact that at Uig they put a Macaulay in nearly every good position except the three key positions of Balnacille, Callernish and Tobson Bernera.

I give you the Uig list of tacks at the date 1725–26, paid in mutton, meal, stones of butter and pounds Scots rental: Donald Macaulay, John Macaulay – Mealista; Malcolm Macaulay – Carnish; Donald Macaulay – Ardroil; Malcolm Smith – Craulista (Crowlista); Alexander and George MacKenzie – Balnacille; Donald Macaulay – Valtos and Pabbay; Rory Maclennan – Kneep; Widow Macaulay – Beirghe (Reef); Widow MacKenzie – Tobson and Bosta; Murdo Maclennan – Ditto; Alexander and Farquhar Maclennan – Little Bernera; Angus MacNicol – Ditto; John Macaulay – Kirkibost; Angus Macaulay – Linshader; John MacKenzie – Callarnish; Aulay Macaulay – Breascleit; Widow Maciver – Tolasta Chaolais; Donald Maciver – Kerivig; Kenneth Maciver – Upper Carloway; Kenneth Mackenzie – Dalamor; William MacKenzie – Dalmore.

This seems a remarkable state of affairs for in 1610 Donald Cam Macaulay was helping Neil Macleod and his followers against the brieve of Ness and the MacKenzies, helped by the Government and northern clans.

Did the Macaulays later turn their coats and go over to the winning side or were they so strong that it was policy for the Kintail invaders to give them good tacks and so win them over? The Macleods, Macdonalds, and the other people who had resisted the MacKenzies and the Fifers were given rough treatment and were forced to work the land for these new lords of creation.

Any solution?

13

John Macaulay of Kneep

I am asked to tell you the story of John Macaulay, Fear a' Chnìp, and the wandering beggar, so here it goes the way I was told it.

John Macaulay was one of the three Lewismen who escaped from the Battle of Auldearn in 1645, and one night while he and his two companions were sheltering in a wood, a shot was fired in among them and they knew they had been followed. They noticed where the flash of the gun had taken place and marked the spot, and as John was the best shot with the bow, and they had only two arrows left, he was deputed to take aim at the assailant. Drawing his powerful bow he let fly his precious arrow at the marked spot, and there was a piercing cry of anguish for help. While the wounded man's friends were attending to his hurt, John and the other two Lewismen made off towards the west.

He got back to his tack at Kneep and settled down peaceably with his wife and children. He had plenty of this world's goods, and no one who called at the big house at Kneep came away empty-handed.

Four years after Auldearn a one-eyed wanderer came along to Kneep and begged for a night's lodging and food, as was their custom, for this was the way news was spread in those days. John Macaulay noticed the man's face was badly disfigured and was very sorry for him and asked the beggar up to the fire to tell him the news of his wanderings. Food was placed before the stranger, and he ate ravenously, and was evidently enjoying the rich fare.

After the meal and when they were comfortable before a huge fire, John delicately enquired how he became so badly disfigured. He said he had been in the army of Alasdair Mhic Colla at Auldearn and that with one or two others he had been ordered to follow up three of Seaforth's men who had made their escape, and on coming upon them in a wood, he had discharged his gun at them, but could not say whether the shot had taken effect or not, but almost immediately afterwards an arrow pierced his eye, and came out through the face causing the hideous disfigurement his host was now looking at.

John of Kneep took the stranger's hand, for he was greatly moved by these words, and said 'It was this right hand that discharged that arrow, and I was one of these soldiers you fired at.' The beggar on hearing this said he was done for now and there was no escaping death, but John Macaulay told him to have no fear. He would be a better friend to him for telling the truth of the adventure, for he was only doing his duty like a good soldier. 'My house and all that is in it is at your disposal and every time you come this way you will get bed and board and we will show you every kindness.'

John Macaulay lived to a good old age after this event and many of the Macaulays of Valtos and Kneep claim descent from him.

14

*The Raid by Hugh Macdonald,
circa 1566*

Uisdean (Hugh) Mac Gilleaspuig Chléirich was a Skye-man who spent most of his life as Macdonald of Sleat's factor in North Uist, on record as such in 1580. He had a very bad reputation in North Uist on account of his having murdered a family of MacVicars in order to gain their lands. It is acknowledged, however, that he was a very formidable warrior in his day. There is a song about him by one of the MacVicar women (about 1566):

> Uisdein Mhic Ghill-easpuig Chléirich,
> Far an laigh thu slàn na éirich;
> Sgeul do bhàis gu mnathan Shléite, *etc.*

Donald Gorm of Sleat was laying claim to Lewis after Torquil Oighre was drowned, and Hugh Macdonald was the leader of the attacking forces. This is told in Morrison's traditions of Lewis, when the men of Clann Mhic Gilleadharain (Maclarens?) changed sides – 140 of them, on the ground that they were Macdonalds: 'Men, act as ye promised to do yesterday,' Hugh shouted across to them. In spite of this extra help he was defeated by the Lewismen. The battle began at Barvas and was continued as a running fight all the way to Loch Seaforth where the Macdonalds had left their boats. Among those who distinguished themselves and helped to beat the Macdonalds was Malcolm Macaulay, an illegitimate brother of Donald Cam's father, and a Macleod known as Torquil MacDhòmhnuill Chis-lich. Hugh Macdonald narrowly escaped being captured and few of his men and of the Maclarens (?) ever reached Skye. The MacGilleadharains demanded their portion of land which had been promised them, but they were given only a cow and a boll of meal each, and told to go about their business, for Macdonald of Sleat could have no trust in them as they had betrayed their country. The Maclarens (?) never had any foot-ing in the island after the Battle of the West Side, and many changed their surnames to Maclennan and Campbell in the Cladach area, and to Macleod in the Lochs area.

15

Zachary Macaulay– Chamberlain of Lewis

ZACHARY MACAULAY WAS THE son of Murdo Macaulay – tacksman of Valtos. His brother John was drowned at Langavat while swimming to or from the Eilean Dubh on that loch. Their summer shieling was at Strome – near the entrance of Little Loch Roag. He went to the university, tradition says St Andrews – where he met the fifth earl of Seaforth, Uilleam Dubh; but the Rev. William Matheson says he graduated MA at Edinburgh University. He was licensed for the ministry, but was never placed in a charge because he was blamed for getting some young woman with child. He was first given the job of collecting the vicarage teinds before being made factor of the Lewis in 1712. He collected the rents and managed the affairs of Lewis during and after the Jacobite rising of 1715 and 1719. In the records of the Commissioners of Forfeited Estates 1726, he is recorded as being the tenant of 'Guringeroy' at a rental of £66 13s 4d Scots. 'Guringeroy' is the Lowland lawyer's clerk's idea of taking down in English Gearraidh Cruaidh where he had his home. He had also a tack of the township of Stornoway at £80 Scots, but MacKenzie of Gruinard bid £100 Scots 'at which rent it continued'.

Donald Morrison (the Sgoilear Bàn) says he died while still Chamberlain, but in 1730 he was so infirm that Alasdair McKenzie of Achilty was called in to help and became joint factor with Zachary.

Uilleam Dubh (Seaforth) died in 1740, and we find that the holding of *Gearraidh Cruaidh* was in the name of Mrs Macaulay, his widow, so he must have died before 1740 – Rent Roll in 1718 was declared and sworn for the Commissioners of Forfeited Estates and gives the following figures for Zachary Macaulay:

For the Garcroy Stornoway,	£5 11 1⅓	sterling
For a small possession in Stornoway,	£0 8 4	sterling.
For the miln of Stornoway,	£1 2 2⅔	sterling.
For the fishing of a small river (? the Creed),	1 barrel of salmon.	

16

John Morrison, Tacksman at Bragar

IN 1653 THE TACKSMAN of Gress was Murdo Morrison, the son of Allan the Brieve, who was killed in a seafight with Neil Macleod. He had a famous son, John, who became tacksman of Bragar, and the people of that village still quote some of his wise sayings, and he seems to have been a good Gaelic poet in his day. He is said to have had 'Ladies' modesty, Bishops' gravity, Lawyers' eloquence, and Captains' conduct'.

In 1653 Col Cobbett of the Roundhead army took possession of the peninsula on which the then town of Stornoway stood, and built a fortress on the site where the Custom House now stands. He left a Major Crispe as governor of Lewis, with six companies of soldiers, two big cannon, and four sling pieces to prevent the Dutch occupying the islands and giving help to the Royalists.

We are told that John Morrison, the future tacksman of Bragar, was in 1654 on friendly terms with the officers of the garrison, and used to visit them, and before Seaforth's attack on the garrison he spent the night with them drinking, and probably playing at the cards. Some seannachies tell us that he took good notice of where the sentinels were usually posted and where the weakest parts of the defences were – all this while his brother Alan was busy in the country areas raising the Lewismen. We also know that Seaforth, even with Sir Norman Macleod's help, was no match for the stern puritans of the Roundhead garrison.

John Morrison betook himself to his tack at Bragar where he had plenty of scope to exercise his poetry, shrewdness, and wit. Once he considered that the factor was demanding too much rent for his holding and refused to pay the sum asked. The factor complained to Seaforth, who sent word to Morrison to come to Stornoway to see him. He set out at once putting the rent into a purse and what he considered the sum overcharged into another. When he arrived at Seaforth Lodge a large watch-dog rushed out at him and barked furiously, on which John Morrison struck him violently on the nose with the stick. The dog set up a dismal howling. One of Seaforth's menservants rushed out to see what was the matter and began to abuse Mr Morrison, who thereupon punished his insolence by striking him on the jaw. He set up such a terrible uproar along with the stricken watch dog that Seaforth soon made his appearance and John Morrison in explanation gave vent to the following quatrain:

> Gille tighearna is cù mór
> Dithis nach còir leigeadh leò;
> Buail am balach air a' charbaid,
> 'S buail am balgair air an t-sròin

Seaforth was very pleased with his impromptu verse and welcomed him into his home. On inquiry it was found out that the factor was exacting more rent than the agreed amount and he was dismissed from Seaforth's service, and ever after this John Morrison paid the rent of Bragar into the earl's own hands.

John Morrison had a red-haired wife, who was said to have a very bad temper, and of whom people said he was a little bit afraid, but upon whom he practised his sarcastic humour in Gaelic verse as follows:

> Fadadh teine ann an loch,
> 'Tiormachadh cloich ann an cuan,
> Comhairle 'ga toirt air mnaoi bhuirb
> Mar bhuill uird air iarann fuar

John Morrison was a very clever engineer and Seaforth took him with him to plan out the attack on Macleod of Assynt's castle at Ardvreck c.1660, and the castle was quickly taken. John Morrison had five sons, described later under Morrisons of Ness (Chapter 18).

17

Hugh the Brieve –
Confession to Parson of Barvas

IN 1551 PATRICK DAVIDSON is paid £10 by the King's treasurer
that he may go to Lewis to charge 'McCleude of the Lews and
Hucheon of the Lews to come to my Lord Governor (Arran) at
the aire at Inverness' (Treas. Accts). This is Hucheon Morrison,
Brieve of Lewis, who was indirectly the cause of the ruin of the
Siol Torquil. The Chief of Lewis, Rorie MacChaluim Macleod
(Old Rorie), married when young a Janet MacKenzie, daughter
of John MacKenzie of Kintail, and widow of MacKay (Reay).
She became the paramour of Hucheon Morrison, and on the
adultery being known, both she herself and the child she bore,
Torquil Cononach, were repudiated by Rorie MacLeod. Torquil
was named Cononach as he was nurtured in Strath Conon
by the McKenzies. Rorie seems to have had good reasons for
putting her away. She went off later with Iain McGillechaluim
of Raasay.

Confession of Uisdean the Brieve, 22nd August, 1566

The which day Sir Patrick MacMaster Martin, the parson of Barvas,
deponed upon his oath . . . that he being in Lewis visiting Hucheon
Brieve of Lewis, who was then on the point of death, and in these
days was confessor to the said Hucheon attending to the custom
in use in these times – that he asked and demanded answer by

the said Hugh about this son Torcuil borne by MacKenzie's sister, as was alleged, to Macleod of Lewis, her husband, what the said Hucheon's judgment was concerning him and to whom the said Torquil, as he believed, belonged. Who [Hugh] answered to the said Sir Patrick that he could not deny but he had carnal copulation with the said Ni Vic Kenzie in her husband's time in due time and season before the said Torquil's birthe. And that the said Hugh's father before him acknowledged the said Torquil to be the said Hugh's son before his death. And in respect that the said Hugh was to depart from this world in paril [fear] of death he could not do otherwise than what his father before him had done, in acknowledging the said Torquil as his son, i.e., that the said Hugh was his natural father and that he could not refuse him to be son to him, in time coming. And this the said Hugh granted and confessed to the said Sir Patrick in his confession being in danger of death.

After Old Rorie had repudiated his first wife, he married in 1541 Barbara Stewart, daughter of Lord Avondale (sister of Lord Methven) by whom he had a son called Torcuil Oighre (heir), to whom Queen Mary wrote that he, being of the Stewart blood, should not marry without her consent, but Torquil Oighre was drowned, somewhere about 1566, when crossing the Minch. Torquil Cononach then made a claim to succeed, receiving the help of Clan Kenneth, and no doubt assisted on the island by the Morrisons. He was also assisted by two of Rorie Macleod's natural sons, Tormod Uigeach and Murdo, which is easily understood if their mother were of the Morrisons. Stornoway Castle was taken, and the chief of Lewis made a prisoner for four years. He gives a miserable picture of the treatment he received from his disowned son. The old chief states that the evil handling he has received from Torquil Cononach and his accomplices these two years bygone is notorious, that his 'Lugeing' was invaded by them at night and burnt, himself held in most miserable captivity in mountains and caves far distant from the society of men, and almost perished with cold and hunger. While still a prisoner Old Rorie was taken to Edinburgh and made, by the friends of Torquil Cononach, to resign his lands to him, Rorie merely holding them in life-rent. As soon as Rorie got back to Lews he repudiated the resignation on the ground of coercion.

In 1576 Old Rorie and Torquil Cononach were summoned before the Regent Morton, when a reconciliation was effected, Old Rorie recognising Torquil Cononach as his heir. In these quarrels three of Old Rorie's natural sons, Neil, Donald, and Ruari Og took their father's part, while Tarmod Uigeach and Murdo sided with the MacKenzies. Old Rorie between 1566 and 1570 had taken a third wife, Jennette, the daughter of Maclean of Duart, and had by her two sons, Torquil Dubh and Tormod.

Tarmod Uigeach, of the Morrison faction, was killed by his half-brother Donald; for which Donald was seized by Torquil Cononach with the assistance of Murdo, and carried prisoner to Coigeach, but he escaped and got back to Lewis. Old Rorie was incensed against Torquil Cononach for seizing Donald and caused Donald to apprehend Murdo and imprison him in the Stornoway Castle. Torquil Cononach invaded Lewis and took the Castle, liberated Murdo, imprisoned Old Rorie, and carried away all writs, charters, etc., which he later gave to Kintail. John, Torquil Cononach's son, was placed over Lewis. This date is fixed by a deed of May, 1583, giving him 'the guidis which pertainit to Rorie Macleod'.

18

Morrisons of Ness

IN 1546 WILLIAM MAC UISTEIN, son of Hugh Morrison, brieve, is mentioned in a remission to Rorie Macleod of Lewis and some of his clan, for treasonable assistance given to Mathew, formerly Earl of Lennox. In 1551 a Patrick Davidson is paid £10 by the king's treasurer that he may go to the Lews to charge McCleude of the Lews and Hucheon of the Lews to come to my Lord Governor (Arran) at the aire at Inverness.

John the Brieve had five sons: Malcolm, Alan, Donald, Kenneth, and Angus.

John Morrison the Brieve captured Torquil Dubh in 1597 and took him to Ullapool. Kintail beheaded Torquil.

John was killed in a fight with John Macleod of Handa, Assynt, at Inverkirkaig and disembowelled at Eilean a' Bhrithimh.

Malcolm Mor, his son, became chief of the Morrisons. He was captured by Macleod of Handa and taken to Norman Macleod at Stornoway where he was beheaded (1601–1605).

Alan, his brother, was next brieve. Neil Macleod killed him and two of his brothers and followers. Their heads were taken in a sack to Edinburgh when Neil went there with Fifers for a pardon.

1630 Donald MacIan Dubh (brieve) is named in the commission of fire and sword given to Rorie McKenzie of Coigeach against last resisters.

1653 Murdo Morrison, son of Alan (brieve), son of John

(brieve), was tacksman of Gress. He had three sons: John, Alan, Murdo. This is the last mention of a brieve.

1654 John Morrison – tacksman – Bragar, is the famous bard and wit already mentioned. He was personally known to Martin Martin and described by him as 'a person of unquestionable sincerity and reputation'. He is still talked about in Bragar and further afield for his poetry, shrewdness and wit. He had five sons:

John, Minister of Gairloch, 1711–1716; Minister of Urray, 1719 (the Indweller), wrote *Traditions of Lewis.*

Roderick, The Clàrsair Dall – harper to Iain Breac Macleod, Skye, c. 1680. He was buried at St Colum's, Eye.

Angus, Minister of Contin, Episcopalian, ejected, lived at Doire na Muic, Loch Broom.

Murdo, Blacksmith, very strong, inventive engineer in his day.

Malcolm, Minister to the chapel at Poolewe.

19

The Brieves of Lewis

JOHN MORRISON, SON OF Iain MacMhurchaidh Ailein of Bragar, 'the Indweller' who wrote a 'Description of the Lews' after 1678 and before 1688, was the Rev. John Morrison, son of the famous John Morrison of Bragar and the father of the Rev. John Morrison of Petty. He speaks of the destruction of Stornoway Castle, which took place in 1645 by Cromwell's troops, as having 'lately' occurred. The writer was intimately acquainted with Lewis and when he was young there were only three people in Lewis who knew the alphabet, but when he wrote, the head of each family at least was usually able to read and write.

The chief of the Clan Morrison, whose dwelling was to Habost, Ness, was hereditary judge or brieve (Breitheamh) of Lewis, and the office was held till the beginning of the seventeenth century. Sir Robert Gordon states 'The brieve is a kind of judge among the islanders, who hath an absolute judicatory, unto whose authority and censure they willingly submit themselves, when he determineth any debateable question between party and party.' In former times there was a brieve in every island, and he had an eleventh of every subject that was in dispute; but from whom there was an appeal to the Chief Judge in Islay. Very exaggerated notions remain of the extent of the jurisdiction of the Brieve of Lewis. One writer asserts that it was a venerable institution that had stood for many ages, and that the jurisdiction extended over the Hebrides from

Islay to the Butt of Lewis, and on the opposite coast to the Ord of Caithness; another that he was invested by His Majesty as judge arbiter from Cape Wrath to the Mull of Kintyre and was absolute in his jurisdiction. It is probable that the brieve in Lewis represented the 'log-maor' of the Norse, and that in the process of time the office changed from 'law-man' or speaker at the 'Thing', to that of 'Domandi' or administrator of Justice, like that of the 'Deemster' in the Isle of Man, one who pronounced doom or judgement. He was judge in cases of life and death, as well as in the most trifling contentions. His presence, whether in house or field, on horseback or on foot, constituted a court; his decisions were guided either by what he could remember of like cases, or by his sense of justice, and this *lex non scripta* was called 'breast law'. On assuming office he swore he would administer justice between man and man as evenly as the backbone of the herring lies between the two sides of the fish. Wherever the brieve or the deemster was present, the aggrieved party could lug his opponent before him. The plaintiff placed his foot on that of the defendant, and held it there till judgment was pronounced. Both in Lewis and the Isle of Alan the decision seems to have been accepted without reserve. King James V in May, 1527, addressed a letter to 'Our Breff of Inverness' where 'breff' is synonymous with sheriff.

It is very doubtful if ever a brieve of Lewis could have spoken a word of English, and as the Scots Acts of Parliament have not been translated into Gaelic the decisions of the judge can never have had any relation to them. Before the utter confusion into which the country fell towards the close of the sixteenth century, the brieve of Lewis, like the bard of Clanranald, may have received some education in Gaelic, but in any case we have ample proof that he exercised his office most unsparingly, for there are few islands or districts in which the Cnoc na Croiche, or Gallows Hill, is not a conspicuous feature. With the judge perished the different records of Lewis and of the countries over which he had jurisdiction, except a few memoranda, or rather scraps, retained by some of the judge's descendants who escaped the fury of the Macleods.

20

Donald Morrison (Cooper)
(An Sgoilear Bàn)

Writer of Conflicts of the Western Highlands

Donald Morrison, although of Lewis descent, was a Harrisman by birth, for he was born in 1787 at Dirisgil on the south side of Loch Resort in the wild deer forest of Harris.

When the Tàran Mór is angry the winds roar and hiss, and the surface of the loch is a whirl of foam and tumult. The boy soon removed to Erista, Uig Lodge area, and was a teacher at Valtos for five years. He went to Stornoway, and was a shopman with Murdo Macleod, cooper and shipowner. He commenced business on his own account, but with no success; then he became a cooper.

About this time he began to write his 'traditions'. He was encouraged to do so by the late Rev. William Macrae, Barvas, and Rev. J. Cameron, Stornoway. Although a Morrison by name he was brought up in the country of the Macaulays, which accounts for the greater fulness and reality of his stories concerning them. Most of this lore he got from his stepfather, who was well versed in the legends of Uig. He married in 1810, had twelve children, and died in August, 1824.

He was three years writing his 'traditions', and he took notes from many people, using a board across his knees as a desk.

One of the missing parts of the traditions he lent to a Dr Macaulay who died at Liverpool, and the other was taken away by Mr H.R. Macleay, Collector of Customs, Sunderland, and they have so far not been recovered.

The late W.C. Mackenzie traced one copy and the manuscript is in the hands of Stornoway Library Committee waiting to be printed and bound in book form.

21

The Morrisons As Ministers

1642 MURDO MORRISON GRANDSON of Brieve Hugh. 1643
Donald Morrison, MA still there on 28/5/56; son Donald succeeded while his other son Kenneth became Minister of Stornoway.

Towards the end of the seventeenth century the whole of
Lewis formed but two parishes – Barvas and Eye. The minister
of Barvas was the Rev. Donald Morrison, 1684, who must have
been born about 1620. He was a grandson of the judge (Alan
or John), was bred an Episcopalian Minister but was won over
to Presbyterianism. He was personally known to Martin Martin
1695, and he supplied that famous writer with information
about North Rona. Mr Donald helped to suppress the sacrifice
to Shony at the church of Teampull, Eoropie, c. 1670, and he
died before 1700 in his eighty-sixth year. He was succeeded in
Barvas by his son the Rev. Alan Morrison 1692–1723.

22

Wild Times in Lewis

FROM 1689 TO C. 1720 THE PARISH MINISTER of Stornoway was the Rev. Kenneth Morrison, MA. He was the son of the Rev. Donald Morrison of Barvas, a descendant of the brieve.

These Morrisons who had gone in for fierce fighting with the Macleods of Lewis, and were partly responsible for the success of the Mackenzies and the destruction of the Siol of Torquil, now went in for religion with the same intense thoroughness; for at the same time Kenneth served in Stornoway, his brother Donald swayed the religious ideas of the people of Barvas parish as far as the Butt and even out to far away North Rona. They gave much information to Martin Martin, when he was wandering about Lewis, gathering facts about the lives of the people which have proved so useful and interesting to us Leod-hasachs.

Kenneth Morrison was a highly gifted man; he lived in his manse at Tong, where the farm of Tong is now. There had been a gradual change in Lewis from the pagan: Culdee, then Episcopalian, then Presbyterianism, and Rev. Kenneth had a difficult time suppressing the brawls between the so-called Papists and the Protestants. He usually carried a sword by his side when he walked from the manse at Tong to the church on Church Hill at Stornoway; when he went inside he left two men with naked swords at the door to keep the Catholics away while he preached.

Mackenzie of Kildun, uncle of Seaforth, was a staunch Catholic, and became very annoyed with the Rev. Kenneth Morrison for preaching against his creed and winning over so many converts to the reformed faith. He had a house at Aignish and was always scheming how he could get even with the minister. So one night, late, a boat manned by six of his men, arrived at Tong and made for the manse. The minister had just gone to bed, but his wife was still up and demanded to know what they wanted. They said they had orders from Kildun to take the Rev. Kenneth back with them to Aignish and they would not take 'no' for an answer. His wife went upstairs and told him what these men wanted, so he told her to send them up. When they told him that he must go with them and see Kildun, he said, 'Very well, but first we will drink to the Laird's health.'

Now Morrison, who was reputed to stand his liquor well, went to a cupboard and took out a horn dram-glass, which held about three of our doubles, and they all drank to the health of Kildun. Then he suggested they drink to the health of his lady; this was done with even more enthusiasm. When the whisky began to warm them he suggested that they should drink his own health and this was, accordingly, drunk with great acclamation. By the time that one was down, they would drink anyone's health, and this went on till each rolled under the table in a drunken coma. The minister then gave instruction to his henchmen to tie their hands and feet with straw ropes and make their appearance as ludicrous as possible – then take them in the boat back to Aignish, carry them up to Kildun's house as quietly as possible and leave them in the lobby as near to the Laird's bedroom as they dared.

This was done, and when Kildun got up in the morning early, he found his six henchmen trussed up like fowls, still in a stupor and unable to explain how they came to be there.

The minister had scored once again and Kildun said they were lucky not to have been left on the seashore to be engulfed by the tide.

23

A Morrison Victory

I DON'T WISH YOU TO think that the Macaulays of Uig always had things their own way, as witness this story from the old seannachie.

The sons of the Brieve John went to Rona to gather eggs and bring back seafowl and wool, and when this became known at Uig the Macaulays made off for Ness to plunder the cattle of the Morrisons. The brieve was old and feeble and there was no one there to oppose the raiders except a few women, weaklings and children, so the Uigeachs had their own way and a big creach was lifted and driven away.

The old brieve sent a youth to watch for the return of his men, and a feast was prepared for them, and taken to the shore to be ready for their arrival. On their return they were told of the foray, and how the cattle had been driven along the coast, making for the west. The Morrisons would not wait to partake of the good food sent to them, but each one drank a large draught of ale, and taking a good-sized lump of beef in his hand, he quickly followed his companions in pursuit of the Macaulays. When the old brieve was told of this he said, 'They will be hearty and strong, and ere they return they will give cause to many of deep sorrow.'

The Morrisons overtook the Uigeachs at Brue, the first village west of Barvas, and attacked them, fiercely killing a great many, and their grave mounds are pointed out till this day at

Druim nan Càrnan. The Morrisons followed up the survivors and another fierce encounter took place at Arnol, so bloody that only three of the Macaulays managed to escape – Zachary, one of their strong heroes, and two of his near relations.

The Morrisons pursued these as far as Carloway, but on the point of giving up the chase they met an illegitimate brother (known in Morrison tradition as 'the wicked incendiary'). He persuaded them to follow on to Callernish as he knew the exact place where they were sure to be hiding.

When they got to Callernish, he led them to the brink of a rock below which there was a scooped-out hollow like a bed place, and there were Zachary and his companions sleeping deeply from exhaustion. It is still called Leabaidh Sgàire or 'Zachary's Bed'.

The Morrisons were for leaving them unharmed to sleep on, but when the brother from Carloway heard this he was very angry, and taking a dagger in each hand he jumped down with all his powerful weight on the chest of the sleeping Zachary, staved in his ribs, and quickly stabbed the other two before they could gain consciousness. Thus died all the Macaulays who took part in that raid.

The old brieve was very angry at the unsportsmanlike way the brother from Carloway had despatched the sleeping Uigeachs.

This name Zachary is peculiar to the Macaulays of Uig, but I am told it is also found in the family of Malcolm of Poltalloch, Argyleshire.

24

The Burning of the Morrisons in Dùn Carloway

DONALD CAM AND THE big smith went one summer to the Flannan Isles, and the Morrisons of Ness, hearing the Macaulays were from home, came and drove the cows from the moor, for they met with no opposition. When Donald and his party returned the women folk told them what had happened, and they set off in their boats direct across the mouth of Loch Roag so as to intercept them, as they would be slow with their spoil. When they got to the opposite shore they sent out parties to reconnoitre, and it was reported that the cows were grazing at the loch not far from the Dùn, so they knew that the Morrisons were resting in this strong fortress. The Macaulays rested themselves by the shore for the night, and in the morning, as they were weak from want of food, Donald Cam and the big smith crept carefully forward, on their guard lest they alarm the Morrisons. When they came near the Dùn they saw a large cauldron over a huge fire with the whole carcase of one of the plundered cows in it, and a man lying asleep near the fire. The big smith held and silenced the sleeper, while Donald Cam drew the meat out of the cauldron, then the smith threw him into the boiling liquid. The smith then rolled the boiled beef in his plaid and carried it to the starving company, while Donald Cam went to the Dùn and surprised and stabbed the sentry on guard at the door. The Macaulays then came up and the big smith was set to guard the door and prevent anyone escaping, while Donald Cam by means of two dirks, which he stuck at different levels into the walls of the Dùn, managed to climb to the top of the structure, which was open. Donald Cam's men gathered bundles of heather which were handed up, set alight and thrown down into the Dùn, and this was repeated until all the inmates were smothered or burnt. So died all the Morrisons of the raid on Uig, and Donald Cam and his men destroyed most of the fabric of Dùn Carloway, which was said to have been built in the fourth century by Darg Mac Nu-Aran.

25

John Morrison –
Son of Hugh the Brieve

HUGH MORRISON THE BRIEVE died about 1566, and his son John succeeded him. He supported Torquil Conon-ach against his father Old Rorie, and later against Torquil Dubh. The Macaulays of Uig were the most ardent supporters of Torquil, about the year 1596. Old Rorie is thought to have died c. 1595 at the age of ninety-four. John Morrison, brieve, mixed his judicial duties with piracy, and once when sailing in his galley to Rona he captured a Dutchman with a cargo of wine. The vessel was taken to Ness and the brieve gave a cordial invitation to Torquil Dubh and Donald Cam to come and share the good things he had aboard. They did not suspect any treachery and went aboard the vessel, and while carousing they discovered the vessel's ropes had been loosened and the ship was drifting out to sea, and found that their arms had been removed. John Roy MacKay Macphail, who lived at Bragar, was the big strong man who tied Donald Cam to the mast with the help of Morrisons hidden aboard the ship. The ship was steered for Ullapool, the residence of the supposed half-brother of Torquil Dubh, and the captives were there imprisoned. Donald Cam and his son-in-law Alasdair (of the small-heel) Macleod, were fettered by a heavy chain to a large block like an anvil, which weighed eleven Dutch stones. All the prisoners were chained in pairs. Alasdair na Sàile Bige had the small foot in

54

the fetter, and he slipped out his heel and placed the block and chain on the back of Donald Cam and both got away. They hid themselves, travelling by night, and at last reached Applecross, where they found an old leaky boat, caulked it with clay, and using bars from a gate for oars, they at last got to Skye, and there a friendly smith took off the chain which was linked round Donald Cam's neck and leg. After resting till their strength came back they managed to get to Harris, from whence they walked all the way to Uig where they had been given up for lost. The Brieve of Ness, when he heard that Donald Cam had got back to Uig, fortified the Ness area strongly, while big John Roy MacKay betook himself to the Dùn of Bragar in which he built a hut for himself and his wife for he feared the vengeance of Donald Cam.

26

The Brieve and Niall Odhar

MANY READERS WILL KNOW the Ness Iorram or rowing song, which is printed in *Eilean Fraoich*, the collection of Lewis Gaelic songs, but few will know that it did not turn out so fortunately for Alan Morrison, the brieve, and his Niseach supporters, as the Iorram would have us believe.

Neil Macleod (Odhar), the bastard uncle of Torquil Dubh, the then chief of Lewis, attacked the Morrisons on Habost moor, but was defeated. Neil then sent to Harris for help and came again to Ness, but the Morrisons had by then taken shelter in Dùn Eystein where Neil besieged them. The Morrisons escaped by sea from Dùn Eystein to the mainland, but Neil pursued them there.

The Morrisons saw Neil crossing the Minch, and slipping out from among the islands on that coast, tried hard to get back to Lewis. The Macleods, however, had ascended a hill and espied the brieve's birlinn and gave chase. Tradition says there were only Alan and two of his brothers in the boat but Alan, as the song says, was very strong and set his two brothers to row against himself and made every effort to outdistance the Macleods.

These Morrisons, with Neil's half brother Murdo, were badly wanted by the Government for their attacks on the supply ships of the Fifers, and we can assume that there were more than three Morrison brothers aboard that day, as the sequel will show.

Tradition says that Neil and the Harrisman overtook the Morrison galley, but Alan was so fierce a fighter and defended himself so well, that they could not capture him or his brothers, until someone fixed a sword blade in an oar. Thus attached, he cleft the oar with his broadsword, but with such force that it went deep into the gunnel of the boat and could not be withdrawn. Thus died Alan and his two brothers, when quite close to the Ness coast.

Neil accepted the terms of the Adventurers and went to Edinburgh with them, taking with him twelve Morrison heads including that of Alan and his two brothers, in a sack, and on the intercession of the Fifers, he received a pardon for his past misdeeds. *Moysie's Memoirs*, p. 165 (Bannatyne Club), states this fact as follows:

> By means of one special Hielanman of that isle there were ten or twelve apprehendit of the special withstanders of that enterprise, and beheadit, and their heads sent here in a poke to Edinburgh which were set upon the ports thereof.
>
> April, 1599.

This was not the last of the brieve for we read that Donald MacIain Dubh – Alan's brother – was wanted for treasonable practices and murders in 1630; and this is actually the last mention of a brieve for Lewis that I can find in the books at my disposal.

27

A Morrison Mixture

W<small>E ARE TOLD BY</small> Sir Robert Gordon that the brieve was a kind of judge amongst the islands, who 'hath an absolute judicatorie, unto whose authoritie and censure they willingly submit themselves, when he determineth any debateable question between party and party.'

The chief of the Clan Morrison, whose big house was at Habost, Ness, was hereditary brieve of the Lewis, and this had gone on from father to son till about the year 1346, when the males of the family ran out in the direct line, and we are left with a Morrison heiress. This young lady was very haughty, and determined she would not marry any man unless he were of the Morrison name. But fate willed it otherwise, and she married a man Cain Macdonald from Ardnamurchan, bringing the Christian name Ceathan, Cennanus, or Cain into the Morrison names – a name which still persists in the island of Lewis, just as Sgàire (tacharg) is peculiar to the Macaulays.

This Cain was a son of Murdo, son of Iain Sprangach of Ardnamurchan, and from him the leading families of the Morrisons of Ness are descended. The badge of the Morrisons is driftwood which the Lewisman calls sgoid, for it used to be driven in great quantities upon the west coast of Lewis.

The old seannachie had his own version to explain how a man from Ardnamurchan went to Ness in the first place, and here is his story.

Cain Morrison was originally a Macdonald, born in Ardna-murchan. It appears that the proprietor of that estate exacted his right to pass the first night with every bride, the *jus primae noctis* which has now gone out of fashion. A vessel had come to anchor in the loch on the day that Cain had married; Cain did not rest at all on the night on which he was married, but wandered about very much upset.

In the morning he was met by the captain of the ship to whom he told of the evil practice prevalent in that country. The captain said that that vile custom should be done away with, and that he would lend him his cloak and sword. He further said, 'You watch about the laird's house, and when he comes out, be looking intently up to the castle, and say that you see a serious crack in the wall. Have the sword ready inside the cloak, and when the laird looks up, and is off his guard, aim at his throat and kill him, then run to my boat which shall be all ready waiting, and I will carry you to where you shall be safe.'

Cain acted on this advice, and escaped with the captain, who landed him at Ness. He was a very handsome fellow, and he soon made himself famous by his skill with the broad sword, and his dexterity in handling ships, and the young heiress fell violently in love with him but would not marry him till he consented to change his name from the proud one of Macdonald and to take the sgoid as his badge. This he agreed to do and they were married, and he became one of the best breithamhs Ness ever had.

They say he was married three times and when his Niseach wife died he went back to Ardnamurchan for the next and took her to Ness as his third wife.

28

The Seer of Petty –
A. Morrison, Sgeulachd

I AM GOING TO TELL YOU about a famous Lewisman – a Morrison of Ness extraction, namely the Rev. John Morrison – minister of Petty, near Inverness, from 1759 to 1774.

This man is known to history as the Petty Seer, because he had that weird faculty of seeing into the future, called in the Highlands the second sight. We in Lewis claim him as he was the grandson of the famous tacksman of Bragar – Iain mac Mhurchaidh mhic Ailein, the direct line from the brieves of Lewis.

John Morrison of Petty was also a Gaelic bard, and he is given the credit of producing that fine song 'Mo nighean dubh tha bòidheach dubh', though some query this.

I would like to tell you of some of the visions which seemed to be forced upon him and which he turned to good account in helping others, and which has left his name well remembered in the Highlands.

One morning a newly born baby was found on the doorstep of the manse of Petty. Mr Morrison was informed and he gave instructions for the child to be brought in and given every care. Weeks and months went by and no one came to claim the child. A year elapsed and the minister called a meeting of the Session at which two of the elders were appointed to go with the minister to find the parents of the child.

They set off one fine morning accompanied by a nurse woman carrying the baby, but none of them knew where they were going except the minister. They walked to Inverness, then to Port Kessock where they got the ferry across to Kessock Village in the Black Isle, and from there they walked to Drumderfit.

At this place they saw three men working near the high-road, and the minister sent one of the elders to ask the middle one of the three to come and take charge of this child, which he had abandoned a year ago on the steps of the manse at Petty.

The man came in fear and trembling and confessed all to the minister. He said that his wife had died giving birth to the baby, and being a poor man he did not know what to do, and got into a panic, and he then remembered the reputation of the minister of Petty for softness of heart, so he carried the baby there and left it on the doorstep where he was sure it would be well looked after at the manse.

There was a special well near the manse at Petty, and Mr Morrison was very fond of drinking its excellent water. One Saturday evening the maids forgot to take in the Sunday water as was their custom. The well was a slight distance from the manse but a good short-cut to it was through the churchyard. On the Sunday night the minister asked for a drink, and one of the maids ran with a pitcher in a great hurry to the well.

The minister asked why no drink was forthcoming – 'You will get a drink in a moment, Sir, it is coming,' said the other maid. 'Indeed, I won't,' says the minister, 'for the pitcher is broken and the water is spilt, and you had better go and lift Mary out of the newly dug grave into which I see she has fallen.'

The maid ran off, and there was Mary in an open grave, dug the day before, just as the minister had said.

One wild wintry night with a depth of snow on the ground the minister ordered his man to saddle his horse and to come with him, but the man, seeing the fierceness of the weather, refused to go, and the minister then set off alone. He battled on towards a small loch on the south side of Petty, called Lochan Duntie, and whom should he see crouching by the lochside, but a young woman trying to conceal a bundle underneath her shawl.

'What have you got there?' says the minister. 'I have got nothing,' says she.

'Don't you tell me any lies, I know very well what that bundle contains,' says Mr Morrison, 'but before you part with him, kiss him and say, "May God bless you" '.

The girl kissed the child and asked God's blessing on it and then confessed that she had come to the loch to throw the child in and so hide the evidence of her sinful folly. She returned home and reared the child with great love and care, and he turned out to be a useful member of the community.

Another piercing frosty night, as Mr Morrison was getting ready for bed, an intense urge came upon him to go out to the stack yard, and on going outside he made straight for a mass of hay in one corner and there he found a man, strange to him, overcome by the severe cold.

'Rise out of there, that is not the kind of bed you should be in on a night like this,' says the minister. 'I know you have been refused a night's shelter, but come you with me, and you shall get food and warmth.'

The man said he was a stranger and had called at a house but he had been roughly refused shelter, and not knowing where he was in the darkness, he had been glad to creep under the heap of hay in the yard.

The minister said, 'I know very well who has refused you shelter,' and led him in the darkness to a certain house. He knocked loudly on the door and when the man came down the minister said, 'You have turned this poor stranger from your door and refused him food and shelter on a night like this. Ministers and elders should show kindness and give hospitality to strangers for they may be sheltering angels unawares.'

The man was taken in and well treated.

One day a group of the women of Petty went into Inverness to sell their fish, and when they had disposed of them they gathered into a pub and drank more than they ought to have done. When they got back to Petty they were well liquored, and when passing the manse they seemed a bit more rowdy than usual. Mr Morrison went out to deliver a homily to them on the evils of excess, but one of them more lively and younger than the rest, asked him to play them dance tunes on his fiddle. Mr

Morrison was a good hand at the fiddle and very musical, so he went into the manse and soon had the whole company dancing reels to his playing.

One of the elders heard about this display and came a few days afterwards to give the minister a piece of his mind, for was it not an awful carry-on for a minister to be playing the fiddle on the high road to a lot of tipsy women?

'How could I refuse to play for the poor woman who asked me to do so, when I know that the holy angels of God will soon be tuning their harps to welcome her home. I wish I could hear the sweet music they will play to welcome her.'

The elder slunk away, still full of self-righteousness, but the young fishwife, who had asked the minister to play for her, was dead within the week, though she looked blythe and bonny when she made the unusual request.

29

Macdonalds (Golliganaich) of Uig

THE REV. MALCOLM MACLEAN, Conon Bridge, seems to doubt the reality of a progenitor of the Uig branch of the clan – viz. Ian Mór an Tarbh. He says the Crowlista people knew nothing of the Uist story.

But John Roy Macaulay, the grandfather of Donald Cam, had a natural son named Malcolm, by a woman called Nighean Mhurachaidh a' Ghabhain who lived in Capadal (Ardroil) in Uig, and this Malcolm was brave and daring and opposed Mac-Conuill, an Uist man who came to raise creachs in Uist.

Surely the Crowlista people ought to know this, for John Morrison, 1787, must have known about it, and Captain Thomas, into whose hands the manuscripts came and who edited them, adds a footnote to this effect in his remarks about traditions of the Clan Macaulay.

No one doubts the veracity and thoroughness of the late Rev. D. Macdonald, Crowlista, as far as his information went, and it may be true that a Macdonald came from the forest of North Harris and settled in Crowlista, but I do know that most of the Macdonalds of that village claimed relationship with the Clann Dhomhuill 'ic Iain as the main stem, but always accepted those who came from Aonghas Mór Mhangursta as newcomers amongst them.

I also know that one of the Macgolligans who lived till he was nearly ninety years of age made arrangements with a Macdonald family of Crowlista to see that he was buried with proper and fitting reverence as became one of his tribe, in Ardroil cemetery, for I was present myself on that occasion.

I am going much further back than the Rev. Mr Maclean. It is a historical fact that when it leaked out that James VI of Scotland gave his consent to the extermination of the Macleods of Lewis, the then chief sent an SOS to Macdonald of Clan Ranald and Macneil of Barra to come and help him, for it might be their turn next. Help was sent, and we do know that these clans made at least one attack on the old castle of Stornoway held by the Fife gentlemen. The Macneils claim that this is the time when their surname got into Lewis.

There is no doubt that when the Campbells seized Kintyre and drove out the Clan Ian Mór, the latter were scattered among clans friendly to them, and some may have found their way to the Lews, and also to Bun Abhuinn-eader and Scarp, but there was an established colony of Macdonalds in West Uig before then who claimed descent from Big Bold John of Clan Ranald.

30

The Cochull Glas

I FIND A GREAT MANY people in Uig would like to trace their descent from the valiant hero, the Cochull Glas; but we seem to have lost most of the tales about him. If there is anyone who reads this article and has other stories or traditions relating to him or his deeds I can assure him or her that there are a great many who would like to see them in print.

According to tradition, the Cochull Glas lived on a holding at Cnoc-an-Ruagain above the head of the Grimersta Bay. The ruins of his large house, with the rigs overgrown with rank heather, are pointed out above the road on the left before one gets to the bridge over the Grimersta as one travels toward Uig.

His name was really John Macdonald, and he was renowned in the Lewis for his natural strength and for his dexterity with the sword, and specially for his skill at wrestling. The Cochull Glas was very much admired by Donald Cam for he had beaten him several times at a wrestling match, and he considered him to be a useful man to look after his interests, especially at a key position like Ceann Thulavaig which everyone had to pass before they could ford the Grimersta River, and he gave him all the support he could when the Morrisons of Ness came down to make a raid on West Uig.

The Cochull belonged to a sept of the Macdonalds called Clann 'ic Gilleadharain, whom the Macleods of the Lews had settled in various colonies along the west coast as far down as Galson, to be a buffer between the Macaulays and the Morrisons. In the neighbourhood of Galson the name Gille Leadharain was rendered in English as Maclaren and it was one of these Macdonald women that Donald Cam married in 1610, when he went north with his brother Malcolm as best man, to fetch back his bride.

The Uig people tell you that the Cochull Glas was one of the MacIans of Glencoe, who escaped from the massacre in 1692, but if that is so, he could not have wrestled with Donald Cam, who died at Valtos before 1640. He may have come from Glen Quoich, others say.

On one occasion the Cochull came on the Morrisons near Garynahine, where they were resting the cattle after a raid on Uig. When it got dark, the Cochull with his sons and helpers crept up to the camp where the Morrisons were roasting part of a stolen ox over a huge fire. The Cochull spread his men around the campfire, keeping well hidden, and the Cochull who was an expert bowman shot an arrow at the cook which pierced him in the heel tendon, and he let out a bloodcurdling shriek of pain, while a shower of arrows landed among the Nessmen, which caused them to panic and seek safety in flight, leaving their wounded behind.

The Cochull and his party then rounded up the cattle and drove them through the ford on the Grimersta River and walked them across the moor till they came to Port-an-Aiseig at the narrows of Loch Roag opposite Unguishader. They were not long resting there when Donald Cam appeared on the opposite side and started shouting across to him, 'O thou pale-coloured Cochull, was it yourself that turned the creach?' 'O, thou turbulent one-eye, thou knowest well it was I that turned the creach – something you were not able to do!'

It was customary in those times to put buffer tribes in between clans that were constantly at feud with one another. The Macphails were settled along the west coast as far as Carlo-way to give information and support to the Morrisons of Ness when they were attacked from the Uig direction.

We have a story of a Macphail having to take refuge in a dùn on a loch near Bragar and how well he defended himself with his bow and arrows from this stronghold.

The buffer watchdogs were known in Gaelic as buannai-chean, and were paid in kind for their services.

31

An Old Uig Tale

WHEN THE MACKENZIES WITH the help of the government forces defeated the Macleods and the other Lewis clans, these were driven westwards and had to take shelter in various parts of the Atlantic coast of Uig – Neil to shelter in Beireasaigh (Berisay), and Domhnull (Donald) Cam to his own stack at Mangursta.

Donald had a well-built dinghy hidden in one of the clefts or geos near Gallon Head, and in this he and Iain Dubh Chròig went out from the headland to set greatlines, and so kept themselves plentifully supplied with all kinds of fish, especially cod and ling.

Donald Cam was subject to changing moods, and had a most violent temper, and so Iain Dubh did all he could to keep him in a good humour. One day when he was rowing the boat for Donald the fish wore scarce and Donald was in a fiery temper, and poor Iain Dubh could not do anything right that morning. When Donald started to abuse him and criticise his rowing he let go of both the oars and jumped overboard. Donald Cam got into an awful state for the boat drifted away and he thought Iain Dubh would surely be drowned, and he made every effort by using his hands to paddle so as to catch up with one oar and then the other, but when he looked around he could not see Iain Dubh anywhere, and concluded he was indeed lost.

After a great deal of paddling and striving against wind

and current he at last got the lost oars aboard, and with a sad heart he pulled for the shore after hauling in his lines. Making the boat secure in its hidden recess, he made for the dùn at Loch Bharabhat, and when he came in sight of the loch, he was surprised to see a large volume of smoke issuing from the outlet that did duty for a chimney, and he then cautiously surveyed the approach to the dùn before venturing to cross by the causeway.

When Donald Cam looked in he found the house in order and Iain Dubh sitting comfortably before a roaring fire. After Donald Cam had warmed himself he turned to him and said, 'Iain Dubh thou foolish fellow, what made you throw the oars out of the boat?' Iain Dubh replied that if he had not thrown the oars out of the boat he might as well have remained there himself, and that it was the only way to escape from the senseless fury. Donald Cam said nothing but smiled and bade Iain Dubh Chròig get ready the supper.

Iain Dubh was one summer fishing in the sound of the Shiants and lived on these islands opposite the Park. It was a time of great scarcity in Lewis, and he brought his old mother along with him to keep house. She had not been there many days when she took ill and died. Iain wished to have his mother buried at Uig, but he was loth to leave the good fishing behind, and so was in a great dilemma. He then disembowelled the corpse, and hung it in a cave to dry. When the fishing was over he had his mother's body taken back to Uig and buried along with her friends and relatives. As the seannachie relates, 'This proceeding was rather barbarous, yet considering the times and the want of culture in uneducated men, we must excuse Iain Dubh Chròig.'

32

More About the Cochull Glas

I GOT THIS PIECE OF INFORMATION from a friend of mine. I was in Inverness and I met a very old friend from Bernera, Lewis, and this was what he said to me.

(a) The Cochull Glas was alive in the time of the famous Donald Cam c. 1600.

(b) It was always on the side of Donald Cam that one found Cochull Glas, ready with his sword, targe, his bow and arrow.

(c) That the Cochull Glas put an arrow through a Nessman and transfixed the man to the mast. The galley of the brieve was driven in a gale into Loch Roag and came close to the shore of Bernera. The Cochull Glas went down to the shore and one of the Niseachs shouted out to him: 'Where can I let down the anchor in a safe place?'

The Cochull Glas put his hand to his ear, and told him to stand in the shelter of the mainmast so that he could hear what he was saying.

No sooner was this done than the Cochull Glas sent an arrow through him and transfixed him to, the must. The place on the shore where the Cochull stood is called Laimrig na Saighde.

(d) The Cochull Glas was second in command with Donald Cam when they captured the pirate ship the *Priam* and took her into the bay at Kirkibost. The spot where two of the crew are buried can still be seen. These two of the crew jumped overboard as they were nearing the shore but were overtaken on land and killed.

Another, who must have had a hump on his back, also made a dash for liberty, but he was overtaken and killed at a knoll called Cnoc a' Ghille Chrotaich, where his grave is still pointed out.

(e) The Cochull Glas was not in Donald Cam's company the time he was captured by John the Brieve and taken to Ullapool. A cowardly plot for which the Morrisons paid dearly afterwards.

(f) Neil Macleod, known as Niall Odhar Bheireasaidh spent his time between that rock and Little Bernera, and when there was anything important doing on the mainland the Cochull used to light a fire on a certain hillock as a signal to warn Neil.

From these bits of information we can gather that the Cochull spent a good deal of his time away from Cnoc an Ruagain, near Grimersta River living in the island of Bernera.

This old man said that it was from Cochull Glas that the Macdonalds of Bernera (the Golliganaich) came, and that, when a boy, he was taken to Little Bernera by his grandfather and shown the exact spot where the Cochull Glas was buried. He thinks he can still find it.

33

The Cochull Glas – Another Variation from the Late Rev. Alex J. Mackenzie, Dun Alasdair.

T HE COCHULL GLAS, WHO LIVED at Cnoc an Ruagain on Grimersta Bay, and Donald Cam Macaulay, who lived at Valtos, Uig, were redoubtable warriors and loved one another and fought for one another like brothers. Donald Cam excelled in swordsmanship, the Cochull in archery and wrestling. When these two heroes stood together in the fight they were more formidable than twenty ordinary men. One day the Cochull Glas went down with a raging fever. His two young sons kept the watch on the pass to Uig the night the Mórthirich slipped into Macaulay territory. There, having discovered that Donald Cam and his warriors were away on a sea foray, they set out to harry the land of the Macaulays. The people of Uig, taken by surprise, could offer little resistance and the raiders lifted a grand creach. Night fell on the raiders at Ceann Thùlabhaig near to the Cochull's abode, so as they could not proceed further till morning; they made a cordon round the cattle. They were ill great jubilation, and here and there a man vaunted and boasted what and how he would do if Donald Cam himself should appear.

The Cochull was still in the throes of his fever and concerned about the guarding of the road to his friend's territory. His two young sons were more concerned about their father, though they pretended they were watching the direction from which an enemy might come. Suddenly the Conchull heard a noise in the distance and knew it was the bellowing of enclosed cattle and that it meant the cows of Uig had been lifted by someone. The stricken warrior at once grasped the situation, and forgetting his aching limbs and giddy head, he flung himself out of the bed, but only to totter a few steps and fall in a heap on the floor. He groaned in despair, but catching sight of his bow and quiver of arrows hanging on the wall, he said to his sons, 'Go take my bow and do something'. The two lads put their father back to bed and set off towards the bellowing cattle. They had not gone far when they saw the watchfires and a great herd of cattle huddled together closed in by a ring of watchfires, round which a number of warriors sat, armed and plaided. Their accent showed them to be Mainlanders and evidently refreshed with Uisgebeatha; there was a great mirth and merrymaking on every side. One great red-bearded warrior in particular caused uproarious laughter showing with his claymore how he would deal with Donald Cam.

It was a hopeless situation for the two lads unless the Macaulays returned in time to save the cattle, but remembering their father's injunction, they tried to shoot an arrow into the circle of light given out by the watchfires. The older essayed a shot but to his extreme annoyance he had not enough strength to bend the bow. They returned home and on hearing their description of the scene the Cochull seized his claymore and bow and quivers and made for the flare of the watchfires. A frenzied and relentless fury came upon him and when within range he shot an arrow at the red-bearded giant, raising at the same time, the cry, 'Domhnull Cam, Domhnull Cam'. The arrow found its mark and the red-beard pitched forward to the ground. The raiders were paralysed by the suddenness of the attack, and suddenly into the circle of light sprang a fearsome figure, claymore in hand and intoxicated with rage and fever. The terrific claymore laid a full dozen low, the cattle stampeded and the Mórthirich made off towards their galley.

AN COCHULL GLAS 'S
CLANN GILLEADHRAIN.

Cha robh an Cochull Glas 'na dhuine tais
Ged thréig e fonn na Mórthir
'Sa shìn e chas air cnoc is glaic
An Eilean ciar donn Leódhais;
Thug e leis ann a dhaoine teann
Is meall de ghillean bòidheach
Nach obadh strì na sgoltadh cheann:
Bha feachd dhiu ann nach sòradh;
An Nis nan stuagh bha cuid de'n t-sluagh
Is chuir iad ruaig air móran,
'S na daoine subba, cnàmhach, cruaidh,
Sin gineal 's dual an t-seòrsa;
Gu ruigeas Uig, no ceò 's nam beann
Cun stad iad ann is phòs iad,
'S an diugh than àl gu lìonmhor dàn
'S gach òb is allt 'sa' chòrsa:
'N uair dhùisgeas pàirt a réir an dàin,
Is fir na h-Iùbhraich* còmhla
Théid iad 'nan deann gu treun neo-ghann
Le Fir Chinn-tìr 'sa chòmhdhail!

*Those sleeping in Tom na h-Iùbhraich (the fairies).

34

Macdonald of the Isles' Bodyguard

SAID THE UIG SEANNACHIE to me in Gaelic, 'It is under this name-title that the story of the Buannas or the selected body guard who for quite a long time settled down and battened upon the people of the Fourteen Pennylands in the Parish of Uig is so often told.'

This was the old name of Valtos, Kneep and Beirghe (Reef) taken as a combined farm holding. These buannas of the Lord of the Isles were a set of picked warriors, who were supposed to keep close to him and protect his person from danger wherever he went, and especially when he left his own district. They were outstanding in strength and stature, very brave, especially expert at the sword play, skilled marksmen with the bow and arrow and with any other weapons of the period.

Macdonald of the Isles visited many of these islands which were his patrimony, to see that law and order were being kept, and also that his rentals were duly paid.

At each place these buannas were quartered out on the people near where the great man stayed. The poor people had to feed them and give sleeping accommodation and keep them amused. One can gather they had hearty appetites, and were a sore strain upon their resources, yet they dared not complain.

These big warriors, in the course of time, got to know the islands where the best food was and where they got the warmest hospitality.

This information spread to the mainland and to the islands further south, and there began to arrive hordes of beggars and sorners seeking food and shelter and pretending they were members of the cut-off bodyguards no longer able to work. They got as far as they could northwards into the islands, and owing to the laws of Highland hospitality it was not easy to get rid of them. The matter became so serious at last that the Government passed successive laws to keep them from coming, and to force them to do some work to support themselves, but they persisted into the nineteenth century.

There were also others wandering from district to district; some sang songs, some told stories, some juggled and showed tricks, and others acted as jesters and clowns to amuse the people, but they all lived off the people who were not too well off in those days and found it a strain. In the end the Gaelic, name Buanna came to mean a mooching sort of fellow, who did not want to work, and who lived at the expense of the natives, on the best he could obtain.

Such a band of quondam buannas must have ensconced themselves in the area of Valtos, Kneep, and Beirghe, then called the Fourteen Pennylands. They stayed far too long and the people were getting very tired of them and their lazy ways, especially the women, while their meagre resources got less and less.

A plan was formed to do away with them or to frighten them out of the area, and this was the way they set about it. It was a very hot bright summer, and the natives, young and old, kept going to the sandy beaches to bathe and keep cool. Everyone knows the sugar-white sands at Kneep. It was fixed that all, young and old, male and female, in the village, on the first hot day would turn out on the beach, and each woman was to pay special attention to a buanna. She was to flatter him and flirt with him and divert his attention, and when one of their number gave a yell each woman was to fasten her arms round the neck of her male stranger, cling heavily to him making a fearful din and keep his head under the water.

The plan was kept a strict secret from the uninvited guests, and when the hot day came, the whole village, young and old, went out wading on the beach. All seemed harmless enough, and for a time there was lots of dalliance and water splashing, till one woman gave an ear-piercing screech and others followed suit, each grabbing a man and holding him under while the strangers tried to throw off the women who weighted them down.

There was one buanna who had not got tied up with a woman and was on the outer edge of the mass, and he asked a man from Kneep what all this yelling and splashing meant.

'They are going to finish off everyone of the strangers, and I would advise everyone of you to get away from here as fast as you can,' he replied.

'How can we do that?' asked the man.

'I will row you myself with my own boat to the mainland on the other side of Loch Roag and then you will be safe,' he replied.

After much wrestling, the unwelcome strangers got the mastery of the women and made for the one talking to the Kneep man, who hysterically explained to them their danger, and said they would get ferried across to the mainland by the Kneep man if they got their clothes on and came hurriedly.

In the meantime the Uigeach went to his boat and got help to push it into the water, and soon he had all the buannas piling into it. They rowed out by the narrows of Siaram and across the sound in the direction of Bernera, but instead of putting them ashore on the mainland of Lewis, as they expected, the Kneep man landed them on Eilean Eunaidh close to Bernera.

The buannas quickly leapt ashore for they thought they had been landed on the mainland, and would be free to go whichever way they liked, but on ascending the rise of ground above the landing place they saw the sea all round them. They were furious with the Kneep man, and quickly ran down the hill towards the boat, but by this time he had pushed off, raised his sail to catch what little breeze there was, and with an oar in each hand was rowing furiously away from the island.

The angry buannas fitted arrows to their bows, and such marksmen were they that they fixed many in the woodwork of the boat and the sail was pierced in many places like a pepper caster until the boat was well out of range, but by the help of providence the Kneep man escaped without injury, and with a following wind was soon back at the white sands of Kneep.

We have no record how long these buannas were marooned on Eunay but they were there for a good while, for there is a well in that island called Tobair nam Buannaichean even to this day.

After that rough handling these wandering moochers never again came back to trouble the people of the Fourteen Pennylands.

35

The Son of Ronald of Keppoch

How many of us in Lewis know that once one of the famous Macdonells of Keppoch found refuge in Lewis and that he came here to save his neck for there was a price on his head?

The tale as told me by an old lady was as follows:

He need not have been ashamed of what he did. One day he came home weary from the hill accompanied by his hound, and he came back empty-handed, for he found no deer in spite of his intense sweep of the mountains of Keppoch. He had a virago of a wife, and when she saw he had no venison, she angrily kicked the weary dog.

He said, 'If you had been at that hound's heels all day it is not kicking him you would be.' She rounded on him and abused him so much with her tongue that he lost his temper, thrashed her and ordered her to be sent back home to her father.

The latter was one of the best swordsmen in the Highlands, and he was so insulted by this act of MacRaoghnaill na Ceapaich that he sent him a challenge to a duel. The son of Ronald of Keppoch was also a renowned swordsman and sent his seconds to see him, and a duel was arranged for a certain date. When the opponents faced each other the swordsmanship was magnificent, but Macdonell deftly snicked off the button below his opponent's chin and then asked him if that would suffice him and he was told no; then they set to again and this time he snipped off the middle button of his father-in-law's shirt – 'Will that not satisfy you?' said Macdonell, but the other again said that it would not. Once more they set upon each other with renewed vigour and the son of Ronald of Keppoch made a large gash in his opponent's abdominal wall, whereupon the surgeon rushed in and the duel was at an end.

Macdonell of Keppoch was warned to keep away from his father-in-law for at least a year, and he seemed to be recovering slowly until one day Macdonell happened to be in the same town at a market, when the wounded man caught sight of him through the window and he grew so excited and enraged that he burst his wound and fell back dead.

The young man was blamed for his death by the law and took refuge in Lewis which was then thinly populated and difficult to reach and made an ideal hiding place – especially among the mountains of Uig. Was it not Mac an t-Srònaich much later in history who said, 'As long as I keep to the Uig hills, the Uig hills will keep me?'

The tacksman of Miavaig at this time was a man called the son of Fair Somerled Mac Shomhairle Bhàin, who also was a famous swordsman and wrestler, and had a great reputation as a hunter in the forest of Uig and North Harris. There is a peninsula on Loch Grunavat called after him. One morning this man got up early and went to hunt rabbits with his bow and arrows in a ravine above Miavaig called Gile Brunnda, and he was very surprised to see a tartan-clad Highlander armed with broadsword and target coming out of the gil to meet him. 'I am the laird of Miavaig. Who is this stranger that so boldly comes to meet me on my own ground?' 'Is dana cù air a shitig fhein,'* said the stranger, 'I am the son of Ronald of Keppoch, are you now not frightened of me, Sir?'

'Indeed I have heard of your prowess and how the law has been hard on your tracks but welcome to Miavaig, and as no-one knows you are here you should fit up a shelter for yourself in the ravine and come secretly to me at night to the house at Miavaig and I shall see you are fed and your clothes dried.'

The two warriors got very fond of each other and for many years they hunted the frìth† of North Harris and the Morsgail and Uig mountains, yet no Uigeach would inform against Mac

---

*'Bold is a dog on his own dunghill.'
† frith – forest.

Ronald of Keppoch or his friend Fear Mhiabhaig, for they respected the property and the cattle of the Uig people on these moors and if by chance they were forced to kill a sheep when lost in the hills, or forced by hunger, they kept the ears for their marks and paid in full the value of the sheep to their owners.

Time rolled on and it was drawing nigh to the date when the proscription against Mac Donell of Keppoch was coming to an end, so the friends one day set out to walk to Stornoway to receive the promised pardon. They did not hurry, but went hunting among the hills at the south end of Loch Langavat, and continued round through the Lochs moor en route for Stornoway when they were both suddenly struck down by a raging fever.

They were weak and delirious, but they managed to creep under an overhanging bank by a strewn where at least they could reach for water to soothe their burning throats. Someone got wind that they were there, and when they found out who they were and that a reward was still offered for their capture or destruction, a Lochsman came out and callously heaved the overhanging bank down upon them, and so they were smothered in their delirium, with only three days to go before they would have received their pardon.

The burial place of Mac Raoghnuill na Ceapaich and Fear Mhiabhaig is still pointed out on the Lochs moor.

The people of Lochs say it was a family of Mackenzies who did this dastardly deed and that it was a continuation of the feud between the Taileachs,* and the Macdonells of Glengarry – a feud which had cost the latter the loss of their castle of Strome to the Mackenzies.

---

* Tàileachs – Kintail men, i.e. Mackenzies.

36

The Seaforth Period in the Lews
1610–1844

1610–1611 – Kenneth MacKenzie – made Baron of Kintail 1608 – received a charter of Lewis under the Great Seal.

1611–1633 – Cailean (Colin) Ruadh – created earl of Seaforth 1623 by James VI for cleaning up the wild state of Lewis – often called the 'Red Earl'. He died in 1633 without male issue and was succeeded by his brother.

1633–1651 – George – 2nd earl – badly defeated at Auldearn 1645 by Montrose – 300 Lewismen destroyed – only three came back.

1651–1678 – Coinneach Mór, 3rd earl.

1678–1701 – Coinneach Og, 4th earl – created Marquis (Irish) by James VII.

1701–1740 – Uilleam Dubh – 5th earl – fought at Sheriffmuir 1715 – wounded in 1719 at Glenshiel – forfeited – fled to France – pardoned – came back in 1726 – lived in exile at Seaforth Lodge, Stornoway – died in 1740 – buried at Eye – had Zachary Macaulay for his factor in Lewis.

1740–1761 – Lord Fortrose – refused to come out for Prince Charlie – died in London 1761 – buried in Westminster Abbey.

1761–1781 – Son Kenneth, who in 1763 received a charter from the crown for his estates – 1766 created Baron Ardelve – 1744 made Earl of Seaforth in peerage of Ireland – 1788 he raised the Old 78th Regiment after 72nd, now 1st Battalion Seaforth Highlanders – financially embarrassed 1779 – sold the estates to his cousin for £100,000 – died without male issue and title of Earl of Seaforth became extinct.

1781–1783 – Thomas Francis Fredk MacKenzie – assumed the name of Humberston – He was the great-grandson of Coinneach Mòr 3rd earl and Col MacKenzie Humberston died in 1783, succeeded by his brother.

1783–1815 – Col Francis Humberston MacKenzie raised two regiments on his estates in Ross-shire, and these are represented by 2nd Battalion Seaforth Highlanders. In 1797 created a peer of United Kingdom as Lord Seaforth and Baron MacKenzie of Kintail, died 1851 leaving daughter. Died after all his male children and title became extinct.

1815–1863 – Mary Elizabeth Frederica (1) Lady Hood (wife of Admiral Sir Samuel Hood, MP for Westminster). Hood died in 1814. (2) Married 1817 James Alexander Stewart of Glasserton (JAS) who afterwards assumed the name of Mackenzie. Lived at Seaforth Lodge. Mr Stewart MacKenzie was Governor of Ceylon and the Ionian Isles. He had a banking house of his own and improved the fishing at Stornoway – put Stornoway on the map and extended the old village of Stornoway. Died in 1843 and his wife sold the island to Sir James Matheson in 1844. She retired to Brahan Castle and both are buried in Fortrose Cathedral.

37

The Seaforth Title and
Why Choose That Site?

A VERY IMPORTANT AND INTERESTING PIECE of Lewis history
has come to light with the discovery of the exact site whereon
the first Earl of Seaforth erected his stronghold in Lewis and
from whence he took his title. As some readers will know, Kenneth, Lord Kintail, died in 1611, a year after he had bought
Lewis from the Fife Adventurers. Colin who succeeded him was
empowered by the Government to clear up the trouble with the
Macleods and pacify the rest of the Lews, for which services he
was rewarded by an earldom in 1623. He looked around the
island and chose a holding at the head of Loch Seaforth and
there he built a stronghold with a round tower to give it further
protection. He was still not very sure of his new dependants,
so to protect himself from those of the Macleod name, who
were very numerous round Stornoway, the Point district, and on
the North shore of Broad Bay, he placed his own MacKenzies,
Macivers and Maclennans in good tacks throughout what is now
the Lochs parish. He had a good hiding place at the head of
the long, shallow and twisting sea-fiord, and he had not much
to fear from the Minch side, for by 1620 the MacKenzies were
powerful from Kintail to Coigeach and across Ross-shire to the
Black Isle.

Danger could come from the west, for the Macleods and
Macdonalds of Uig had backed the losing side, and to keep

their old enemies sweet, the Macaulays were given good tacks all over the Parish from Mealista to Carloway, but taking good care to put a MacKenzie into the key positions of Balnacille, Tobson, Callernish, and Dalbeg, in order to keep the chief or his factor well informed of any threat or trouble from that area. The Pàirc area was full of deer, and its rivers also were well stocked with salmon and sea trout, nor was the big Laxay water far away, and by building a high turf wall between Loch Erisort and Loch Seaforth, called Gàradh an Tighearna, and also by shifting some of the cottars in the peninsula to other areas, he could have a private sporting preserve at his own door.

How do I know it was here Clan Kenneth had their first abode in the Lews? I read as a footnote to an old paper given to the Society of Antiquaries that the first Seaforth who settled in Lewis on a small farm on the North of Loch Seaforth, could not have been very reverent or superstitious, for he had built three standing stones of a druid circle into the walls of his new castle; so if I could find a building with standing stones built into its walls in this area, I would have discovered the actual site. Mr Duncan Macrae, Eishken, went on the hunt, and he found such a site on what is now croft No. 6 Seaforth Head; and as he is very interested in this topic, he found out quite a lot of detail about the old castle for me.

The farm of Seaforth Head was broken up in the 1880–90 period, and the daughter of the tenant, Mrs Morrison, No. 1 Balallan, says that she had been told by old people that there had been a castle with a circular tower, and that standing stones had been built into the walls of the building. There is a heap of rubble there now, and at least one of the monoliths is still in position. This is proof that we have located the actual site of the stronghold, and the heap of rubble is still called the Seann Chaisteal.

When did the MacKenzies leave this place, and have the elegant mansion known as Seaforth Lodge built on the Gear-raidh Chruaidh overlooking the beautiful harbour of Storno-way? We know that the third earl – Coinneach Mór and Col Norman Macleod of Bernera, Harris, came from the Loch Seaforth direction to attack the Cromwellian garrison in 1654. They were badly defeated, and if Seaforth Lodge had been in existence it would have been occupied or destroyed. From the rent roll for 1726 there was a tacksman called Donald MacKenzie in possession of the farm of Seaforth – probably some relation of the chief; and we also know that William Dubh, the fifth earl, entertained Marischal Keith and his brother at Seaforth Lodge in 1719; for it was there the plans for the '19 Rising were prepared, and it was from Stornoway they sailed for the ill-fated skirmish of Glenshiel. Brahan Castle has now been demolished, and the pictures and papers have been given into the keeping of the Town Council of Fortrose, and I have no doubt that given time one can get the exact date of the construction of Seaforth Lodge. Mr Stewart MacKenzie died in 1843, and his widow, the last of the direct line of Seaforth, sold the island to Mr (later Sir) James Matheson in 1844, when Seaforth Lodge was demolished and the magnificent Lews Castle was built on the site.

38

The Shoeburn Hoard of Silver Coins

IT HAS BEEN SAID of the hoard of coins found in the Shoeburn gorge that they might have been part of the money used by the Seaforths to finance their various attempts to help the Jacobite cause, but there might be another and simpler explanation.

Now these coins were of many countries and had been in circulation a long time, and were well worn. Stornoway from about 1820 to 1843 was a very busy port and as we may read from descriptions of these times, ships from Norway, Sweden and Denmark kept calling in on their way to Liverpool, and also from Spain and the Mediterranean ports. Did you know that Mr Stewart Mackenzie had a large distillery built in the Shoeburn gorge below where the clay bowl containing the coins was found? The distillery was built at a cost of £14,000 to stop the excessive illegal distilling of whisky in all parts of the Lewis. Many people, including the sailors from these foreign ships, went to this distillery and got a supply of liquor, and good measure was given for cash, Tomhas mhór Mhic Nith as it was called. Could some dishonest person from the distillery keep on pilfering and hiding in this clay vessel coins from the till? Or was this a form of honest saving for a rainy day? Why did the owner not come to unearth it? Your guess is as good as mine! No one in those days trusted to such banks as were then in existence, and a favourite way was to hide your treasure in a clay crock and bury it. Many of these clay crocks with gold and valuable jewellery have been buried, and come to light from time to time. One of these was once unearthed at Kirkibost in Bernera. One can meditate on this theory of the burial of the ancient coins, and I hope we manage to keep some in the island for our Lewis Museum.

39

The Seaforth Title –
Castle of Seaforth Head

MR DONALD MACKINNON, 43 Balallan, writes that he has asked Mrs Morrison, 1 Balallan, who was brought up at No. 6 Seaforth Head, and she says that the original site of the home of Clan Kenneth in Lewis was on the present croft of No. 6 Seaforth Head. The building was of the castellated tower type, and one of the three original standing stones can still be seen upright in the wall of the circular base of the tower; the others may be hidden in the debris which piles up to seven or eight feet. He says that at a later date, probably about 1800, another MacKenzie occupied the cottage on the site. (In the 1726 Seaforth Rent Roll the tacksman of Seaforth is given as Donald MacKenzie, who paid £40 Scots and meal, mutton and butter.) An old lady, Miss MacKenzie of the Applecross Mac-Kenzies, says that her grand-aunt lived at Seaforth Head at that time. She came from Tattenhall, Wolverhampton, and was a great friend of Mrs Platt. This lady took with her to England some slabs from the top part of the tower (which had fallen and had been unearthed), and also some heather from the area, and built a miniature Seaforth garden at her English home with them. The late Mr Allan Macmillan had visited the site on two occasions and took copious notes from Mr and Mrs MacKinnon, the first crofters who went into No. 6 Seaforth Head when the farm was broken up 1884–1890. These notes would make interesting reading.

Mrs Morrison, No. 1 Balallan, may have further information about the stones. The Morrisons took down the south end of the house and erected a gable about 1928–29. Some parts of the old erection may have been removed. Her husband had told Mr Macmillan, previous to this date, that there were stones in the building that were not supposed to be removed. The house there now is a ruin – only walls – and they are not the original walls; but one can see that they were built on the site of the original castle (tower), commanding a magnificent view down to Airidhbhruach towards the west and eastwards towards Gravir.

40

The Island of Lewis Before Being Bought by James Matheson in 1844

LORD SEAFORTH DIED IN 1816. Mr and Mrs Stewart MacKenzie resided now and then at Seaforth Lodge, Stornoway, and in 1838 Mr S. MacKenzie was made Governor of the Ionian Islands and the Island of Ceylon. The management of the Lews was for many years in the hands of trustees, and their local factor did almost nothing for the benefit of the tenants, large or small. The annual value of the property returned to parliament in 1843 – counting the feus of the town of Stornoway it was £10,110. The 1841 census gave a population of 17,037. Sir James bought the Lews from the Seaforth family in 1844 for £190,000. The area was 417,469 acres.

When purchase was completed, Mr Scobie of Sutherland was appointed factor, and under his superintendence was commenced all the improvements and expenditure. When the potato famine came on in 1846 Sir James took on himself the burden of relieving the starving poor upon his estate, and imported large quantities of meal to be paid for by labour or in money. The potato crops of 47 and 48 likewise failed, and the proprietor's charitable supplies of meal had to be carried on as before. Mr Scobie resigned the factorship in 1849 during the famine, and was succeeded by John Munro MacKenzie, 'a gentleman respected by everyone who knows him'. The improvements were carried on, but involved an expenditure very considerably in excess of the revenue of the estate, and in 1850 had to be brought to a close.

In January, 1851, the four parish boards of Lewis presented a memorial to Lord John Russell backed by a letter from Sir James – that the potato crop had failed again and praying, (a) that the Government would grant relief and give help to emigrate, and (b) give financial aid to those left who required it, till the next crop was harvested. Sir James's letter says 'the redundancy of population is notoriously the evil, emigration is the only effectual remedy to afford elbow-room and fair scope for the success of the antecedent measures which from over-population have hitherto proved unavailing.'

The Government sent Sir John McNeill, Chairman of the Board of Supervision for the Relief of the Poor, and of Public Health for Scotland, to question and report on the conditions and examine sundry witnesses in the Lewis. Sir John McNeill estimated the Lewis crofters and their families in 1851 at 14,000 souls, and that a croft did not provide food for an average family for more than six months of the year. Till the autumn of 1846, the produce of their crofts, and of the fishings at home and in Caithness (Wick), generally sufficed to maintain them, but on the failure of the crop of that year they were in distress as already stated, and in Lewis as elsewhere, the circumstances and conditions of the working classes had declined from year to year; for exclusive of paupers on the roll, there were in 1850, in Lewis, 11,000 inhabitants receiving relief from the Destitution Fund. Sir John McNeill states that for six years from 1844–1850 the proprietor of Lewis had expended on improvements £67,980 more than the whole revenue derived from the property, which it is presumed includes a sum of £30,000 borrowed under the Drainage Act, expended on trenching, drainage and fencing; £4,000 of which was expended on crofters' land, for which they paid interest, the balance being expended on the large farms, the tenants of which had been paying 6.5 per cent for the sums so expended; and by this time they had redeemed the loan in terms of the Drainage Act.

Mr Smith of Deanston said that he would make the moor he treated at Loch Ganvich with sand and drainage, 'blossom like the Carse of Gowrie' but it appears from Sir John McNeill's report that 'the block called "Deanston", after having been cultivated by the proprietor for four years, was abandoned or drained again to a greater depth with tiles'. And now the traveller may, on passing from Stornoway to Garynahine see 'Deanston' going back to its original moss and heather. Mr Munro MacKenzie was of the opinion that if the potatoes continued to fail, the inhabitants of Lewis could not be made self-sustaining 'unless a considerable number of them remove elsewhere'. He also stated that Sir James offered to provide a thousand free passages to America 'and relinquish his right of hypothec over their stock, and to cancel all the arrears of rent due to him'. Only 112 families consisting of 653 souls had consented to go, their arrears of rent at Whitsunday, 1850, being £672. A suggestion to emigrate was made to 184 more families consisting of 1,126 souls, with £1,951 of arrears of rental, but they having refused to emigrate, summonses of removal were served upon them, as well as on a number of other crofters who were in arrear of rent, but who could find the means of liquidating the arrears.

41

Rev. Malcolm Macphail – Kilmartin

I SEE THAT MY FRIEND Mr Mac Gille-Chaluim has written about the poem 'Clach an Truiseil', and he also has a good word to say about the late Rev. Malcolm Macphail of Kilmartin.

On going through the pages of the proceedings of the Society of Antiquaries for the period 1860–1880 I find him often quoted as an authority on things Lewisian especially by Cpt. F.W. Thomas, who did such a lot of good work for the Society.

The present generation of Gaelic enthusiasts owe a great deal to this clever son of Lewis, for he was a pioneer for Gaelic survival before the days of 'An Comunn', at a time when it was not fashionable to perpetuate the language, and when the then mandarins of Stornoway were trying to forget they came from black houses, and were aping the ways of the south.

Calum Aonghais 'ic Dhonnachaidh was born in Shawbost and by his own industry educated himself sufficiently to get to college. During his holidays he taught for the S.P.C.K. School at Ness, and his sister, Marion, my maternal grandmother, used at these times to keep house for him. She had many stories of the good times she spent among the Niseachs, and I wish I had had the sense then to take a note of the tales she told me of life at Ness as it was lived then.

She always prefaced her stories with 'When my brother Calum was teaching "Sgoil nan Ladies",' and explained that this he did in order to get money to complete his studies to become a really fully-fledged minister. It was while doing this duty at Ness that he got in touch with Norman Murray, Habost, and Angus Gunn, North Dell, two very old seannachies, and from their dictation he wrote down old history, stories, poetry and songs that had come down the ages in Lewis. He compiled a small booklet called *The Traditions of the Morrisons of Ness* – I wish I had a copy of it now for myself!

Rev. Malcolm Macphail wrote a great deal to the papers in his day, mostly on Gaelic subjects and archaeology, especially to the *Oban Times*. He spent his life as a minister in Kilmartin, Argyllshire, and there he is buried. He had a large family, who all did well, several of them were doctors of medicine. While at the recent Oban Mod I went to see his grave to pay homage to his memory and for the great work he did on behalf of the Gaelic cause.

If Mac Gille-Chaluim will follow up the introduction I gave him to a certain erudite lady in Edinburgh who has inherited most of her father's Gaelic manuscripts, he may still retrieve some of the sgeulachds and historical lore which are fast disappearing from the Gaelic landward parts of Lewis.

Here for Mac Gille-Chaluim and others is a portion of a Gaelic poem I got from a Bernera man about Clach an Truiseil, when I showed him a copy of a painting of the monolith done about 1819, when there was peat surrounding its base 6–8 feet deep.

> Co aig tha fhios an ùin a thriall,
> 'S an cian tha mi 's àn aite-sa?
> Bho chunna mi air tùs a' ghrian
> Cur sgiamh air feur nam blàth
> A nis ged tha mo cheann cho liath,
> 'S mi faicinn triall gach àl;
> An so bidh' mise gus an téid
> An cruinne-cé 'na smàl.

I thank Mac Gille-Chaluim for giving me this opportunity of putting a stone of appreciative remembrance on the cairn of my late grand-uncle, Calum Macphail.

42

The Macphails of Lewis

HERE ARE A FEW BITS of information I have gathered about the Clan Macphail.

This tribe goes very far back in connection with Lewis tradition and history. They must have descended from some progenitor called Paul. There are a set of drystone bothies in the Flannan Isles – said to be prehistoric – known as Bothain Chlann 'icPhail – built on the bee-hive system, but tradition does not tell us who were these children of Paul.

There were Macphails in various parts of Scotland, and when one looks up a book on the clans and septs of Scotland one finds them listed under Cameron or Mackay. This is not likely to be the case for the Lewis Macphails, who are more likely to have come from one or other or both of two famous progenitors called Paul.

There was Paul Mactire, a warrior Pict who lived in northwest Scotland, and was the terror of the neighbours to the south and east of him. The Rev. William Matheson tells me that 'Mactire' is an old Celtic word for the wolf, so he must have been 'Paul the Wolf' and evidently true to his name.

There was another Paul from whom they might have come, namely, Paul Balkesen, who ruled parts of Lewis and Skye under the authority of the king of Norway. This Paul quarrelled with the Norse power that held sway over the Hebrides from the Isle of Man, and he was finally slain in a sea-fight near the coast of Skye.

The Macphails made their power felt through the ages, and we find that they were used as wardens by the Macleods of Lewis and placed along the west coast, especially at Carloway, Shawbost and Bragar, to prevent the Macaulays of Uig from passing north to raid the Morrison territory. It was big John Macphail from the three-storied dùn at Bragar, the strong man of the west, that Brieve John hid on board the ship when he treacherously lured Torquil Dubh and Donald Cam Macaulay and their followers to drink the wine of the prize he had captured. This John Macphail paid dearly for his support when Donald escaped and got back to Uig, but that is another story.

In the forfeited estate papers 1726, we find three brothers sworn in as paying rent at Shawbost, where they are still known as Clann 'ic Dhonnachaidh, going back to some warrior called Duncan Macphail. Then we have the famous Peninsular War hero who came back with the scarlet silk shirt that had marvellous properties and who for years defied the press gang that often tried to lift him again for more service.

When the Macphails ceased from their wild ways, we find them, like the Morrisons, taking to the Church. There were three Macphail ministers outstanding in their day – Calum Macphail, minister of Kilmartin, who took down the traditions of the Morrisons of Ness from Angus Gunn of North Dell, for Captain W.F. Thomas, the archaeologist and surveyor; John Macphail, who was parish minister for so long at Balnakil, Uig, and Cross, Ness; and also Murdo Macphail who was for many years minister in Benbecula.

Air mo shon fhéin cha do thachair aon de Chlann 'ic Phàil rium, boirionn na firionn, nach toireadh sgarbh as a' chreig dhaibh fhéin, and I had a granny Macphail on my maternal side.

43

Iain Dòmhnullach a'Chaolais – Born 1800

JOHN MACDONALD WAS ENGAGED as a subfactor in Bernera. His grandfather was Niall Bhearnaraidh Bhig, on record as tacksman from 1773–1787 and married to Catriona nighean Dhòmhnuill Mhic Dhùghaill, an aunt of Dòmhnull MacSheòrais, tacksman of Linshader (Doctor Ruadh). They had a son Donald who succeeded at Little Bernera. His son was John Macdonald who built Tigh a' Chaoluis, worked for Donald Munro, and married Catherine Stewart of Hacleit. He had a son Murdo, who went to Mauritius, and his daughter, who married Dr Ross of Borve, was the prototype of the heroine of the 'Princess of Thule' in William Black's famous novel of that name.

44

'An Leine Shioda Sgarlaid'

A SEANNACHIE WHO HAD CONNECTIONS with Shawbost in his younger days gave me this story which he heard from his granny.

About the year 1780 there lived in Shawbost a warrior of the name of Calum Macphail, one of the tribe called Clann 'ic Dhonnachaidh, whose reputation for strength and ingenuity in getting out of tight corners had spread all over the Lewis of his day.

He had been one of the soldiers who had served overseas with the Seaforth Highlanders in Spain, and by some means or other had managed to get back to his native village. He had brought back with him among his belongings a silk shirt of a scarlet colour, and when he wore it on special occasions, he was the admiration of the ladies and the envy of the young men of the village.

This shirt began to have legends of the virtues and luck it would bring the wearer, and the young men vied with one another to get a loan of it to wear at a wedding or other gala occasion.

At this time there was a sabhal dannsa or special dance hall in Shawbost, which was much frequented by young and old – one must remember the Calvinist type of religion did not start in Lewis till 1824 when Rev. Alexr Macleod came to Balnacille.

Calum took full advantage of the reputation of the scarlet silk shirt, for there was none other of its kind then in Lewis. On one occasion he got one of the gallants to go to the Beinn Mhór to rescue a sheep that had fallen on to a ledge. He climbed down the rock face and draping the injured sheep round his neck and shoulders, he lowered himself with his burden to safety, and walked the four or five miles home with it to the village.

Calum got all sorts of messages and unpleasant chores done for him for a loan of the scarlet garment.

The press gang came to Lewis looking for Calum Macphail, and he had to take to the moor and hide himself in a concealed bothy he made in one of the deep clefts high up on Beinn Choinnich. From there, for a whole spring and part of early summer, he used to come at night and turn over with the cas chrom the parts of the croft which his wife and family had spread with manure during the day. He had periods of fasting and discomfort, but when he got a meal, a gigot of mutton was just an ordinary helping for him, and a portion of fish was on the same lavish scale.

He got very tired of this hide and seek sort of existence, and one morning when he landed from his boat on the sands below Loch a' Bhaile after an all night fishing, four of the press gang surrounded him, and advancing on his would-be captors shouting 'beatha na has bhios ann' he laid about him with the oar, cracking heads and delivering fearful punishment, so that they were forced to retire, and ever after this he was left unmolested.

He was known in Shawbost by the nickname of 'Beatha na Bàs' after this fight.

The seannachie's granny was very proud of the fact that he was one of the best whisky distillers in the west, and many a drain did Calum Macphail give to his cronies. But a day came when he, along with two others, was caught red-handed with their black pot and copper worm in a cave in the rocks below Fivig, for the gaugers had either spotted the smoke of their fire or someone had informed.

Calum Macphail and his pals were sentenced to a whole year in Inverness for making whisky from his own barley and God's water percolating through the cave at Fivig. But for all this the granny was very proud of her grandfather Calum Macphail.

45

The Men Were Precious

WHILE ON A HOLIDAY in the Black Isle I paid a visit to the ruined Cathedral of Fortrose where the Seaforths lie at rest.

From the inscriptions on their tombstones I was set thinking how little we Lewismen know of what they did for us and our town, especially the last and 7th Lord Seaforth, his daughter and son-in-law, James Alexander Stewart Mackenzie.

This Lord Seaforth succeeded his father in 1761 – he was called Francis Humberston Mackenzie. He is the subject of Coinneach Odhar's famous prophecy, and he is also Sir Walter Scott's 'high chief of Kintail'.

He was a soldier, rising to the rank of Colonel, and in spite of severe deafness he did much useful work for the government of the day. According to Lord Teignmouth, his acquirements, classical taste and erudition, powers of conversation, urbanity and liberality, rendered him the delight of every society in which he appeared, the pride of his clansmen and the ornament of his country.

The principal residence of Lord Seaforth was Brahan Castle near Dingwall, but this Seaforth took more interest in his island possession and came frequently to live at Seaforth Lodge overlooking the town and harbour of Stornoway.

He visited the country areas of Lewis and saw that it was in a very backward state. He got an expert geologist, the Rev. Mr

Headrick, to write him a full report on the rocks, soil, fishings and hunting possibilities of the Lews. He also personally went among the people, and with his winning ways coaxed many of them to enlist in a regiment he was raising called the 78th, and which afterwards became the Seaforth Highlanders.

An amusing story is told of him about this time. The women of Lewis were compelled to submit to much drudgery from which the women of the south were exempt. It was then the practice in this island for the men to be carried on the backs of the women across the fords so that they would not wet their feet while paying a visit to the big town and so remain in wet socks all day. The men were very precious to the women! Lord Seaforth arrived at a stream on horseback while a peasant so mounted was very contentedly crossing. He rode up to the man just as his fair hack had reached mid-channel, and then laid his whip across his back and shoulders with such vigour that he quickly dropped off, clad in all his finery into the water.

It was this Seaforth who started the first road across the island in 1791 – that was to Barvas, but Hogg, the Ettrick shepherd, tells us in 1803 that only ten miles of it was made and that it petered out in a morass and left him to walk the rest of the way to Barvas across difficult and boggy moor.

The ways of the Leodhasachs were very crude in those days and their houses were wretched, and to give him credit this chief tried to improve our manners and set up a school in Stornoway to teach us the fine ways of the better classes in the south, especially those of the elite of Edinburgh. He had a large family of sons and daughters, but they all died before him except his daughter, Mary Frederica Elisabeth.

Lord Seaforth died in 1815 and was succeeded by this daughter Mary.

46

James Alexander Stewart Mackenzie

FRANCIS HUMBERSTON MACKENZIE, 7th Lord Seaforth, died in 1815 leaving his daughter Mary Frederica Elizabeth as the head of Clan Kenneth. She was known to the people of my grandfather's time as Lady Hood Mackenzie, for in 1804 she married Admiral Hood, a naval friend of Nelson's, who had fought with him at Trafalgar. He died in 1814.

She married, as her second husband, James Alexander Stewart of Glasserton, a grandson of the 6th Earl of Galloway, and he took on the surname of Mackenzie to please his wife, and so that there might be male heirs of the surname of Clan Kenneth carrying on the proud name of Kintail at Brahan Castle.

This is the man that Stornoway has to thank for putting our town on the map, for it was a little village when he came to the island. It was he and his lady who started the great improvements and progress which are still going on. Lord Teignmouth tells us that the business men of Stornoway, who had their big houses on Point Street then, were not applying themselves to the pursuit of the fishing as they ought, and tended to be lazy and put things off too often till another day, and so the fishing was at a standstill and the kelp industry had failed also.

Mr Stewart Mackenzie, no doubt profiting by the Rev. Mr Headrick's report to his late father-in-law, took the superintendence of the fisheries of the island into his own hands and started to fish herrings by the drift net system in the Minch. He also built the first cod smack to take fish alive in salt water in its hold direct to London. Teignmouth says – 'The cod smacks are capital sailing vessels well manned and well appointed; they vary in size, from 50 to 60 tons, and are rigged as sloops, and the crew are well accommodated on board. Each vessel contains a well for the reception of live fish, of which the cargo sometimes amounts to ninety score.' Seven trading vessels belonged to Stornoway and their captains were Liverpool-trained seamen.

Lewis had been a bit of a poor Cinderella to the Seaforths, but now Stewart-Mackenzie and his lady spent less time at Brahan Castle and stayed for longer periods of the year at Seaforth Lodge where Lewis Castle now stands.

Great stretches of peatmoss near Stornoway were dug and drain-pipes laid down, so that new arable ground was formed – the ground behind Newton, and along the canal by the Sandwick road, and out to Mossend, must have been reclaimed at this time. Many short roads and paths were made or improved leading to the country villages. A distillery which in those days cost £14,000, was constructed at the Shoeburn, in order to stop the excessive illegal distilling that went on all over the island and which was ruining the health and morals of the people. This distillery went on for quite a number of years. The manager was a Mr Macnee who must have been generous and given good measure, for the phrase 'tomhas mhór Mhic Ni' persisted in Gaelic in Stornoway until my time, when anyone gave extra measure of anything; and a man in my youth who had a wholesale business in liquor, was known as 'Calum an tigh-staille', for he had worked in the distillery.

The Mackenzies tried to improve the manners and education of the Stornoway youth by setting up a school of the higher and more genteel kind; this was apart from the existing church schools. They also taught the spinning and weaving of linen cloths and the country people were encouraged to grow flax for this purpose, but the scheme never caught on. It was Mrs Stewart-Mackenzie who was the means of sending to Balnacille in Uig, Alexander Macleod – the first evangelical minister who did so much to stir up the people with his fiery eloquence. He is also the minister who sold the ivory chessmen in 1831 to the British Museum.

Mr Stewart-Mackenzie had a bank and counting house of his own, and we can still see a few of his £1 notes payable at Stornoway – good currency of that day, preserved as curios in several offices and homes in town. He became MP for Ross-shire, and made a name for himself as an orator and administrator at Westminster, and he was appointed governor of Ceylon.

There were great assemblies of the mandarins of Stornoway and their ladies in the Masonic Hall of the day, and I am sure the residence of the laird for such long periods at Seaforth Lodge did a great deal to tone down the rougher methods inherited from earlier and more uncertain times. Our James Street is named in his honour, as Francis Street is named in memory of his father-in-law.

Mr Stewart-Mackenzie died in 1843, and is buried in Fortrose Cathedral. Next year, 1844, the widow sold Seaforth Lodge and the island of Lewis to Mr James Matheson of Jardine Matheson and Company, for the sum of £190,000. He had come home from China with a million of money to spend. There was no male heir left to become the chief of Clan Kenneth, for they all died in infancy, and Mrs Stewart-Mackenzie betook herself to Brahan Castle where she died in 1862. She is buried beside her husband in Fortrose Cathedral.

47

The Inn at Loch Shell

I HAVE READ WITH great interest the letters which have appeared in the recent issues of the *Gazette* about the Inn at Loch Shell, and I wish to add what I have read about it and the Park area, and also to correct some of the dates given.

When the Mackenzies first settled in Lewis the chief built himself a stronghold at the head of Loch Seaforth, and when the earldom was bestowed the title of Earl of Seaforth was taken from this place. The residence known as Seaforth Lodge, near where Lewis Castle now stands, was not built till long afterwards.

One writer about 1680 tells us that MacKenzie who then owned Lewis had a high wall built across the neck of land between Loch, Erisort and Loch Seaforth as he wished to shut in the Park area and reserve it as a private hunting forest for his own pleasure. I am told the ruins of the old stronghold at Seaforth Head and the remains of the deer wall can still be seen.

Were some of the little clachans cleared then to give solitude and sanctuary to the animals Seaforth wished to hunt?

In 1797 Mr Simpson wrote the Old Statistical Account of the parish of Lochs. In 1800 the Rev. Mr Headrick wrote a report for Lord Seaforth, and he advised getting the natives to go out into the Minch and fish the herring by drift net (Dutch fashion), for he had seen vast shoals in the Minch, and for several seasons the fishing in the Lochs had failed.

Anyone who has seen the etching by Daniell of Stornoway Bay with Seaforth Lodge in 1819 cannot but be struck by the great number of sailing ships which are in the harbour. Most of them were on their way from Norway to Larne in North Ireland, and put into Stornoway for shelter, and also to buy stores of salt pork, which was a speciality of the butchers in the town. These ships when met with contrary winds often put into Loch Shell, and you may be sure that the crews went ashore and called at the inn.

Lord Teignmouth was in Stornoway in 1829, for he was at the famous funeral of Mary Carn, and visited the Rev. Mr Simpson at Keose and from there he went to Valamas and thence surveyed the Shiants, and it was then, and not in 1841, he landed at the inn, where he got such an inhospitable reception.

The Rev. Mr Simpson died in 1830, and so Lord Teignmouth could not have been entertained by him in 1841. I know that Lord Teignmouth's memoirs were printed in 1836.

The heads of Lochs Isginn and Shell are quite a distance apart, but Loch Shell Head is stated by Lord Teignmouth to have an inn where whisky might be obtained. The Rev. Robt Finlayson was transferred from Knock in 1831 and it was he who wrote the Second Statistical Account of the Parish in 1833, and he definitely says there was a slated roof on the inn at Loch Shell.

Capt. Otter's map was quite correct in showing a house at Eishken where the boathouse is now, for the late Mrs Platt, who was a good friend of mine, told me that she and her husband lived in it when first they came to Lewis, and that her husband had built the present lodge to her own design.

If Loch Isginn was called Loch Shell in those days then the inn may have been that house, but one would think that the Rev. Mr Finlayson would not have mixed them up.

Mr Roderick Macrae, the brother of the keeper, says there are ruins at Shell Head which he heard old men calling 'làrach tigh-òsda Loch Sheilg'.

48

At Seaforth Lodge, Stornoway –
August, 1786

Hᴇʀᴇ ɪꜱ ᴀ ꜱᴛᴏʀʏ that may be of interest, for it gives us a peep at the ways of the gentry who lived at Seaforth Lodge in the year 1786.

A certain Mr John Knox had been sent 'to investigate and report on suitable bays and islets on which to erect fishing stations along the west coast of Scotland and in the Hebrides', by the gentlemen of the British Society for Extending the Fisheries, etc., and he became a guest of Lord Seaforth at Seaforth Lodge in August 1786. He tells us that Seaforth Lodge is built on a lawn that rises gradually from the head of the bay, and being perfectly white, produced a good effect.

Stornoway was divided into two towns, one for traders and the other for fishermen. The first was built upon a peninsula jutting into the bay, with the houses close to the beach and 'is accommodated with a church, custom-house, and a good inn'. The population of the whole island was about 9,000.

'The Lewis now pays £2,500 rental by means of improvements in agriculture, fisheries, and kelp, of which about 200 tons of excellent quality is made chiefly on the west side of the Lews.'

Seaforth's principal residence was at Brahan Castle, near Dingwall, but he resided at Stornoway with his family two or three months every summer, 'where he enjoys more than Asiatic luxury', in the simple produce of his forest (Park), his heaths and his shores. His factor had a long lease of the Creed fishery, but Seaforth was supplied from the bay called Loch Tua (our Stenish and Tong pools) with salmon. An expedition led by the proprietor was set on foot, nets were provided, and Mr Knox and some other gentlemen accompanied him to Broad Bay.

Here is an extract from the journal:

August 17th, 1786 – Hauled only the Little Pool once. Caught – salmon, 29; trout, 128; flounders, 1,468.

August 18th, 1786 – Hauled both Great and Little Pool once – Great Pool, 139 salmon; 528 trout; a few flounders. Little Pool – 5 salmon; about 100 trout; 500 flounders.

August 23rd, 1786 – Hauled both pools once. Did not count the fish separately, but the whole were – 143 salmon; 143 trout; and the flounders I did not count, but they were a great heap, about 7 or 800. Every day an immense number of herrings, sprats, and cuddies were caught.

How do these numbers compare with the totals in 1958?

From what Mr Knox tells us they seem to have fed very well at Seaforth Lodge. He gives the items for breakfast:

A dram of whisky, gin, rum or brandy, plain or infused with berries that grow among the heath. French rolls, oat and barley bread; tea or coffee; honey in the comb; red and blackcurrant jellies; marmalade, conserves and excellent cream. Fine flavoured butter, fresh and salted; Cheshire and Highland cheese, the last very indifferent. A plateful of very fresh eggs. Fresh and salted herrings broiled. Fresh and salted haddocks and whitings, the skin being taken off. Cold round of venison, beef, and mutton hams.

Besides these articles which were placed on the table there was usually cold beef and moor-fowl for anyone who wished to ask for them.

After breakfast the men amused themselves with the gun, fishing or sailing, till the evening, when they dined, at which meal even more luxurious and elaborate food was produced.

A packet went from Stornoway to Poolewe, on the opposite coast, every fortnight, but when Seaforth was in residence it went once a week. Mr Knox took the opportunity of getting to the mainland of Ross by this vessel.

49

Suggestions for Stornoway – 1800

MANY OF THE IMPROVEMENTS to our town and harbour were discussed in a report by the Rev. Mr Headrick to Lord Seaforth in 1800.

Read what he says:

> The increase and prosperity of the town of Stornoway must contribute much to raise the value of your Lordship's property. The Stornowayans should bring water into the town by pipes laid across the bay. A proper mill to make pot-barley would prove highly useful there. Were the country opened by roads, weekly markets should be established, and no article of provisions permitted, under severe penalties, to be sold in the town, except in the public market. Were regular markets and the fattening of cattle and hogs established, vessels could depend upon a supply of meat either fresh or pickled, and on cheaper terms than they could get in the port from which they sailed.
>
> At present the people of Stornoway keep too many hogs, which literally devour each other, and are a great nuisance. At the fishing-places many hogs might be reared on the garbage of fish, and fed off on yams or potatoes.
>
> But what would crown the prosperity of Stornoway and contribute highly to the improvement of the Island of Lewis would be the construction of a proper harbour or quay to which vessels of all magnitudes might lay their sides.

In a footnote I found out that in 1814, '15, '16, a quay of very handsome dimensions, and very efficiently built, was erected by voluntary subscriptions among the merchants of Stornoway, unassisted by any public or outside aid whatsoever. This was made easy, for there was a natural ridge of rock stretching from the old castle of the Macleods to what is called the Stone point today, which only required the smoothing of the face of rock and filling in a few gaps to make a natural quay. A few jetties were also built along the west side of the town.

He further adds:

> If afterwards found requisite to accommodate more shipping, the Green Island might be joined by a jetty to the mainland, and the whole eastern basin converted into a harbour encircled by a quay.
>
> Should such a project be entered into, the first thing that should engage the attention of subscribers is the erection of a buoy or perch on the point of the rock which runs below the sea from Arnish and another on the sunken rocks* in the northern entrance of the bay. These would render the harbour at all times accessible, even to the most ignorant strangers, and without the aid of a pilot.

I find that Mrs Stewart Mackenzie in 1816 got the Board of Lights to send Mr Stevenson, the father of R.L.S. and the builder of the Skerryvore Lighthouse, up to survey the reef sticking into the bay from Arnish point and that a beacon was to be erected on the outermost end.

---

* The Sgeir Mhór.

50

The Lewis Chessmen –
Recovered in 1831 at Ardroil –
by Rev. A.J. MacKenzie

THIS STORY USED TO BE TOLD in a ceilidh house near the old
sanctuary of Balnacille when Rev. MacKenzie was a boy, but
there are other variations of the tale:

The beginning of the seventeenth century saw the end of
the war between the Macleods and the MacKenzies for the
possession of Lewis. Neil Macleod had been beguiled from his
island fortress of Beirisay, taken to Edinburgh, and executed at
the market cross in 1613, and the direct line of the Siol Torquil
came to an end soon afterwards.

When the MacKenzies took over in 1610, clansmen from
Kintail followed the chief who gave them farmlands, and among
them was Calum Mór, noted for his skill as an archer and swordsman. To him the chief gave Baile-na-Cille (Balnacille), and also
some rough pasture in the Ard Mhór beyond the mountains
which shut in Uig, and here in summer his cattle used to graze
in a long glen strewn with great boulders through the hills all
along to Loch Hamnavay. The cattle were in charge of the Gille
Ruadh or red gillie, and on one of the days he was herding
the cattle he climbed to the top of Ardmore, and lo! he saw
a ship riding at anchor in the loch below. There was no sign
of life anywhere. He hid himself in an alcove in a cairn, and
watched to see what would happen. At moonrise he noticed a
small dinghy being rowed to the shore, from which a sailor boy

jumped to land holding a weighty bundle. The place where the boat came ashore is still called *Gleann-na-Curach*. The red gillie watched the boy and from his movements judged he wanted to get away from that ship. The red gillie left his hiding place and by a roundabout route met the boy at the bend of the glen where the river sweeps past the great boulders of Diuire (Guire).

The red gillie spoke to the boy, who told him he was tired of living with a rough crew and had made up his mind to escape though he did not know what kind of country he was in, but he thought any land would be better than living with the kind of drunken sots that comprised the crew. As he had no money, he had taken away the playthings with which the sailors amused themselves, hoping to be able to sell them later on. The red gillie was most kind and took the boy into the shelter of the cave formed of boulders where he was told the boy's story about the bundle, and 'once again as ten million million times it had happened before and as ten million times it will happen again, the wicked prospered and the righteous suffered: but the wicked shall not prosper for ever, says the Great Book.' The herd servant, overcome by greed and a desire to own the bundle, attacked the boy, killed him and buried him in the cavern.

The red gillie set out for home and arrived just as the first pale gleam of dawn was tingeing the sky. He hid the bundle of treasure, and some time later when his master appeared, he told him about the ship at Ard Mhór and suggested that he – the master – should take some of his men and plunder her before she set sail again for the open sea. The master, Calum Mór, was horrified, and sternly commanded him never again to show his face within sight of the lands of Balnacille. Thus he was prevented from unearthing his treasure, which he had buried in the sands of Uig, for he never saw these sands again. He tried his fortune around Stornoway, where he was caught redhanded in a dastardly deed for which he was hanged on Gallows Hill. The Lord Kintail raised this new erection – the gallows – on the hill across the bay opposite the ancient stronghold of the Siol Torquil. Among a long list of crimes to which the red gillie confessed was the story of the sailor boy and his treasure bundle. No one would believe his story and so the sand dunes of Uig kept the secret of the buried treasure.

Then one day in 1831 Malcolm Macleod of Penny Donald, known as Calum nan Sprot, was herding his cattle amongst the sand dunes when he saw one of the beasts rubbing itself against a baca gainmhich and acting in a queer manner, so he went along to investigate and saw her pull out some whitish objects with her horn. He lifted some of them up and examined them, and took them to be idols or graven images of some kind which he did not understand. A gentleman from Stornoway heard of the discovery and came over and dug out all the pieces, for Calum nan Sprot would meddle no more with them. There were eighty pieces in all, and when they were put into a creel they made a substantial burden for a man.

They were taken to Stornoway, and at length found their way to the museums of London and Edinburgh where they can be seen to this day. Incidentally, Calum nan Sprot, who showed some scruples about having the 'idols' in his possession, had no scruples about taking a reward for his discovery. He received thirty pounds! Thus after the lapse of more than two hundred years, the hidden treasure of an unknown sailor boy who had been treacherously done to death by the red-haired handyman in the fastness of the Ard Mhór, was again brought to light, and the truth of an old sgeulachd substantiated.

There remains now to add a coincidence to this tale. Nearly another century passed, and one wild winter's day the writer, the late Rev. A.J. MacKenzie, and a friend were exploring the Ard Mhór, and while a violent storm was passing, they took shelter in a cave formed by a cairn of glacial boulders. The curious arrangement of the stones on which they were sitting caught their attention, for it was obvious they had been placed there by human agency. They began to remove them one by one, and presently they came upon a human skull and a heap of bones. Two jagged holes in the top of the skull showed clearly the owner had met with a violent death. There was only one conclusion to be drawn; they had discovered the grave of the sailor boy, in which he had lain for three hundred years. Unknown to the men of old, in the midst of whose bounds he had met his death, the cavern in which the grim tragedy had been enacted kept its secret well. Then after three hundred years his grave opens and he comes into the ken of the living. Truly a remarkable instance of the truth of that saying, which belongs to a sacred context, 'He being dead yet speaketh.'

The Uig Chessmen – Na Fir Tailisg

Bha sinn sàmhach fo'n an tom
Gus na lorg bó na h-adhairc sinn,
Tha sinn a nis fada thall
'Nar call aig Eilean Leódhais!
'S gur call do Eilean Leódhais e
Rìghrean, ridirean, easbuig is ban-rìgh
'S gillean beag ann 'n am pàin,
'S gur móir an call e Leódhas!

Calum Maclean, Conon Bridge

51

The Eleven Chessmen in Edinburgh

Proceedings of the Society of Antiquaries Scotland,
1888–89, page 9

THIS VERSION SAYS THAT the chessmen were found in a chamber built of drystone in a sandbank, Uig Bay. The chessmen, seventy-eight pieces, fourteen draughtsmen, one buckle, all carved out of walrus tusk ivory, were partly covered with sand on the floor of the chamber. There was also a quantity of ashes with them. They came into the possession of a Mr Roderick Pirie, Merchant, Stornoway, by whom they were brought to Edinburgh and exhibited to the Society of Antiquaries Scotland at their meeting 11th April, 1831. The natural result would have been for that society to acquire the whole hoard, but *Arch. Scot.*, Vol. IV, p. 376, says:

> It was proposed at the time by a few of the members to make a joint purchase of the entire collection, and after setting aside a certain number for the Society's museum to apportion the rest among those contributing. By some oversight this arrangement was not carried out, and a dealer in curiosities in Edinburgh purchased them. The greater number of the hoard were afterwards sold to the British Museum [the ticket on those in the British Museum says, 'sold by Rev. Alexander Macleod, Minister, Balnacille, Uig, Lewis, 1831']. Ten of the pieces had, however, been selected from the collection by a Mr C. Sharpe before being offered to the British Museum. An additional piece, a bishop, was sent on to Mr Sharpe from Lewis, making the collection in Scotland, eleven pieces, ie.,

two Kings, three Queens, three Bishops, one Knight, two Warders (Castle or Rook). On the death of Mr Sharpe his collection was put up for sale in Edinburgh, and the eleven pieces were bought by Lord Londesborough. When Lord Londesborough's collection was exposed for sale in London, the eleven chessmen were acquired by the Society of Antiquaries Scotland and are now in the National Museum, Edinburgh. Forty-eight chessmen in the British Museum are described by Sir Frederick Madden in *Archaeologia*, Vol. XXIV, p. 203.

52

Seanchasan

THA NA SEANCHASAN SO AIR an aithris mu Bhan tighearna Siophort agus a fear-tagraidh glic, Iain MacGillinnein. Bha a' Bhan-tighearna ag agairt gum biodh teanga ùr mairt aice air a dìneir gach là de'n bliadhna, Shaoil MacGill Innein gu robh sin ro-chosdail agus bha e airson dearbhadh a thoirt di air an. anacaitheamh a bha i a' dèanamh. Shaodaich e leis a Cinn t-Sàile, dròbh chruidh anns an robh trì chiad, trì fichead 'sa cóig, agus chuir e iad cruinn còmhla air lianaidh mu choinneamh Caisteal Bhrathainn. Ghabh a' Bhan-tighearna iongnadh mór an uair a chunnaic i an dròbh mór chruidh sin an aon àite agus thubhairt Mac G-I. rithe gum be sud dìreach an àireamh chruidh a dh'fheumte mharbhadh anns a' bliadhna airson teanga ùr mairt a chumail air a bòrd gach là. Chan 'eil e air aithris ciod e a'bhuaidh a bha aig an achmhasan sin air a' Bhan-tighearna.

B'e Murchadh MacGillinnein aon de thriuir bhràithrean aig an robh Beàrnaraigh Bheag agus Croir eatorra. B'iadsan mic MacMhurchaidh Mac a' Chléirich, a bha fuireach an Cinn t-Sàile Mhic Coinnich, agus a thaobh is gu robh iadsan glic seaghail agus tùrail, bha meas mór aig Siophort, uchdaran Chinn t-Sàile orra. Bha eud aig Siphort ris na mic aig MacAlhurchaidh, agus do brìgh sin is ann a thogair e MacGillinein a dhol gu fearann an Circibost am Bearnaraigh, agus thug e Tolostadh a' Chaolais da airson fiarach samhraidh, agus Beàrnaraigh Bheag is Croir do a thriuir mhac. Bha aramach eadar an dithis a bha am Bearnaraigh Bheag agus bhuadhaich bean an fhir a bha an Croir air airson imrich a dhèanamh gu. Nis, an t-àite anns an deachaidh a togail. Air an t-slighe an sin le bàta lan eòrna, chaidh am fuadach o'n chladach le stoirm agus bha dùil gun do chailleadh e. Fada, fada an déidh sin choinnich Captein soithich a Steòrnabhagh e an Gottenberg agus thug e stocain làn de bhuinn òir do'n Chaiptein airson an toir do a bhràthair Murchadh ann am Beàrnabhaidh Bheag. B'e Murchadh sin sì-seanair Iain agus b'e a phiuthar sì-seanamhair Ruairidh MhicNeacáil fear luingeas an Steòruabhagh, 's b'e a mhac a thug pàirt de'n airgiod a chuir air bonn Sgoil MhicNeacail ann an Steòrnabhagh, sgoil a thug cothrom fòghluim luachmhoir do òigridh Leódhais.

B'i Catriona Stiubhairt, nighean Choinnich Stiubhairt, Fear Hacleit, Bean Iain Dòmhnullaich a' Chaolais. Is ann as an Eilean Sgitheanach a bha Coinneach, agus bha e 'na dhlùth-charaid do'n Urr. Uisdean Macleòid a 'na bha 'na mhinistear an Uige. B'i Màiri, nighean Fhearchair Mhic a' Ghobhainn, Fear Iarsiadar, a bu mhàthair do Bheann Ian D. B'e Fearchar sin mac Dhonnachaidh Mhic-Fhearchair Ghobhainn a thàinig as na Lochan agus a phòs Barabal nighean Iain MhicIllinnoin à Cinn-t-Sàile air an d'rinn sinn iomradh cheana. Mar sin bha Iain agus a bhcan càirdeach da chach a chéile, troimh nan Linneineach: a bharrachd air sin bha fear bho na Lochan càirdeach do theaghlach mo mhàthar (an Dotair Ros) clann Mhic-Leòid, Bhaltois, agus mar sin bha càirdeas fad' as eadar mis (Ros) is Bean Iain Dòmhnullaich.

(The following lines are from a poem composed for the late Gia MacKenzie's granny, who was one of the Stewarts of Hacleit Farm in Bernera, Lewis. Gia's father was Mac Chaluim mhic Ruairidh – Siadair. Another of Stewart's daughters married Iain Macdonald of the Caolas, and another one eloped to Canada with her father's grieve. Their grandson came over with the Canadians. Mrs Maclean, the Coffee House, and the first wife of Peter Smart were sisters of Gia's father (a Mackenzie), and daughters of the subject of the song):

Horó cha bhi mi 'gad chaoidh nis mò
Ma thréig thu mise cha lughaid orm thu;
Nan tigeadh tu fhathasd bu tu m m'aighear 'smo rùn,
'S nam faighinn do litir gu ruiginn thu'n Uig.
Ged tha mi'n Ardhàsig fo shàile nam beann
A' cur a bhuntàta 's ag àiteach gu trang,
Chan 'eil mi fo thàire do 'n té bhàin a tha thall,
Ged ghabh i fear-ceird' bhios a ghnàth ris an dram.
Thoir'n t-soraidh, ceud soraidh,
Thoir an t-soraidh so bhuam
A null air an linne,
Far 'eil osnaich a' chuain,
Far na dh 'fhàg mi mo leannan
Caol mhala gun ghruaim
'S gur cùbhraidh leam t'anail.
Na'n canach 'ga bhuain.

53

The Ship with the Cargo of Iron

THIS IS THE WAY an Uig seannachie told me the story of 'Long an Iaruinn', in the Gaelic. In the year 1775, two cailleachs were admiring the physique of a big negro who was lying before the fire in a house in Carnish. He was in a sleep of exhaustion, snoring fit to drive the cows out of the corn.

The poor man was among the few survivors from a ship that had gone aground during the night on the skerries at the point of Carnish.

All night the people round Uig Bay had listened to their cries of woe and to their frightful screaming, as piece after piece broke away from the ship and the crew were being washed overboard; but they could do nothing to help them, for no boat could live in those awful waves and the night was inky black. She was a big ship, and had come into Camus Uig the evening before, and had taken shelter in the lea of an islet called Sgeir Sheilibhig, putting out two anchors for further safety. She probably needed a quiet period to mend her sails after battling with the wild storms in the Western Ocean, or for some other reason. Anyway the wind began to get stronger as night came on, and by midnight it was blowing a howling gale right into Uig Bay. She began to drag the two anchors until she scudded before it, gaining momentum all the time, until she struck on a sunken 'bogha' with such force that she gave off a loud clang as of metal being struck, so that all in the houses of Carnish and Crowlista heard the noise. This was a mortal blow for it ripped part of her timbers off, then she scurried with renewed force on to the sharp fangs of the skerry at Carnish Point, where the mighty billows kept on tearing her asunder, but she was well out from the land, and no human being could get to her on such a night of doom. Most of the crew perished, but as any survivors were rolled up on the beach they were immediately taken up by the Uigeachs above the wave's force, as much water shaken out of them as possible, and if any sign of life showed, they were chafed and rubbed and wrapped in blankets and carried up to the houses in Carnish, where they were laid on pallets of straw, which had been prepared for them in front of big blazing fires. They seemed to be of different nationalities, and among them was the handsome black man, who had caused so much admiration and astonishment in the village of Carnish that morning, yet on recovering they could not make themselves understood, for none of the survivors could speak either English or Gaelic. The people of Carnish did all they could for them in the way of food, warmth and clothing. The ship is one of the mysteries of Uig folk lore, for her name was never found out, nor where she had come from, nor where she was going.

For several days after that disaster the sea kept giving up the bodies of the poor, unfortunate seamen, for many more were drowned than were rescued. They were gathered together and taken to a very ancient cemetery within the bounds of Timsgarry, not far from Balnacille, called Cladh a' Ghàraidh Mhóir, and were all buried in one big grave. There they lie, at rest in a beautiful green spot, looking across the great sands of Uig with Mealasbhal and the hills of Ardroil in the background; a haven anyone would like to have reached as their last port of call. The seannachie was wondering why they were not buried in the consecrated ground at St Christopher's at Balnacille. The reason was that Daoine uasal Uig, the males of the Clan Macaulay, looked upon this cemetery as their own sacred private burial ground, and when they insisted that their own womenfolk should be buried in Valtos cemetery, they were certainly not going to have the bodies of drowned strange foreign sailors interred within that special sacred acre of theirs. The real name of the ship will never be known, but the wreck on the skerries of Carnish disclosed that she was loaded with iron hence she is handed down as Long an Iaruinn and the sunken rock which caused such a metallic-sounding crash is called Bogha an Iaruinn, and the sharp fangs of rock off Carnish Point upon which she was beaten to pieces belong to Sgeir an Iaruinn.

54

'An T-Ainmean' – A Blood Libation

A MAN FROM THE UPPER END of Uig has told me about a curious ritual that used to be practised in the Brenish area called 'performing the t-ainmean'. His grandfather knew the last man chosen to offer the libation, a man of the surname of MacKinnon. This offering was made to a god of the sea, so that this powerful deity would send abundance of fishes close inshore where they could be caught from the rocks by rod and line.

The performance of the an t-ainmean was carried out at the end of the summer, and the blood of the first animal slaughtered that season was collected in a vessel, and one of the villagers was chosen for dèanamh an t-ainmean as it was called,

This individual walked out to the extreme tip of the longest peninsula carrying the vessel of blood, and baring his head he said a weird incantation, poured out the sanguinary libation, and hoped Manaan mac Lìr would answer his request for plenty fish for the coming season.

Compare this ceremony with the worship of Shony at the Teampull Mor at Eoropie as told us by Martin Martin, but there the libation was of home-brewed ale in exchange for plenty of seaweed to fertilise the land. This ceremony was a survival from the pagan times and would have been carried out behind the ministers' backs.

Was the ceremony of performing the t-ainmean known in any other part of our island of Lewis?

The surname of MacKinnon was scarce in Uig, and my informant tells me that it was introduced by Donald Cam MacD-hùghaill, when he saved the life of a man and woman and a male child from a ship, which he and others had captured and plundered, as they were the only ones aboard who could speak Gaelic and their surname was MacKinnon. He gave them a portion of land in Brenish for their support. The child was very intelligent and was taught the arts of swordsmanship and archery by Donald himself, and he afterwards became his close friend and bodyguard, and was known as Iain Dubh Chròig.

55

A Peep at Uig, 1749

YOU WILL BE INTERESTED to know what the minister of the parish of Uig wrote to his superiors in 1749 when there was a movement to increase the stipend of parish ministers in the Highlands.

He says that the stipend of the parish amounted to 800 merks Scots money, paid one half at Martinmas and the other at Whitsunday by Lord Seaforth, sole heritor of the parish. No allowance for the Communion elements was granted to the minister, so thirty shillings of his stipend was used for that purpose.

The fuel for the manse was difficult to obtain and made big inroads into the 773 merks left of his stipend.

Secondly, he says his parish extended to eighteen miles from Mealista in the west to 'Dunmelossie' on the east side, and ten miles from Balnacille on the north side to Kinresort on the south side, where it terminated with the country of Harris. In the parish there were four islands, namely: Bernera Mor, Bernera Beag, Bhuidha Mhor and Pabbay; the passage to these was at all the seasons of the year very dangerous, and on that account in order to discharge his duties the minister was forced to keep a large boat with a crew of six men, which every year cost him not less than 160 merks Scots and so reduced his stipend to about 613 merks Scots per annum.

Two great arms of the sea, he writes, divide this parish. One of them called Loch Roag runs ten miles long up towards the mountains at Kinloch, and the other seven miles long running eastwards to Kinhulavaig, and both these arms of the sea 'are very throng inhabited on all sides and corners'. He also says that in his parish there were 'three broad rivers seldom passable but in summer time of the year'.

He does not mention any paths, bridges or roads anywhere, and makes the picture as gloomy and as difficult as he can. He says that he has to preach at Little and Big Bernera on every third Sabbath, and that there are sixty-seven families with 180 examinable persons living in them. In Bhuida Mhor and Pabbay in the bosom of Loch Roag where the sea can be mighty rough, he has to attend to five families and eighteen examinable persons. There are in his parish, counting the inhabitants of these four islands, 259 families making a total of 1,247 souls, and of these 1,053 were examinable persons, but of that whole number

> there are not eight souls young or old that can read the scriptures, and have neither school nor catechist, or never had in my time among them, nor could I have obtained it, although I oftener than once made application for it, as this being the most remote parish on this side of Scotland.
>
> The case of these starving souls might challenge sympathy and charity at the hands of the managers of the Royal Bounty, and the members of the Committee for Propagating Christian Knowledge in our Highlands and Islands.

In the third place he says the tithes of the country are paid in cows and sheep distinct from land rent and tack duties, and are all let out to a tacksman, one John Maciver, living at Dalmore, who pays the rental in Scots money to my Lord Seaforth, and there are three years yet to run of this tack agreement 'from Whitsunday last 1749'.

> The King is patron of all the parishes in the Island, and the whole land rents and tack duties of this parish from the tithes and casualties amount to the sum of 6,239 merks 12s and 4d Scots money. There are no vacant parishes in this country; all our parishes are planted.

This is the substance of the report signed at Uig on the 15th day of October, 1749, by 'your affectionate brother and most humble servant in the Lord, Norman Morrison.'

56

The Wizard of Holm

A BOUT THE YEAR 1800 there lived at Holm an old man whose reputation for white wizardry and wise forecasts had become known all over the Long Island. He was known in the Gaelic as Fiosaiche Thuilm (the Holm Wizard).

At that time there lived in the hamlet of Miavaig in Uig a very knowing man of the name of Iain Macaoidh, who in his young days had been a sailor and had visited most of the countries of the world. He it was whose cows one morning suddenly went dry and acted in a peculiar manner without any visible cause. The evil eye of some neighbour or passer-by was suspected, and after a family conclave had discussed the loss of the milk for some time, it was decided that Iain Macaoidh himself must go and put the case before the skilful Wizard of Holm.

There was no road from Uig to Stornoway in those days, but he set out to walk all the thirty-nine miles to Holm to consult the famous fiosaiche. Making for Port-na-h-aiseig at Unguishader, he got a ferry to the Scaliscro shore, and from there he made his way to Linshader where again he got ferried across to the point of Callernish, and you may be sure he did not waste much time in getting to Stornoway, sixteen miles across a moorland track, well marked from ancient times as the shortest route to the headquarters of the Chief of Lewis.

He soon got to Holm and found out where the wizard lived. He told him what had happened to his cattle and wished him to give him a cure, and if envious eyes had caused the trouble would he please name the party who had so badly treated him.

The wizard said to him, 'You are a sensible man, and have met many people in your travels, yet you have never harmed anyone knowingly, so I can tell you that your cows have been subjected to the black bad magic, but I will not tell you the name of your envious enemy, for that would do no good, but I can tell you he lives in the township of Crowlista.'

The old fiosaiche went to a battered ancient sailor's chest, and took out a packet from which he extracted roots, pliable stems, leaves and other vegetable products, and with these he made an entwined circlet, which he handed over to Iain MacAoidh, saying an incantation in Gaelic over the circlet at the same time. The story does not tell whether MacAoidh crossed the Fiosache's palm with silver or not. He returned to Miavaig and put the circlet given him by the wizard in a large wooden cist where the milk basins were usually kept, and soon the cows received back their milk and everything in Iain MacAoidh's household went on as before, but the magic circlet of stems and leaves was always kept in the milk chest.

After many years the good wife of the house noticed that the circlet was becoming damp and sticky, so she had a brainwave, and hung it on the slabhraidh or pot chain that hung from a rafter above the fire so as to dry it. She was very busy with her household duties and for a time forgot the precious circlet of leaves given to her husband by the famous wizard, and then with a shock she remembered it, but when she went and took a hold of it to put it in the chest it suddenly crumbled into nothingness; but the milk was never again taken from these same cows.

57

The Jetty of the Uig Men

'Seachain laimhrig fir Uige, tha droch rath air.' ('Shun the rock jetty of the Uig warriors, there is bad luck on it.') Why was this advice given by the older men of each generation to the young fishers who pursued their calling among the islets and skerries of Loch Roag?

This natural rock embarking-place at Reef point has been avoided and disused ever since 1645, for it was noted that not one of those who went aboard the ship there ever came back. John Macaulay of Kneep, a son of Donald Cam, had gone aboard at another point nearer his home, and he along with Angus Macleod, Kirkibost, and a man from down the west coast, were the only survivors of the three hundred that went to join George, the 2nd Earl of Seaforth. This vacillating leader was at that time on the side of the Covenanters, and along with General Hurry he came face to face in battle with Montrose and his redoubtable lieutenant Alexander Macdonald (Alasdair nan geur lann sgaiteach) at Auldearn near Nairn.

The story of the fight with its terrible carnage is given by MacVurich, the historian. The brunt of the battle fell on the Lewis Macaulays to whom Seaforth had entrusted his standard and they fought on till they all perished but one. Among the heap of slain round the standard was found the body of Angus Beag of Breanish, the little lion-hearted warrior who would insist on going to join his fellow clansmen in spite of their decision that he should stay behind.

In the final assault on the standard John Macaulay of Kneep found himself borne back contesting every inch of the ground, and on realising that all his kinsmen were slain, he retreated with two other Lewismen into a wood where they were pursued by some of Montrose's troopers, but managed to escape and finally got back to Lewis, but not before enduring many hair-raising experiences.

This tragedy of Auldearn made such a deep impression on the folk memory of the people of Lewis that it is still talked about and the rock of departure is marked in the mind of the Uigeachs for all time.

58

The R.N.R.s in Stornoway, 1900

THE MALE NATIVES OF THE Island of Lewis were encouraged to join the navy as reservists, but instead of going to Chatham, Portsmouth and Devonport as they do now, they were drilled at a battery on the shore on the north side of Sandwick Bay, looking straight down the Minch.

The drilling took place from the late autumn till early in the spring, as the men were then free from the serious working of their crofts, and the fishing for herrings was mostly in the sunny months from the 10th of May till the end of August, after which the herring have become spent and not worth curing.

One can understand the stir all these hundreds of men caused when they came into the town of Stornoway, each one looking for lodgings, and for shops where they could find a shop-keeper to agree to let them have provisions, all to be entered in a little book, till they discharged their debts on each pay day.

Stornoway was a much smaller place then than it is now, and the sanitary and other arrangements for human comfort were not as up to date as we are fortunate in having, so you can understand there was many a scramble as to who would be first at the sink for washing and shaving – a cause of much bickering.

The elite of Stornoway would not give them houseroom, so they had to pack in among their relations in the poorer quarters of the town: Point Street, Murray's Court, Pringle's

Close, and other salubrious quarters in Maciver's Buildings, and the Havelock Lane – famous places, which are now no more, or are rebuilt under much grander names.

The townsfolk who kept cows for milk for sale or for their families, used to go round collecting the broken scraps of bread, potatoes and herring remains, to make swill for their beasts.

I well remember seeing houses where bunks had been rigged up – three tiers, like those in a ship, one above the other, in order to accommodate as many Reservists as possible. The landladies did not charge them much and made little profit on them in those days, for many of them had their own sack of potatoes, and a firkin of salt herrings.

The evening was the time for us boys to go ceilidhing into these houses, and many a tale we heard from some of these bearded R.N.R.s about Mac an t-Srònaich, Donald Cam, Niall Odhar Macleod, the Morrisons of Ness, and other warriors of the past.

The battery skailed its reservists about the same time as we got free from school, and if the snow lay on the ground it was great fun pelting these big reservists in their naval uniforms, but they often gave us better than we gave them and put us to flight, unless we were cowardly protected by a high garden wall. They were a fine body of men when fully dressed and on parade.

There were a great number of Petty Officers and Instructors from the Royal Navy to teach the men of Lewis, and many a Stornoway girl found a husband from among these smart Sassenach sailor lads.

The Stornoway of those days was kept at high pitch, and it was a busy place, full of interest for us youngsters; and at many a fight we looked on with excitement and admiration when the Leodhasachs fought with the balaich ghorm, as they called the Englishmen. On pay night, when the daorach was on them and the courage was of the Dutch variety, it was Bannockburn refought all over again for us. There were very few police in Stornoway then.

Firing practice at the battery was a great day for us, and we used to go down, playing truant from school, to watch the results of the shooting, and we enjoyed the bangs. The cannon were probably a bit old-fashioned, but they made plenty of noise. The targets were towed by a ship across the bay, pretty far out and well behind its stern, and we could see by the splash how near each gunner got to the target, but it was not often the target got knocked to smithereens by a direct hit.

There was rifle drill and also revolver shooting practice, and the cartridges that misfired were thrown down the shore, where we hunted and retrieved them. It was one of our exciting games to lay these cartridges on a flat slab, and explode them by hitting them violently with a heavy ulpag which we dropped upon them, and they often made a bang.

The reservists had a full parade once or twice during the period of training, and they marched through the town to show how smart they had become. There were also competitions at the range of the little battery, between the Cockle Ebb and Steinish, where the various sections competed against one another, and the bull's eyes, inners and outers scored, kept them interested and arguing for days afterwards. There was sometimes a shooting contest between the R.N.R.s and the local volunteers, which was of great interest to us boys, for we were nearly all of us on the side of the town squad.

Once there was a grand inspection by the then Duke of Edinburgh, and he was very taken with the fine appearance and size of the men, and as he passed along the lines, he kept on speaking to one here and one there, saying 'You would make a fine soldier in the Guards'. That was in the year 1889. He stayed at Stornoway Castle.

The battery ceased gradually and the naval authorities began to order each reservist to put in his drills in the south of England, for the mechanism of the guns had got so intricate and they also wished the new recruits to get accustomed to a life among the bluejackets on board the modern warships. When there was no longer any Battery, the town of Stornoway lost a good deal of interest for us young lads, and the merchants and other townsfolk lost a good deal of income that used to be expended each winter by the R.N.R.s.

59

Norway and the Isles

IN THE PAST OUR HISTORIES of the Highlands and Isles have been written and forced upon us by south of Scotland historians who did not speak Gaelic, and who looked upon us as the 'hairy wild Hielanmen, ignorant of grace and of culture', so I think readers might be interested in the following:

An assault was made on the Norwegian kingdom of Man and the Isles, known to the Norsemen as the Sudoreys, by Fearchar, the son of the Red Priest of Applecross, who was the first Earl of Ross of that family. He was knighted by Alexander II for quelling an insurrection in Moray, and then made Earl of Ross for quelling another rising in Galloway. Mac-an-t-Sagairt and his men made a ruthless descent on Skye, destroying with rapacity and violence, and so rousing the islands' chiefs, that they sent for help to King Haakon of Norway.

Roderick Macdonald of Bute, who had been badly treated by King Alexander, needed no great spur to urge him to go as envoy to Norway to plead their cause. Haco sailed with a large fleet from Herlover on 7th July, 1263, calling at the Nordreys on the way and taking reinforcements and fresh supplies aboard. He arrived in the Isles, calling at the Bay of Stornoway about the middle of August.

Sailing to Skye the barons of the Northern Hebrides joined him there, and he was piloted by the envoy, Roderick of Bute, southwards through the treacherous skerries till they anchored off Kerrera opposite Oban.

All the princes of the house of Somerled joined him there except Ewen of Lorn (Macdougall). The combined host devastated the coast of Argyle, and then penetrated inland as far as Loch Lomond and the Lennox, for the forces of Alexander could not withstand the fierce onslaught.

The expedition restored Bute and the Hebrides to the Norse rule once more. Overtures for peace were made between Haco and Alexander but with no result. The Battle of Largs – though claimed as a victory by the Scots, was not decisive though a storm destroyed a good many ships and men. The cession of the Sudoreys was accomplished by diplomatic negotiations and brought to a successful issue three years later in 1266. Four thousand merks were to be paid in Norway, and an annual tribute of 100 merks was to be paid to the Church of St Magnus in Orkney, while the Pope was to be mediator in case of non-payment of the annual tribute.

Alexander III seems to have treated the island chiefs, who had sided with Haco, very leniently. They were left in possession of their lands and acted as if they were a separate kingdom ruled by the progeny of Somerled. The Norse among them could emigrate to Norway or remain under the altered condition, but no vengeance was to be exacted upon them. It would be about this time that the more Gaelic-speaking Gall-Gael moved to the northern islands, and that the Gaelic language gained the mastery, though the Norse names of the islands, lochs and headlands etc. were retained.

60

'Plocs' Thrown at Sheriff Officer, Bernera Riots Recalled

F ROM EARLY TIMES THE CROFTERS of Bernera had as their summer grazings the moors called Mòinteach Beannaibh a' Chuailein, stretching from the Uig road to Loch Bruiche Breiavat, Loch Langavat, and Loch Coirgerod.

In 1872, after the sporting estates of Morsgail and Scaliscro had been formed, these grazings were taken from them, and they were offered the moorland between the road and the sea which had previously belonged to the tack of Earshader. These summer grazings they did not consider to be as good as the old ones, but when James Macrae, the ground officer, came with a paper which he read to them, they agreed to accept this moor, and also to build a dyke between themselves and Scaliscro.

They all signed or put their cross to the agreement, for it said that as long as they paid their rents in Bernera and behaved themselves they should have these Earshader moors for summer grazings. They set to and built this dyke nearly seven miles long, with their own labour and at their own expense.

They had been in possession of this sheiling-moor but a bare year and a half, when the ground officer came again and told them that the chamberlain had sent instructions that they were to be deprived of the new grazings and that they were not to take any stock across to the mainland, but that he would give them in exchange the farm of Hackleit.

The Bernera folk were furious and even the ground officer thought it was a raw deal they had got, and so they refused to

137

accept, especially as they had built such a long wall. Hackleit was a grassy arable farm, but there was no wintering for stock.

Donald Munro, the chamberlain, went to Bernera to talk to them, and he tried by alternate wheedling and bullying to get them to sign a paper agreeing to take the farm of Hackleit, but they stubbornly refused his offer. The Bernera men were then told that he was going to summon them out of the Earshader moor and also out of their crofts in Bernera as well, though they were paying their rents regularly.

On the 24th day of March, 1874, the Earraid or sheriff officer, accompanied by the Maor or ground officer, landed in the isle of Bernera to deliver the summonses (there was also a customs official on business with them). They went first to Breaclete, then to Vallasay, and finally to Tobson, where they delivered the summonses, except to three householders who were not at home, all without any molestation.

It was getting late, and the three men proceeded in the direction of Hackleit where they were to lodge for the night. They had not gone far when a crowd, said to be mostly boys and girls, followed them, shouting and yelling and throwing clods and sometimes stones at them, and the darker it grew the more they were plastered with the plocs. They said they were hit and hurt many times, yet they could not show any serious injury or effusion of blood, nor could they identify any of their aggressors, but they finished the final lap in hasty retreat. The sheriff officer was said to have shouted at them that if he had his gun many a mother in Bernera would be lamenting for her son.

Next morning the trio proceeded to Tobson and delivered the summonses not yet served, and the Earraid is said to have repeated his threat about the gun, and what he would do.

They then set off in the direction of where they had left their bout, between Kirkibost and Breaclete, and they noticed some individuals moving furtively in the same direction, and dodging behind knolls. When they had got a little way past Breaclete a company of people, thirteen to fifteen in all, rushed from behind a hillock and barred the way, one of them shouting 'Are you the fellow that was threatening us with a gun?'

The sheriff officer, in evidence, admitted he was very frightened and said one of them got him by the neck and tore his coat. The land constable advised them to disperse and go home, but they said their business was with the Earraid, and they asked him to repeat the threat he had made.

There was a lot of shouting and yelling, the customs officer had his oilskin taken and thrown up in the air, and the sheriff officer's oilskin jacket, which was over his arm, had the sleeve badly torn. One of the Bernera men admitted that he put his hand on the sleeve of the oilskin and that it was roughly snatched in the opposite direction by the Earraid. The three were allowed to proceed to their boat after the sheriff officer gave an undertaking never to come back to Bernera to deliver ejectment summonses.

In evidence, all three admitted there was no injury to their persons. Some little time afterwards one of the Bernera men who had been conspicuous in the argument with the sheriff officer, had occasion to go over to Stornoway on some business, and while walking along Cromwell Street, he was identified and pointed out to the police, and after a charge was made against him, he was arrested and taken to the police station, but not before a fierce struggle took place in which he lost most of his clothes.

Word was quickly sent to Bernera that this man had been lifted, and the people who were already exasperated with the raw deal over the land, went riotously mad with loyalty to their imprisoned comrade.

A band was formed and it was determined to march to Stornoway to lay their grievances before Sir James. Some men from the mainland of Uig joined them.

Word was sent to Stornoway that they were coming, and that they were determined to get a ship's mast and batter in the door of the jail, and so liberate their fellow islesman. The prisoner was washed and given a new suit of clothes and set at liberty, and he met the oncoming procession with a piper at their head halfway to Garynahine.

When they arrived at the Porter's Lodge, they were met by the chief constable, who asked what they wanted and what they intended to do. They told him they had a petition for Sir James's own hands, and that they did not want any dealings with the chamberlain. They were then taken up to a field at Goathill to rest, while many sympathisers from the town brought them food. Meantime a message had been sent to the castle, and Sir James consented to see a small deputation.

These men were well received, and they told him the full story about the breaking of the agreement, the building of the dyke, and the summonses for eviction against them. Sir James said that he had not been told about these matters, and that he would take it up with the chamberlain, and promised to do what he could for them and so they departed in peace to their island home.

The chamberlain had, however, picked out three of the agitators whom he considered most aggressive in the affair with the sheriff officer, two from Tobson and one from Breaclete, in order to make an example of them and a warning to others and they were indicted for 'wickedly and feloniously assaulting Colin Maclennan, Sheriff Officer, in the discharge of his duties, etc.'

The case was tried at Stornoway on the 17th and 18th July, 1874, before Sheriff Spittal and a jury of the business men of Stornoway. The three men pleaded not guilty, and were defended by a very clever lawyer from Inverness called Mr Charles Innes.

Mr Donald Munro, chamberlain, was a witness for the prosecution, and during cross-examination Mr Innes got him to admit that he was in charge of nearly all the worthwhile posts in the island, numbering between twenty to thirty, and this included the Procurator Fiscalship. He denied that there was ever an agreement about the Earshader moor, yet the ground officer admitted that there was, and that he had sent it to the chamberlain. He admitted he had sent summonses of ejectment to fifty-six families in Bernera, and that he had not told Sir James about this as he considered it a small matter.

Asked if he considered rendering fifty-six crofter families homeless with nowhere to go a small matter, he said that was so. Many other items of his autocratic way of dealing with the crofters came to light during the evidence, and we now cannot understand the fear he instilled into them or the absolute power with which he ruled them for over twenty years.

The sheriff officer made a great deal of the fright he got, and the way they had used him and torn the sleeve of his oilskin, but had to admit he had received no bodily injury nor was he prevented from delivering the summonses.

The ground officer and the customs official both treated the affair much less seriously, and gave away that the Earraid had boasted that if he had had a gun he would have used it against the Bernera men.

All three accused denied that they had used violence and asserted that they had told the sheriff officer and his friends that they had no intention of injuring them, and that the oilskin was torn by the sheriff officer violently snatching the garment away. They also wanted to make sure that he would not use a gun on them, and would not come back to deliver any more summonses in Bernera.

Mr Innes made much of the autocratic methods of the Chamberlain on a simple people, the awful fear he instilled, the unfair exactions, till they were goaded to the point of exasperation.

A verdict of not guilty was returned against all three.

The chamberlain never got over the disclosures at the trial. He was stripped of his posts and died a very poor man. He seems to have been a man to whom power was everything, and he did all he could to raise the revenue of the estate for Sir James. When his books were examined they were all in order and he does not seem to have amassed anything for himself.

61

Clach Aonghuis Bhig

A MONG THE UIG PEOPLE there are many tales of bloody battles of long ago which their forefathers fought with neighbouring clans. In every part of the island there are stones and mounds and river fords, whose names signify that once upon a time warriors had met there in deadly conflict, and if one makes enquiry at the local ceilidh, the tale of what happened there is sure to be told. Some tales go as far back as the time of the feinne, i.e., 'in the first centuries of the Christian era'. Yet, of the great battles fought outside of our island, in which Lewismen must from time to time have taken part, there is only the memory of one, and that one has persisted only because there are two topographical features which have acted as a perpetual reminder of the event.

George MacKenzie, the Second Earl of Seaforth, owned Lewis, and by signing the National Covenant, had to join forces with the other clans who resisted Charles I's efforts to force his own religious opinions on the Scots. So he sent round the fiery cross to rally his followers and Lewis had to send its quota as well. Donald Cam, head man of the Macaulays, was still alive, though very old, and could not lead his men. His eldest son, Angus of Breinish, had none of the physical qualities that make a leader of men, for he was small of stature and known as Aonghus Beag, and although he had the blood of kings in his veins through Olaf the Black, he got little respect from his fellows, and his wife was a virago. He welcomed the chance of getting away with the other men to the war, but on account of his large family and the puny size of himself, he was persuaded to return home and look after the harvest, etc. As soon as he appeared at home his wife laughed at him in mocking contempt and said 'Ho, ho dh'fhalbh na fir, is dh 'fhuirich na fideachan dig'. This was more than he could bear and he turned on his heel and took to the road. He never stopped or looked back till he reached the distant height which shuts in the village, and there he sat down on a large boulder to consider his next course of action. He made up his mind to follow and overtake the other members of the clan and do his share of the fighting. The stone on which he sat is called to this day 'The Stone of Anghus Beag'.

The Uig contingent embarked at a natural jetty at the point of Reef, since called 'Laimhrig Fir Uige' – The jetty of the warriors of Uig – and it is still shunned by the fishermen of Uig as a point for landing or going aboard their boats, for of all the warriors who set out for the war that day, only one returned, and he had gone aboard the boat from another part of the shore (i.e., John Macaulay of Kneep, one of the sons of Donald Cam). The tragedy made so deep an impression on folk-memory that it is still remembered. Montrose met the forces of the Covenant at Auldearn (Allt-Eireann) in 1645 near Nairn, where Seaforth was badly beaten, Alexander Macdonald (Colkitto), Montrose's Captain, making great havoc on that day. Three hundred Lewismen were there, and only three came back – namely, one of Donald Cam's sons (John of Kneep), Angus Macleod of Kirkibost, and a man from the west side.

The brunt of the battle fell on the Lewis Macaulays to whom Seaforth entrusted his standard, and they all perished around the standard. Amongst them was found the body of Angus Beag Macaulay of Breinish, the little lion-hearted warrior, who would insist on going to the war. One man, however, got separated from his kinsmen in the heat of the battle and it is natural to suppose that the sole survivor of the Macaulays would have a tale to relate. In the final assault on the standard he was borne back, contesting every inch of the ground, and on realising that all his kinsmen were slain, he retreated with two other Lewismen into a wood, but not, however, until he had tried conclusions with Colkitto himself, who, finding three warriors too formidable for him single-handed, and, after John Macaulay had transfixed his target with an arrow and caused him to be unhorsed, left them severely alone with the remark 'That is enough of you, ye men of Lewis.'

Soon afterwards they were pursued by some troopers, and when on the point of being captured John discharged his one remaining arrow at the leading trooper. The shaft was seen to take effect, and while his companions attended to the wounded man, the three fugitives got away. It seems remarkable that bows and arrows as a weapon of war were still used in the middle of the seventeenth century. John Macaulay of Kneep, the sole survivor, who left Uig for the battle of Auldearn, and whose memory is kept green in folklore by the associations that centre round the 'Jetty of the Men of Uig', eventually returned home. Long years afterwards a travelling packman called at the house of John of Kneep. His face was terribly disfigured by a scar that scarcely left him any resemblance of human features, but he was made welcome at the hospitable fireside and food and drink were put before him. The man's sore case aroused John's sympathy, and he asked him how he got his terrible disfigurement. The answer was an unexpected one. When young he was a trooper in the squadron of Colkitto and fought at the battle of Auldearn, and when pursuing three Highlanders, one of them turned and discharged an arrow which hit him full in the face so that he never recovered his normal features again. The warm-hearted Highlander took him by the hand and said, 'The hospitality of my house and board is always yours for the asking, come when you wish, and go when you wish, for know this; mine was the hand that discharged that arrow.' Angus Beag (Fear Bhrenish) was the eldest son of Donald Cam and he was killed at Auldearn, as previously stated, and the fifth in direct descent from him was the Zachary Macaulay, who as governor of the West Indian islands became the pioneer of the 'Anti-Slavery Movement'. His son, Thomas Babington Macaulay, sixth in descent from Angus of Brenish, surpassed his father in fame, as scholar, poet, historian, high councillor of state and peer of the realm. Father and son are buried in Westminster Abbey.

62

How Coinneach Odhar
Got the Seeing Stone

KENNETH'S MOTHER WAS WATCHING the flocks by night, and as she sat on Cnoc Eothail, which looks down on the ancient mound and commands a wide view of sea and moorland and mountain, she occupied her time by spinning with her distaff and spindle. As she watched her flock, looking over the grave-yard, she saw the graves open and the ancient mound became thronged with a great concourse of spirits. Then one and all sallied into the stilly night in all directions. Before cock-crow the spirits returned, fluttering into their own places, and then she noticed one grave was still open. The old lady decided to watch for the late-comer and put her distaff across the open grave, and at last she saw the spirit approaching from the ocean regions to the north. In a moment a vision of beauty stood before her, and a young woman, graceful as a fawn, 'golden-haired and fair as the young morn', entreated the old lady to allow her entrance. 'Remove I pray thee thy distaff from my grave and let me enter into my rest.' 'Neither prayer nor pity,' the old lady replied, 'will make me remove my distaff until you tell me who you are, and where you have been.' 'In the days of my earthly life,' said the wraith, 'my name was Gradhag, the daughter of the King of Lochlinn. In those far-off days my people ruled the seas, and few were the dwellers in the Southern Isles who had not reason to dread when the white sails of the ships of Lochlinn appeared on the horizon. There were burnings and slaughter and spoils wherever my fierce kinsmen descended, and often my heart was sore within me at the thought of the red ruin these sea-reivers left in their wake, for I had the gift of seeing the dreadful things that were done. One day when the croaking ravens moved the warriors to leave the fiords to make a descent on the coasts of the land of the Scots, I hid myself on board one of the ships, hoping that being a king's daughter, and favoured of the gods, I might perhaps be able to stay this senseless slaughter. The voyage was not favourable to the Northmen, for before they sighted these Southern Isles (Sudreys), our ship went down and all perished. My body floated about the ocean currents until it was left at the foot of this mound by a high spring tide. When it was discovered by the people, they carried it up here and buried it among their own kindred. That is why I have been so long in getting back to my place of rest, for I have to travel far over seas and through gales and currents of air to distant Lochlinn, to commune with the spirits of my own people. One thing more let me tell you. When I was in the world of living breath, the gift of vision which I had was in virtue of a stone of prophecy which was given to me by an ancient Sgald. This stone fell from my bosom as I lay in yonder pool, and there it still is with all its pristine virtue, waiting for a finder who is worthy to look into the things that are hidden from the natural vision of man. He who seeks will find it and he will be a famous man, but he who will neither seek for it nor find it, will be a much happier man. Now, I beseech thee, remove the distaff from the mouth of my grave and let me enter into my rest.'

When Coinneach came to relieve his mother at sunrise she told him of the strange happenings of the night. Scarcely conscious of what he was doing he searched diligently amongst the pebbles in the shallow pool putting each one to his left eye; but no vision came. Eventually he picked the fatal talisman, for an agonising pain shot through his eye and to his dismay he discovered that his sight was gone. The sight came back gradually and whenever Coinneach put his left eye to the hole in the stone lie could see what was happening in other places or what was to happen in the future. The foregoing is the version current in Uig at ceilidhs in the old days.

63

Feannag A' Chlarsair
(The Harper's Rig)

D O YOU KNOW WHERE Feannag a' Chlàrsair is and why it got
that name? Well, it is in the south-east corner of the park
at Gisla, nearest to the wall beside what is still called Lios Iain
Mhitchell, and there is another story attached to that patch but
of a different kind.

Tradition has it that in the long long ago it was customary
for a visiting Irish packman to wander from village to village
with his wares, and to pay for his keep he played music on
the harp, sang old ballads and recited the tales of the ancient
warriors which he had probably learned in Ireland. His wife
was an exceptionally fine-looking woman, very gifted, and she
accompanied him about Lewis in his wanderings. Many a one
cast envious glances at this beauty, and rumour had it that she
and her husband often quarrelled in public.

At this time there lived in 'Penny Donald' in the Ardroil
peninsula an eligible man getting on a bit in years who seemed
to prefer his mother's care and cooking to that of any of the
women of his acquaintance. His mother was always at him about
getting married but to no avail. He is said to have been one of
the Macaulay clan.

One day the Chlàrsair and his wife came the way, and sang
and recited to the members of the Clachan of Ben Domhnuill
as the Uigeachs called it. He was fascinated by the beauty and

the charm of the woman, and his mother was quick to notice this. On the morning when the Irish harper and his wife had departed the mother started on him about lack of manliness and his allowing her, an old woman, to carry the burden of the housework. 'If some people were worthy of the ancestors from which they have sprung they would soon provide themselves with a wife of their bosom.'

This so infuriated the son that he set out after the pair who were making towards the east and overtook them at the hamlet of Gisla. He picked a quarrel with the Irishman and killed him, and then brought the woman back to his mother's house at Ardroil. It was discovered that she was expecting a baby, but when the baby arrived he reared it as his own and gave it his own name.

There were other children from this union, but those descended from the first child were known in Uig as Sliochd a' Chlàrsair.

That is why that rig at Gisla is called Feannag a' Chlàrsair, for it was on that spot that the Irish harper was despatched and sent to play his harp in another sphere. In those days, apparently, in Lewis, the end justified the means.

64

The Irish Harper's Rig at Gisla

THE STORY OF THIS IRISH harper's murder at 'Feannag a' Chlàrsair' – Gisladh, was supplied to the *Stornoway Gazette*, and when it appeared it gave great pleasure and interest to the Rev. Calum Maclean of Conon Bridge who wrote the following verse in Gaelic:

Feannag a' Chlàrsair

Ged tha mise 'san uaigh
Is mo chnàmhan ro fhuar,
Cluinnidh fear a bhios buan mo sgeul;
Gun do ràinig mi Uig,
'S gun do stad mi 's an uìr,
Fo làmhan nam brùid gun spéis.
Air mo chéile laigh sùil
Is theann iad orm dlùth
'S chaidh a' bhiodag gu cùl, 'nam chré;
'S tha mo shliochd ann an Uig
'S mi an Giosladh 's cha dùisg,
Ach rùisgear duibh rùn mo dhroch-éig.

Seanchas

Fios agus fiosachd is fàisneachd,
Fìrinn is faoineas is feart,
Faigheam is faiceam is fuaigheam
Furasda suas gu ceart; is feàirrd an Gasaet
Seo pàirt diubh
Is ruigidh iad càch gu beachd,
Eadar Ucon is Patagonia
Eadar Pomona [Orkney] is Peairt.

65

The Marie *of Dunkirk*

THIS IS THE WAY I got this tale in Gaelic, from a seannachie of Crowlista.

It was the time of planting the barley in the year 1874 when the bodachs of Crowlista saw a beautiful full-rigged ship coming into Uig Bay and then letting her anchor down in the Poll Gorm, the worst anchorage in Camus Uig.

The men of Crowlista went out to her in a small rowing boat and hailed the ship. The crew came to the rail and started to shout to them in the most awful gibberish that not even the Man in the Moon could understand, and the Crowlista men tried out the few bits of English they had, but neither could understand the other.

The captain suddenly appeared at the rail. He could speak English and told them that she was a French ship and that her name was *La Marie de Dunquerque* and that they were on their way to Iceland.

The bodachs told him that he must not stay where he was but when the tide was at its highest later in the day they would guide him to a safe anchorage in the shelter of Creag Reidhmoil near their village.

They returned to their labour of spreading the manure on the feannags; working with renewed vigour waiting for the high tide and the excitement of piloting in this mysterious vessel to a place of safety, for they were not hoping for something stronger than water as reward for their efforts.

Unfortunately it was not to be like that, for as they gazed they saw the ship had dragged her anchors and was drifting over towards the dangerous skerries at Tràigh a' Chidhe on the Carnish side.

Out they pushed their boat, but by the time they got across, the current had drawn the vessel on to one of the skerries; there she sat on even keel jammed in one of the clefts but holed below the water-line and the water pouring into her. The wind was not very strong, and for the time she was not in immediate danger, and none of the crew was hurt, but she was full of cargo and the sea might get angry any moment, so it was decided to take the crew and distribute them among the families in Crowlista, at the same time sending word to the custom house, Stornoway, and asking for instructions.

Orders came back that the cargo was to be unloaded and taken to the store at the quay at Crowlista, and that a guard was to be set over it, and when the ship was lightened she was to be patched sufficiently to get her dragged up on the Carnish sands after a squad had managed to ease and push her off the skerry, and there proper repairs were to be made of the damage she had sustained.

All this was done by the crew of the small boat with the French sailors lending a hand as well.

It was found that this ship was laden with provisions, fishing tackle, lines, ropes and all sorts of gadgets, and much brandy and wine – in fact she was a supply ship for the French cod and ling fishery off the Iceland coast. For some reason the skipper and mate did not want to go so far, and put into one of the worst sheltered and most unsafe anchorages on the coast of Lewis, for the sea rises suddenly and the anchors do not grip the hard sandy bottom, yet no one could find out what was in the captain's mind.

For six weeks the repairs to the vessel went on and the sailors lived as best they could among the villagers. There was no lack of food and drink during this time in the township of Crowlista, and they were very open handed with the contents of the vessel. When the bodachs would be busy on their crofts the French sailors would come around and a small piggy was pulled out from the oxter pouch of the blue blouse each wore, and they were encouraged to take a good swig of the brandy or wine, and then pass it around the company. Many a stomach, on many occasions, had a warm glow put into it, and the work was resumed with heightened vigour, many blessings and lightening cheery songs.

One thing that astonished the folk of Crowlista was that the Frenchies were in the habit of shooting seagulls, plucking them, and cooking them in olive oil and vinegar and eating them with great relish. It nearly made the housewives of Crowlista sick to watch them – fancy anyone drinking seagull broth! The Frenchmen had plenty of good things, and they did not need to eat such a vulgar low-down bird.

Week after week went by and many a container of spirits and wine was drained to the bottom, yet the people of Crowlista were not making much progress in conversing with the Frenchmen, though the latter seemed to pick up a few words of Gaelic and seemed to get along not so badly. They could be seen in groups of twos and threes entering or coming out of the houses, out on the hillocks or sunning themselves down by the shore.

On one of these days a group of girls was busy washing clothes in the burn and who happened to come on them but a band of Frenchmen. Whatever was said or whatever banter or language of the eyes was used, up started the girls and made off as fast they could run, and soon the sailors were in hot pursuit of them.

The girls arrived breathless at the house of an old maid named Peggie Donald and explained to her why the haste and the excitement. Peggy sent them to the upper chamber of her house and told them to hide, while she herself waited at the fire to deal with the situation, looking as unconcerned and innocent as she could.

Soon the Frenchmen rushed in asking if she had seen the girls, and she by signs, grunts and shakings of the head denied all knowledge of them; at the same time she shouted loudly in Gaelic, 'Dead silence up there, ye that are in hiding!' The Frenchmen went outside still suspicious of Peggie and her house, so they pretended to go away, but actually returned and hid behind a knoll close to the house.

After a reasonable time the girls came out of their hiding-place, and soon from behind the hillock the Frenchmen rushed upon them with great delight. The biggest and strongest of them seized a girl called Annie Ruari – she who was the prettiest and most lively of the bevy, but the others managed to escape. Anna was there in the embrace of the Frenchman and he would not let her go. When it was realised that he was serious and that this was no boyish ploy, news of the affair spread like wildfire through the village. Strong measures must be resorted to in order to free Anna, but no one made a move.

The other Frenchmen by coaxing and threats did their best to get him to set her free, but the more they pleaded and reasoned the more madly he clung to her. His companions were ashamed of the way he was acting, and the poor way he was returning the hospitality of the kind folk of Crowlista, but he was so strong and they were all afraid of him.

During the evening it was whispered that he had taken her to Murchadh T . . .'s house on the hillock, and that he still had no intention of setting her free. Some of the men were for using violence but others advised patience for they did not wish the lassie to get injured in the melee.

About ten o'clock at night the widowed mother of the girl came into the shop of George Macleod, shoemaker, her brother-in-law, who was still working along with his apprentice, Donald, and with exasperation and weeping said, 'George, do you think that the one that is dead would sit there calmly at work while his daughter is still in the clutches of a frenzied Frenchman, and not get up and batter in his ribs and set her free?'

Throwing off his apron and accompanied by his strong-armed apprentice and a band of young men who were ceilidhing at the shoemaker's house he made for the house where the girl was restrained by the Frenchman. They all formed a circle round the pair, gibbering and trying to distract the attention of the foreigner with Gaelic imprecations.

Donald said quietly, 'Anna, give me your hand,' and she stretched forward and clasped his broad one while the rest of the Crowlista band increased their antics to distract his attention even more, and at one point when his attention on Anna was relaxed, Donald made a sudden supreme effort and jerked Anna away from him, and that was the last he saw of Anna Ruari.

He was furious and admitted defeat, and had to listen to the uncomplimentary baiting of his fellow sailors about the ungrateful way he had treated the kind folk of Crowlista and caused them so much alarm.

The ship had by now been repaired, and word came to the crew to be ready for sailing any day. The cargo was put aboard, the fishing requisites and other gear, and the remainder of the food and drink which was still unused.

A skilled pilot was chosen to guide the vessel away from the dangerous rocks of Lewis. On the day of departure a steady and favourable breeze blew from the mountains of Uig as the ship hoisted her sails on a flood tide. Out she sailed past the dangerous Poll Gorm till she reached the larger waves of the Atlantic proper, and soon she was lost to the sight of the Crowlista folk who had gone up to a hill to bid her farewell for ever.

The vessel paid off the pilot on the east coast of Lewis; she did not resume her voyage to Iceland, but went back to France whence she came.

In time the end of the story got to Lewis. When the stern laws of the Republic got the captain and mate within their power, they were both tried for neglect of duty and disobeying orders, and causing hardship to the French fishermen at Iceland who were patiently waiting for the rations of food, wine and fishing gear which never arrived. The fishing fleet went to Iceland as usual but there was no *Marie of Dunkirk* to minister to their wants in that summer of 1874.

In the course of time Anna was married, but not to her Frenchman. She was chosen by a wise well-beloved member of the village of Crowlista. They had several of a family, and were very happy together, and they died in the process of time, both living to a good old age.

66

A Crowlista Folktale

IN OLDEN TIMES TWO MEN were held in great esteem, the bard and the man gifted with exceptional strength, and both these were combined in Dòmhnull Aonghais Buachaille, Crowlista. Here are some of the stories about him told me by a very good seannachie from Crowlista. Donald was a man of a quiet disposition, well behaved and a good man in a neighbourhood.

He seems to have been one of the Uig soldiers who had later enlisted in the Seaforths, and he lived on the outskirts of a place called Bàstair, as he himself tells us in one of his poems, a verse of which I shall translate freely:

> Though I now live on the edge of Bàstair,
> I much prefer it to service in the King's army,
> with my gun to my shoulder,
> While the hail of lead cuts chips of flesh from my sides.

Donald, though he never looked for trouble, was not one to put up with insults, nor could he suffer a bully to oppress the weak ones, and he always protected his village friends against injustice. He must have lived in the period 1820–1856 from the stories one hears about him and the people he came across in his time. Was not this the strong man who carried the big lintel, still pointed out at Baile na Cille (Balnacille), on his back from the rock face behind Tolanis, a long distance away, a slab that few men could move single-handed?

A story is told about him and the parish minister of his day, the Rev. David Watson, who came to such a tragic end at Balnacille afterwards. It seems a meeting of ministers, officers and adherents of the parish churches had been called to meet at Ceann Langavat Miavaig where the Church of Scotland now has a church, and one of the ministers had been holding forth on some touchy and debatable subject. Rev. Mr Watson got up and brandishing a stick in the direction of the chairman shouted at him, 'You are a liar.' Donald Aonghais Buachaille, who happened to be sitting in a pew behind him, leaned forward and grabbed him by the collar of his clerical coat and violently jerked him back into his seat, shouting in English, 'Sit down, man! Sit down!', a very daring thing to do to a minister in those times. The minister was so shaken and astonished at the way the strong man had treated him that he dared not move for the rest of the discourse. Donald produced the famous four lines which are still quoted in Uig:

'Cha chuala mi an eachdraidh,
'S chan fhaca mi ri'm linn,
 Ministear is bat' aige
 Air tharruing bhos a chinn.

The people of Uig had for a long time been thinking that the parish ministers were paying more attention to their glebes and stock than to their people. This discontent had smouldered into flame when Mr Watson's predecessor arrived at Balnacille in 1824, the first evangelical minister for Lewis. Donald was in the habit of going with his fishing rod in the evenings to fish off the rocks at Fibhig Tarras behind Crowlista, and no doubt many a good basket was caught, for I am told that even the ling and the cod came in close to the rocks in these days. Now at Carnish lived a wicked imp of a man, always playing practical jokes on his neighbours so that he got the nickname of the crosd one. It happened that this man from Carnish came along one evening to fish at these same rocks, and who should happen to be there before him but Dòmhnull Aonghais, who was not feeling in a good humour for he complained that he had a painful boil on the posterior aspect of his body and that the rocks were hard and painful to sit down on. They went on fishing for some time, but when the Crowlista man turned his back on the other and bent down to put fresh bait on his hook, the Carnish crosd one lifted his foot and kicked him hard on the area where the painful boil was, and gathering his rod made off in haste towards the Tràigh Mhór and Carnish. Dòmhnull Aonghais Buachaille was so shocked with the pain and the unexpected attack on his person that he collapsed for a time. Then recovering he determined he would get his man, and made after him, but the latter was crossing the cockle ebb, known as Tràigh nan Strùban, between Crowlista and Balnacille, before he got a hold of him. Dòmhnull Aonghais caught him by the scruff of his neck and shook him as a terrier shakes a rat, and administered a thrashing he never forgot for many a day, and he had a wholesome fear of Dòmhnull Aonghais Buachaille for the rest of his life.

On another occasion our hero set out to walk across the moors to Stornoway accompanied by two Macleods from Crowlista; one was Iain Slaodach and the other was Iain MacAonghais Ruaidh. They were barefooted and carried shoes made of untanned cowhide with the hair still on it. No great weight on their shoulders and one may suppose they would cover the distance at a good speed. When they came to the bridge at the little village of Bayhead, where the Porter's Lodge now stands, there was the big pullaidh of Stornoway shouting defiance at everyone and inviting any who dared to come and try a fall with him at wrestling. When the pullaidh called Donald a coward he said he would not mind trying a bout with him.

When the two Macleods saw what was happening, one of them, Iain Slaodach, ran and hid himself under an upturned boat on the shore, while the other, Iain, ran to a shop nearby and came back with an armful of reaping hooks (corrans) so that the Stornoway partisans who had gathered would show fair play.

The affair ended with the bragging pullaidh being beaten into an inert mass, while Donald of Crowlista had his knee well sunk into the stomach of his opponent, who was crying and begging for mercy. The crowd cheered and Donald was acclaimed as the strong hero of Uig. We are told that they were well feted with whisky and other good things, for there were eighteen licensed drinking places in Stornoway at this time, besides many shebeens which were called pràbans.

This fine young man from Crowlista was carried off by small-pox in the fullness of his strength, but they still talk about his mighty deeds in Uig, just as if they had happened only yesterday.

67

The Evacuation of Pabbay and the Sergeant Mor

I HAVE A STORY FROM a Valtos seannachie of how the Island of Pabbay came to be evacuated – that rich fertile isle of Dean Munro, 'wherin there was a sanctuary temple where Macloyd of the Lewis used to go when he wished to be quate or was fearit.'

About a hundred and ten years ago there were four families living in comfort in Pabbay, and prominent among them was one of the old soldiers of Uig – the Sergeant Mor, who had got a holding in Pabbay, a son of Tarmod Mor Maciver of Beirghe (Reef). These old soldiers used to be given a small sum to act as coast watchers, etc., to the customs authorities of the day.

It seems a ship put into the shelter of Pabbay, and the sailors, on coming ashore, disclosed to the islanders that she was loaded up with whisky and that the captain was doing a roaring trade in this smuggled whisky.

After the ship set sail the members of the boat's crew of Pabbay saw that she was becalmed in the sound of Bernera, and they set off in pursuit armed, and the seannachie says the sergeant shot the captain through the head. We are not told what they did to the others aboard, or to the ship's cargo of whisky, but we can understand that they did not pour it all into the sea.

A good many months afterwards the rumour reached Uig that the relatives of the dead captain were coming to wreak vengeance on the dwellers in Pabbay. A panic set up in the island, and they hurriedly gathered all their worldly possessions and made for the mainland where they got pieces of land from the Valtos people. One woman, whom the story-teller knew when he was a boy in Valtos, was only one year old when she left Pabbay and was known by her contemporaries as Bliadhnach Phabaidh – she was a sister of Mairi Dhall (Maciver), the author-ess of the song 'Och nan och tha mi fo mhulad'.

We are not told whether the ship ever came seeking revenge upon the Pabbay crew led by the Sergeant Mor, whose ruined house wall is still pointed out on Pabbay by the Valtos people, who now use this lush island as winter grazing for their stock. This is the reason given for the clachan on the island of Pabbay being denuded of its people, but I have a more mundane tale to tell.

At the Crofters' Commission it came out in evidence that the people of Valtos, Kneep and Reef were complaining that the peat banks were too far from them, and that the winter gales were shifting the sand dunes and burying their agricultural patches deep under sand (the bent grass had not then been planted in the sandy areas of Lewis) and also according to the factor, they were badly in arrears with their rents. It was determined by the trustees of the Seaforth estates to remove all the inhabitants of these villages and the adjacent islands to other and more suitable holdings somewhere else in the Lewis.

With this end in view in 1843 a lease was granted for fifteen years to Dr Macaulay (An Dotair Ruadh) of these three town-ships along with the farm of Ardroil. When Sir James bought the island in 1844, the position of these crofters was pointed out to him, and on his appealing to Mrs Stewart Mackenzie she arranged with Dr Macaulay to break the said lease, for which he was paid upwards of £4,000 to which Sir James on the score of goodwill contributed £500, and besides took over the stock of Ardroil from the Dotair Ruadh at a cost of £933 4s 10d, in the hope of improving the condition of the crofters.

The Reef crofters, who had refused to take part in the works provided near them, such as draining a lake at Kneep, and the making of a road in Glen Valtos, and who were also, by

1850, £231 88s 6d in arrears with their rents, were removed by the factor, Mr J. Munro Mackenzie, who had them dispersed among other townships where they probably became more co-operative.

68

Murt Fir Mhealastaidh
(Murder of the Mealasta Men)

Here is another story I got in the Gaelic from the Uig seannachie.

In the long, long ago, there was a boat, manned by Mealasta men, that went for a load of timber to the woods in the neighbourhood of Gairloch, and no doubt they had permission to do so, for was not friendship cemented by the marriage of Angus Beag Macaulay of Brenish, and the big daughter of MacKenzie of Achilty. They got their cargo of timber and then set off to return to Mealasta, but in the Minch they were driven southwards with a strong north-east wind, and then it came on to blinding thick snow, and finally they lost their way, and did not know where they were. When most of them were overcome with the intense cold and hunger, someone managed to guide the boat into one of the fiords in the Park area of Lochs, which afterwards was proved to be Loch Claidh. The natives of these parts, seeing their weakened condition, frost-bitten and unable to defend themselves, and envious of their boat-load of tree trunks, killed each in turn by hitting him on the head with a large stone contained in the foot of a stocking. They were strangers and the Park men did not know them anyway. Wood was very useful, and 'dead men tell no tales', was their creed. Days went by, then weeks, and finally a year passed, and the poor women of Mealasta waiting anxiously for the return of their men shed many a tear. If only they could get any news of what happened to them. The suspense was awful!

One night the spirit of one of the missing men came to the bedside of his sweetheart, and he sang to her the verses of this song – trying to explain to her what a cruel fate had overtaken them. The title of the song is 'Bàgh Ciarach'.

> 'Se nighean mo ghaoil
> An nighean donn òg,
> Nam bithinn ri taobh
> Cha bhithinn fo leòn.
> Tha m' chuideachd am bliadlina
> 'G a m' shireadh 's 'gam iarraidh,
> 'Sa tha mis' am Bàgh Ciarach
> Aig iochdar an lòin.
> Tha fearaibh na Pàirce
> Air tomhadh na lamh-thuagh,
> Ach's e sinne bhi gun thàbachd
> Dh'fhàg iadsan gun leòn.
> Bha Donnachadh 'g am fhaire,
> Fear-siubhal nam beannaibh;
> Tha saoghal ro-charach,
> 'S gur mealladh an t-òr.
> 'S ann-dìreadh na bruthaich
> A chaill mi mo lùths,
> 'S fo leacan an Rubha
> Tha ''m Fear-Buidhe 'g a leòn.

The young fiancée wakened up with this song on her lips, for she could remember every word of it, and she sang it to the tune which the spirit of her dead lover had sung to her in her sleep. This was the way the knowledge of their cruel fate was first made known to the people of the upper end of Uig. A year after this the fiancée attended the Dròbh or yearly cattle market that used to be held on the first Tuesday of July, and what did she see there but a man from Park wearing the exact geansaidh (jumper) which she had knitted with so much love and care for her missing lover.

The seannachie does not tell me whether the law was set in motion, or whether the Uigeachs made a foray into the Park to avenge their murdered kinsfolk. Another version says that it was a shoulder plaid of Nicolson tartan which she had woven with her own hands for her lover, that she saw exposed for sale in the Dròbh by a woman from the Park, and that she went up and challenged her for it, and said that it was her very own handiwork.

69

The Snake and Stones (Clachan Nathrach)

ONE OF THE COMMONEST objects found in the debris from ancient dwellings of prehistoric man is a small circular whorl of stone or bone, perforated in the centre. These seem to have been used by the female of the species ever since wool began to be twisted into the form of thread by means of a spindle. The perforated whorls were used to give weight, and balance the wool she took off a stick called the distaff. Why then call them snake stones?

In my young days in Uig I knew an old woman who had six of these small steatite whorls tied on a string. What did she do with them? Whenever an animal like a cow or a sheep showed a swelling on one of its joints, it was taken to the house of this old crone for her to see and examine. She then took a bowl of water from a well and the whorls were taken off the string and immersed in the water, while an Abracadabra rune was said over them. I am sorry I don't know the rhyme. They were allowed to remain in the water for about an hour, then the old woman went with the bowl and washed the injured or swollen joint with the water, and she stated firmly that a snake had bitten and poisoned the joint. The remainder of the water was put into a bottle and the owner of the animal took it home and continued to bathe the injured joint with it for several days.

As a rule the animal recovered from its malady and no doubt the old lady got some gift from a grateful owner. The natives of this period got quite annoyed when you told them what these perforated discs were originally used for, and said that each was formed by a female snake twisting itself into a circular coil, and that twenty male snakes kept passing through the loop thus formed until they had left enough of the slimy mucus from their bodies to form the whorl, which was then discarded and left to harden in the sun – hence its efficacy against snakebite.

Lewis has no poisonous reptile, and the only animal that looks like a snake is the blind worm or limbless lizard called Anguis Fragilis, which is quite harmless. Now that bunch of snake stones can no longer be traced and has possibly been taken south, when they should be on show in a museum here for the enlightenment and amusement of future Lewis boys and girls.

I am glad to say I have a specimen given to me, cut out and bored from a soft stone called steatite and I know where there are several made from the vertebrae of various animals waiting to go into our promised museum.

Solus an Dealain bho Ghrunnabhat aig Giosladh

'N uair a bhios Abhainn Ghioslaidh gun lann
Cha bhi an solus gann
O cheann gu ceann de Leódhas.
'N uair a théid an t-allt' 'na steall gu solus
'S a gheibhear an connadh á Grunnabhat Mór
Bidh rathaidean an Uig cho ùr (reidh) 'sa thogras tu
'S drochaid 'si farsuing air abhainn is òb (or òs).

               Calum Maclean, Conon.

Bha mi'm Barabhas air an fhalbhan
Is bu chearbach a'treabhadh iad,
'S cha do chuireadh riamh am shealbh
An eachdraidh gharbh aig Torcull Og [i.e. T. Cononach].
Bha MacCoinnich air a thaobh
Bu chaomh leis ann an Conan e
Is gun fhios aig luchd-nan-arm
Nach bu dhearbh-mhac do Mhacleoìd e,
'N uair a theann e ris an uaigh
Mo thruaighe! ghabh an Niseach ris [Confession of Hugh
the Brieve re Torcull Cononach]

'S ann air sliochd a' Bhritheimh Ruaidh
A fhuaras Torcull Og-so!

> Rev. Calum Maclean, Conon.

An uair an lionas iad gach loch 'sa chuirear gàradh air gach allt
Bidh Giosladh dhuinn 'na sholus is na bothain air an geall;
C'àit an togar bradan agus c'àit am faighear breac?
Thig air gillean caol an Rudha nis dhol an taobh nach
do chleachd;
Ach bidh Tamnabhagh 's Ceann Reidheasort làn gu bac!
(An latha nach bitheadh!)

> Calum Maclean, Conon.

Urnuigh Cailleach An Rubha

O Thì! cuir MacCoinnich air tìr!
Làn phrìs air a'mhairt!
Bliochd is dàir air an nì,
'S meadair blàthaich anns gach àit
an tachair sin.
An Tì a chuir an seip so oirnn
Cuir seip eile oirnn!
'S bho sheip gu seip
Cuir seip eil' òirnne,
'S biodh e mar sin gu
Siorruidh suain!

> Amen

Ioghnaidhean

Chunnaic mis' ioghnadh an diugh
Mactire a' bualadh,
Fiadh a' tarruing mònadh,
'S mòinteach air a ghuailinn,
Calaman a' treabhadh,
Seabhag a' cliathadh,
An dreathan donn an cairt

Cur an each a riaghailt,
Fiadh a' bualadh dhòrn,
Ròn a' séideadh bhalg,
Cuileag 'si ri pìobaireachd
'S an fhiodhall aig an sgarbh.

These Gaelic lines were sent me by Mr Malcolm Macdonald
(MARA), 23 Holly Street, Toronto, Canada.

Letter and Ode on my visit to the Perth Mod, 1954, by Rev. Calum Maclean, Conon Bridge.

Dear Dolly,
    Here is the annual ode which may find you in Perth with all
the other warriors:

Clann Dòmhnaill am Peairt

Mur 'eil mis' aig a' Mhòd
Bidh tus' ann a sheòid,
Le breacan Chlann Dòmhnaill ùr dlùth,
Bidh na Caimbeulaich òg
A' ruith do gach fròg (far 'eil na sgillinnean)
Is t'inneal 'nad phoca dlùth [my pocket scissors].
Tha mi an dòchas gu dearbh
Gun till thu gun chearb
Is tu luath mar an earb as ùr,
Mur dèan casan duit deann,
Chan 'eil dìth air a' cheann,
Cum suas gu teann do chliu!
Mo thruaighe 's mo leòn,
Am fear a ni 'g . . . t'
Cha 'bhalach' gun treòir
A ni chùis!

70

An Iorram Niseach

The chorus 'Nàilibh i's na-ho-ro' is repeated after every line:

Iomair a Choinnich fhir mo chridhe,
Iomair i gu làidir righinn,
Gaol nam ban óg 's gradh nighean.
Dh'iomrainn féin fear mu dhithis
'S nam b'éiginn fear mu thrithir;
Tha eagal mór air mo chridhe
Gur i birlinn Néill tha tighinn
No eithir mhic Thormoid Idhir.
'S truagh nach robh mi féin 's Niall Odhar
An lagan beag os ceann Dhùn Othail.
Biodag 'nam làimh, is e bhith fodham –
Dhearbhainn féin gun teidheadh i domhain
'S gun bìodh fuil a chleibh 'na ghobhail.
Dhèanainn feòil is dhèanainn sithionn
'S chuirinn biadh fo ghob an fhithich.
Cha d'rinn mi fhathast beud do bhuar
Mur do leag mi fiadh fo bhruthaich,
No biast mhaol an caolas cumhang,
No dubh sgarbh an cois na tuinne.
Chì mi nise tighinn air fàire
Gob an Rubha 's iodhlann na h-Airde [or is lagan beag eile]
Anns na mhilleadh mo dheagh chàirdean.
Cha tàinig mi riamh an cuan so
Gun bhall taobh 's gun taod guaille,

'S gun a rac a bhith 'sa bhuaraich,
 Cupaill ann am bòrd an fhuaraidh,
'S fiùrain dhìreach sheasadh suas innt'
'S cranna fada rachadh mu'n cuairt orr'.
'Nàilibh i's na-ho-ro.'

Tenants in Tobson in *1787*

John McCoil vic Gilliechalluim (father of Donald na Mòintich,
  my granny's ancestor)
Neill MacEan
Normd McDonald
Angus McEan
Normd McBeath
Mary Macleod
Murdoch McCoil
Malcolm Macleod
(There is a Domhnull MacGilleChaluim in Baraglaum in 1766
who is probably father of John.)

71

Tenants and Populations

Tenants in Carishader

1754 Donald Macaulay – names of other tenants not given
1808 Duncan Maclennan
      Norman Matheson
      John Macleod
      Neil Maclennan
      Malcolm Macdonald (Calum MacDhomhnuill 'ic Iain)
          (pullaidh mór Uige)
1819 Norman Matheson
      Angus Matheson
      Donald Matheson
      (The Pullaidh) Malcolm Macdonald
      Murdo Macleod
      Angus Martin
      Mary Macdonald

1890 William MacNeil
      Uistean Ian MhicAoidh
      Ian Sheoc (John Mackay who saw the eachuisge on
          Loch Suainabhat
      Margt Carstiona nic Iain 'ic Coil
      Angus Macdonald (grandfather)
      Murdo Macdonald
      Murdo Matheson

Calum Gillies
Alasdair Ban (Macdonald)
Donald Macneil (Domhnull Aonghais)
Iain Gobha (Ferguson)
Iain Moireastan
Bairney O'Hare

Population of the Parish of Uig – August, 1792

Families, 387
Souls, 1,898
Males, 898
Females, 1,000
Persons under six years old, 314
Persons under fourteen years old, 342
Persons between fourteen and sixty, 990
Persons above sixty years old, 252

In 1755 the population according to Dr Webster was 1,312 souls.

There are in the Parish:
275 netmakers
299 kelpmakers
 26 weavers
  9 wrights
  7 tailors
  3 blacksmiths.
Calves being reared, 641
Milk cows, 914
Other cattle, 2,007
Sheep, 5,044
Goats, 304
Horses, 682
Fishing boats, 73

The Minister, Mr H. Munro, says:

> There are at present more instances of longevity here (as is always the case) than in any other parish in the island, several near ninety, and some above that age alive. They marry very young and barren-

ness is scarcely known. All the people live in little farm villages, and they fish in the summer season. The women do not fish, but when there is occasion to go to sea they never decline that service and row powerfully. When they go to the hills with their cattle, all description of sex and age angle on the fresh water lakes. All the woollen and linen cloth used for common purposes is spun and wove in the parish. There is only one surgeon in the whole island. All the inhabitants are of the Established Church. In the parish are four or five boat carpenters, and several persons who make broags of leather tanned by the inhabitants with tormentil roots. There are no instances known of suicide. Many of the people in the parish are employed in manufacturing kelp, and many of them go for the same purpose to Harris and Uist. There are no trees, etc. The parish never supplies itself with sufficiency of provisions. The people have lately acquired a superior knowledge and practice of the culture of potatoes to what they formerly had. About fifteen years ago the present Minister (i.e. himself) was obliged to give over the cultivation of potatoes except a little for his own private domestic use, because prejudice hindered the people from eating them. A small quantity of flax and hemp is sown in different parts of the parish.

72

Cattle Raiding in the Highlands

CATTLE RAIDING, TRADITIONALLY KNOWN AS 'Lifting the Cattle', Togail nam Bó, was a common custom in the Highlands for many generations. It was common to every race of mankind, and probably dated back to the days when men ceased to be primarily hunters and began to be more and more dependent on their tamed herds for subsistence. Wherever men were grouped together in tribes, mutually exclusive, there arose inevitably a conflict of interests and rights, real or imaginary, and as a consequence, there followed blood-feuds which recognised no law but retaliation on life and property. To this day in the Arabian deserts, where the tribal system still survives in its original pastoral form, raiding is still carried on – though the livestock 'lifted' are usually camels and horses. Cattle raiding was a natural consequence of the right of feud – the right to protect oneself and one's kinsmen and punish injuries received. In the prosecution of feuds between rival clans it was obvious that as pastoralists, one of the most vital forms of retaliation was an attack on the livestock of the hated rival tribe.

One of the most heroic exploits in the sagas of the Gael is the famous 'Tàin bó Cuailgne' – The Cattleraid of Cooley, which took place in Ireland in the opening of our era. The story is found in the eleventh and twelfth century manuscript – 'Leabhar na h-Uidhre', 'The Book of the Dun Cow', one of the finest and most extensive pieces of Gaelic literature in existence.

Thogail nam bó, thogail nam bó,
Thogail nam bó, théid sinn,
Ri uisge 's ri ceò, gu monadh Ghlinn Chrò,
Thogail nam bó, théid sinn.
Thogail nan creach, bhualadh nan speach,
Thogail nan creach, théid sinn,
Ri uisge 's ri ceò, gu monadh Ghlinn Chrò,
Thogail nam bó théid sinn.

These are the words of a very old pibroch – 'Lifting the Cows'. Cattle lifting was a task for the strong and the brave, demanding courage, skill and daring, and the exercise of the most warlike qualities. The time usually chosen for these forays was the second full moon in September, and was traditionally known as gealach bhuidhe na saille – the fattening yellow moon. Cattle lifting can never be placed in the same category as sheep-stealing. The sheep-stealer was a man of treachery and deceit: his was a nefarious trade, carried out in secret and darkness, demanding not the heroic qualities, but the base and the mean. Sheep are weak, timid and inoffensive creatures, incapable of putting up a fight to save themselves. In the case of cattle-lifting, to the natural stubbornness of cattle themselves, their tendency to stampede at critical moments, their noisy bellowing which would prevent the raid from being carried out in secret, add the possibility at any moment of armed retaliation by the raided; so it can be understood that a cattle raid was an enterprise demanding courage, skill, daring and the exercise of the most warlike qualities. It is no light task to drive half-wild Highland cattle, and it can be appreciated that to try conclusions with the horns of a fierce Highland bull can be as terrifying, as paralysing to mind and muscle, as any encounter with any other wild beast in a hunter's paradise.

73

The Churches of Lochs

A CORRESPONDENT, LEÓDACH, INVERNESS, wishes to know
something of the history of the church on Eilean Chalum
Chille in Loch Erisort.

He says he is surprised that I said that little Bernera in Loch
Roag was the Iona of the west coast of Lewis, with its name
for sanctity. I did not say of the whole of Lewis, for I had read
that Eilean Chalum Chille was also a consecrated island; but
its fame depended more on its fertility and its famous orchard,
which, like that at Rodil in Harris, had a reputation for fruit
growing given it by the early monks from Iona.

There were two pre-Reformation churches in the Lochs area:
St Colum Kil in the island of that name, and St Pharaer in
Kaerness, as Martin Martin tells us in 1695.

Was there an old religious ruin on the island of Tabhaigh
in Keose Bay before the present parish church was built there?
Was this St Pharaer, and was the Swordale peninsula called
Kaerness in olden times?

The priests in pagan times always picked on a rich piece of
ground to build their religious temples, and I have no doubt
there would have been one on St Colum's Isle in Loch Erisort,
with its rich soil and facilities for catching the abundant fish
that swarmed around it.

One may be sure that after the death of St Columba in 597
and onwards, the big colony of Celtic monks at Iona sent out

exploring missionaries, who fixed up a religious establishment on this island, and like the one set up at Aignish, the site of St Catan's temple, dedicated to the much venerated St Colum, and the island in Loch Erisort, became known as Eilean Cholum Chille.

The monks introduced fruit trees and better forms of intensive tillage, and the island got a great name for its fruitfulness; but as a religious establishment the priory church at Eye became better known, especially after the Benedictines ousted the Celtic monks from Iona in 1204 and forced them to get back to Kells in Ireland.

We have no history that St Cholum Cille was ever looked upon as the parish church in Lochs, though it had a great name for sanctity, and the people around Loch Erisort and in the Park area all wanted to be buried there, even up to recent times.

In 1549 Sir Donald Munro, who had himself been rector at St Colum's, Eye, and came as Archdeacon of the Isles to inspect and report on the religious houses held under Iona, says nothing about the church at the time, so one concludes its power in spiritual matters had become small. Yet he enlarges on the fertility of the soil of Eilean Cholum Chille, and says that Macleod of the Lewis used it as an orchard and market garden, and possibly a granary, to supply his wants at Stornoway Castle, and that he kept a gardener there to look after his interests, and 'he that is gardener hes that isle free, guid in mayne land for corne, and gressing and fishing, pertaining to McCloyd of the Lewis.' Dean Munro says there were four parish churches in Lewis.

In 1626 there was a minister at Barvas (including Uig) and another at Eye (including Lochs) – each living being worth 2,000 merks; the population of the island being then only about 4,000.

Martin Martin in 1695 says there were only two parishes – Eye, which took in Lochs, and Barvas, which included Uig.

The ideal after the Reformation was to have a church, a manse, and a school in every parish, though this took some time to come about. The parish church of Lochs was probably fixed at Swordale, Keose, because there was a fertile piece of land there for a glebe and it was near to the Laxay river for the Friday fish dinner. It was probably erected in Seaforth times, as being central for the people around Loch Erisort from Arivruaich to Grimshader, and being on the mainland of Lewis one could walk to it on a Sunday even with a gale of wind and rain, when one would not venture to use a boat for an island like St Colum's.

I cannot find any date when the transfer took place to Keose, but no doubt there was a missionary or a catechist sent to Lochs early, from St Colum's at Aignish.

The minister of Lochs in 1820 was a Mr Simpson, very famed for his strength of body and for being a good agriculturist. He was an old man in 1836 when Lord Teignmouth called on him at Keose, where he entertained him royally on salmon and venison.

Lord Teignmouth was making for the farm of Valamus in the Park, the only sheep farm then in Lewis, and as there were no roads in Lochs at the time, he had to walk most of the way. The farmer of Valamus took him to the Shiants which belonged to Valamus.

He says Mr Simpson had to walk miles to the outer fringes of his large parish, and always carried his own bedding to ensure cleanliness and get a comfortable sleep while away from home. He died at Lochs, and Mr Finlayson who preached in the new evangelical style of Rev. Alexander Macleod of Uig, succeeded him.

At the disruption in 1843, Mr Finlayson came out, and took the Lochs congregation with him to Crossbost as a Free Church. Mr MacCallum was minister of the Parish church at Keose in our day, with few members, but the adherents of the reformed Church of Scotland at Laxay (Kinloch) are the actual successors now of the congregation of the once venerated Eilean Cholum Chille church if it ever was the parish church in olden times.

74

Lewis One Hundred Years Ago

Here is a description by one in authority in 1855 and who had access to the figures I am going to quote. 'The number of fishermen and boys employed in manning the boats was 2,982; persons employed in gathering bait, baiting lines, as carters, etc., 2,900. The Port of Ness is the great centre of the Lewis deep-sea fishing.'

The quantity and estimated value of the exports from Lewis in 1855 were as follows:

	Quantity	Value
Smoked Haddocks (Barrels)	800	£1,600
Herrings (Barrels)	40,000	£60,000
Cattle (Number)	1,700	£6,800
Horses (Number)	100	£400
Sheep and Lambs (Number)	4,000	£3,000
Eggs (Numbers)	1,507,400	£2,617
Cod and Ling (Tons)	900	£13,600
Salmon (Boxes)	400	£8,006
Lobsters (Number)	41,900	£1,396
Rags, Bones (Tons)	80	£800
Wool (Tons)	90	£5,400
Whelks (Tons)	22	£110
Oil (Tons)	20	£800
Hides (Number)	650	£450
Old Cordage and Canvas (Tons)	30	£400

On 31st December, 1855, the number and tonnage of vessels registered as belonging to Stornoway not above 50 tons burden, 38 – tonnage 989; above 50 tons, 12 – tonnage 1,245.

Only a small fraction of the people remained with the Established Church at the Disruption. More than nineteenth 20ths of the inhabitants of Lewis belong to the Free Church. The population of Lewis at the 1851 Census was 19,711.

Stornoway, the only town of Lewis, and the capital of the Western Hebrides, is situated on the head of a bay on the east side of the island. It is well and regularly built, and its streets are lighted with gas. Most prominent of its buildings are the Parish Church, Free Church and Episcopal Chapel, several schools, jail and the Masonic Lodge. On an eminence overlooking the town is the magnificent mansion of the proprietor, recently erected in the castellated Tudor style. The castle grounds are extensive, and laid out with great taste.

The industrial female seminary in Stornoway is a neat and commodious building, erected and endowed by the proprietor and his lady in 1847, at a cost of more than £2,000. It is attended by about 150 girls of the poorer classes, who are instructed in Ayrshire flowering needlework, domestic millinery, and laundry-work, as well as the elementary branches of education.

The masonic lodge contains elegant assembly rooms, reading rooms and a public library. Stornoway has a branch office of the National Bank of Scotland, customs house, a savings bank, sailors' home, hospital and a gas and water works. There are also commodious piers and a building dock, with a Morton's patent slip worked by steam, and fitted to haul up ships of 800 tons burden. The entrance to the harbour is marked by a lighthouse and beacon.

This description was written eleven years after Sir James came to this island and will be of interest to many readers, and a comparison will doubtlessly be made with our present position.

75

Kidnapping in Skye and Harris, 1739

H OW MANY READERS KNOW that in 1739, i.e. six years before
the year of Prince Charlie, the following disgraceful deeds
were enacted in our islands? The facts are verified from the
Irish state-papers No. 408.

In September, 1739, a vessel named the *William* from Donaghadee, William Davidson, Master, put into Loch Bracadale in
Skye on the pretence of discharging some brandy there. The
real purpose of her visit was soon made apparent, when about
sixty persons, men, women and children, wore torn from their
homes and bundled aboard like cattle.

Then the vessel went to Finsbay and Loch Portan in Harris,
at each of which places she received on board some twenty
or thirty persons, similarly forced from their homes; in some
instances from their beds.

In all, the *William* had on board about 111 persons, compris-
ing men, women, and children, when she sailed from Loch
Portan to Donaghadee where she arrived on 20th October with
about ninety-six so-called felons on board. Of the remainder,
five boys and girls had been put ashore at the island of Rum,
four persons and the body of a young woman, who had died on
board, were landed at Canna and an old sick woman and two
pregnant women were put ashore at Jura. All these people were
dumped down on the islands named, without (so far as the
evidence shows), the slightest provision being made for their

sustenance. They were thought to be too weak to endure the voyage to Pennsylvania.

On the arrival of the *William* at Donaghadee, to rig and victual, the men were taken up from the vessel's hold where they had been stowed, and the women and children from her tween-deck. They were marched ashore under guard to two barns, the men being put into one barn, and the women and children in the other. The barns were guarded, but the prisoners, by some means, managed to escape on Sunday, 4th November (one suspects with the connivance of their guards), and dispersed throughout the country.

They were pursued by Davidson and men employed by him, and some of them were captured, bound, and brought back; Davidson cudgelling brutally those who failed to move as quickly as he wished. They were labelled as convicted felons fleeing from justice, and the magistrates had therefore issued warrants for their arrest, and as a result, there appeared before them on the next day nearly thirty women and children. Many of the children did not seem to be over ten years of age, and on the whole they were the most miserable objects of compassion, and the most helpless creatures that had ever appeared before the magistrates.

They told their tale of woe to what were obviously sympathetic ears, and later an official inquiry was set on foot, which could only have one result, namely – the captive Highlanders were released and allowed to go where they chose, and they as well as those who had dispersed themselves about the country 'are now at perfect liberty to be employed by the country people in their service according to their several abilities'. Probably there are descendants of these Highlanders in County Down at the present day, whose Irish brogue shows no trace of their Hebridean descent, and who are completely ignorant of the story of the *William*.

The chief partners in this iniquitous scheme were William Davidson, the master of the *William*, and Norman Macleod, son of Donald Macleod of Bernera, Harris, and when a warrant for their arrest was made out, after the official inquiry, it was found that they had both fled the country and they were never brought to justice. It seems that people convicted of crimes for which the penalty was death, could be sent at the whim of the chiefs, as felons, to work in the plantations, on signing a paper that they consented to go. Two purposes were served at once, viz: the getting rid of troublesome fellows, and making money of them at the same time at so much per head.

The story of the *William* created a great stir in the South and many people whispered that people in higher authority than Davidson and Macleod were implicated in this transaction.

76

Venison Galore in 1887

W<small>E ARE TOLD THAT</small> the Uig Macaulays came over past Loch Langavat with their cattle in summer, and had their sheiling on a site overlooking Loch Seaforth, which is marked on the map of the Park as 'Airigh Dhòmhnaill Chaim'.

The Mackenzies built their first stronghold at Seaforthhead and Colin, the First Earl, took his title from this place or the loch. A wall was built from Loch Seaforth to Loch Erisort called the 'chiefs wall', in order to keep the deer within and marauders without.

In 1716 there was only one tack in the Park, namely Habost, held by a Mackenzie, who was probably a near relation of the laird. By 1780 we find that people had built houses at Shield-inish, Isginn, Stiomrabhaigh, Leumrabhaigh and Oransay, which would not have been allowed in previous times.

Then the whole of the Park was let early in the century as one large sheep farm to Mr Lachlan M'Kinnon of Corry, in Skye, who put in a Donald Stewart from Perthshire as manager, and he afterwards became tenant until 1842. The farm continued under different tenants down to 1883 when it was given up by Mr Peter Sellar.

The people in the villages mentioned were shifted to other villages or were given assisted passages across the Atlantic to the States or to Canada.

When the lease ran out it was advertised again as a sheep

farm but no offers were forthcoming, and it was then let in 1886 to a Mr Joseph Platt from England, as a deer forest.

The condition of the people of the rest of Lochs was considered to be the worst in the island. The number of squatters had increased enormously, and hunger stalked the land. In 1881 and 1883 petitions were sent to Lady Matheson asking her to grant portions of land for crofts and winter grazing on the south side of Loch Erisort to these wretched, badlyhoused cottar-fishermen, but their petitions were refused. The papers in the south sent up reporters to investigate, and they sent word back that conditions were even worse than had been described, 'wretched hovels, filth and hunger everywhere' (though I cannot see Mac nan Loch dying of starvation while there was so much fish in the sea).

Fair Rents

The Crofters' Commission helped a great deal and fair rents were fixed. Crofters had been grossly overcharged, specially in Balallan and Airidhbhruach, and it was at these two places that the discontent found its greatest outlet.

There was a Mr Donald Macrae, headmaster at Balallan at this time, and he was a very ardent supporter of the cause of 'land for the crofters', and for many years meetings were held at night in the Balallan school, where people from all the villages in Lochs came to air their grievances and discuss ways of obtaining land to apportion amongst the people.

These meetings were opened with the singing of a psalm and then a long prayer delivered in very good idiomatic Gaelic, asking for God's blessing on their deliberations. Then someone would shout out that it was time to purge the meeting, and a committee of strong young men was chosen, who went round and lifted bodily anyone who was lukewarm or suspected of being a Castle spy, and with shouts of 'Mach leis! mach leis!' he was pushed through the door into the outer darkness.

This went on till 1887, and from nearly every village of Lewis any kind of musket, gun or rifle that could shoot was collected secretly at the Balallan Schoolhouse. Then on a Tuesday early in November, 1887, the raiders were summoned by the blowing of a horn, and from each township went forth its little army of starving, ragged men and women, headed in some instances by a piper.

There never was witnessed in these islands a more grotesque spectacle than this army of poachers, strung out in a long thin line, as they marched towards the haunt of the deer in the Park. It is reckoned that there were 1,100 people out for the hunt.

Mrs Platt went to meet them and reason with them, but all they would say was, 'No English, my lady', and when the Chamberlain went to speak to them in Gaelic he got no further than 'An ainm Dhé bheil an caoeh oirbh?'

The Poachers' Camp

On the Tuesday night they encamped in a sheltered place in the heart of the forest, but on the Wednesday the camp was removed to Airigh Dhòmhnuill Chaim where it remained until a storm of rain drove the raiders home.

There was a great slaughter of deer in the two days. The raiders admitted to 200, but from the number of skins the total was much more.

The camp on the Tuesday night was described by one who was present as follows:

> The camp was a huge rectangular pavilion facing leeward, and made of cabers covered with old sails. A long way before arriving at the camp its blazing fires were sighted, and the sounds of music were wafted over the gentle breeze. There would be in the tent at this time, considerably over a hundred persons, and five large fires of peat were burning brightly.
>
> The night was one of the loveliest, and in every respect favourable to the raiders. The interior of the camp was of such an extraordinary character that there is no other probably in Highland history, at any rate since Culloden, to compare with it. Imagine a tent one hundred yards long, with its open face illuminated by five peat fires, each as large as an ordinary hayrick. Over the one in the centre there was suspended a magnificent specimen of a royal stag. Within ten yards of this fire there was another of equal size, above which was the carcase of a deer broiling, and there was also

an immense cauldron containing another stag reduced into chops, or what is known in the south as 'Irish Stew'.

Immediately behind these fires were the raiders in their wild attire, either reclining on couches of heather or sitting upright on stones or boulders, pretty much in the fashion of their forefathers when they roamed the ancient forests of Caledonia before the Saxon set foot on British soil. Some were eating, others attending to the fires, and a considerable number of them chanted Highland songs mostly from 'Donnachadh Ban nan Oran', such as 'Chunna mi'n damh donn 's na h-eildean, direadh a' bhealaich le cheile'.

On the approach of strangers to the camp there was not the slightest attempt to prevent their entering. On the contrary, they were asked to listen to the causes which induced them to resort to this method of hunting for food, and to partake of a share of what was going. I and others did not hesitate to accept the invitation, and we sat down on a huge boulder close to one of the fires. One of the raiders said, 'Our forefathers selected Park Forest as the spot above all others in Lochs where God our Father in Heaven intended that we should dwell, but now we are slaves, while the land that is ours by right is consecrated to deer.'

What is to be the end of the whole business? you ask. Does any man in his senses suppose that this country will stand by and see a whole parish slowly starve to death, merely because a few Highland lairds are determined to turn fertile lands into deer runs and sheep walks?

The Patriach's Grace

There was the grace of the white-haired patriarch, who, standing bare-headed, with his back to the blazing peat fire, with uplifted swarthy hands, invoked the blessing of 'God the Father and God the Son' upon the venison festival. In rich sonorous Gaelic the old man asked a blessing 'upon each and all who were that day engaged in the holy crusade', and expressed the hope that 'a church to the glory of God would be erected on the sacred spot upon which the camp stood, to commemorate the event'.

The newspaper reporter and Mr Donald Macrae returned from the camp at Airigh Dhòmhnaill Chaim late in the morning to the schoolhouse at Balallan. They had not been there long when a loud rat-tat was heard on the door, and then the face of a man, white as a sheet, and he himself shivering with fright, appeared. He said that while returning to his home with a deer's head slung over his shoulder he had been hotly pursued. He had thrown down the deer's head and stood at bay, pointing the muzzle of the gun at the nearest oncoming man, who turned out to be the superintendent of police. He was thus guilty of a serious crime he knew, and was in a fever of excitement, and his whole body shook with fear.

He was advised to hide himself until all the disturbance was over, but instead he lost his nerve and went straight to the castle and made full confession, and gave the names of the ring-leaders of the raid. This was the only man who turned informer during the whole of the eleven years of the land agitation.

The newspapers of the day made a great deal of the raid and sent representatives to investigate the reports of the destitution in the parish of Lochs and other parts of the island. In a month a sum of £4,000 was subscribed to a 'Lewis Destitution Fund'.

Sheriff Fraser and Supt Gordon, when driving through the forest, were met by a party of cottars, several of whom were armed with guns. The sheriff requested them to return peaceably to their homes, but they refused, so the sheriff was obliged to read the 'Riot Act' and warn them of the consequences which would follow should they persist in disregarding his counsel. The ring-leaders were arrested, and many exciting incidents followed before every one of the raiders quitted the forest.

The trial of the alleged raiders took place in the High Court in Edinburgh. They were defended by a very clever lawyer, a Mr Shaw, who understood the crofters' needs, and had the sympathy of the nation in their favour, and in spite of all the evidence led by the Crown and the information supplied by the informer, who himself admitted shooting deer and pointing the gun at the super, a verdict of 'not guilty' was returned by an Edinburgh jury. The judge declared that deer were not private property, neither were grouse nor any other wild animals but that the proprietor had the right to prevent strangers coming on to his grounds.

Mr Donald Macrae got a great reception on leaving the court. He was carried shoulder-high down the High Street amid cries of 'Down with the tyrants'. The verdict had an immense effect all through the Highlands. On the way home Mr Macrae was feted by the Glasgow Highlanders, and in the Waterloo Rooms, he addressed a packed audience and made the most eloquent speech of his life. He was known ever afterwards as 'Balallan'.

77

The Highlander in War

PEOPLE WITH ONLY A SUPERFICIAL knowledge of Scottish
history think the martial exploits of the Highlanders were
entirely confined to conflicts caused by feuds between rival
clans. This is quite erroneous, for the clans played a most important part in the historic battles which moulded the destiny of
Scotland, and when the unity of the nation was at stake the
lesser differences of the clans were forgotten. When the King
of Alba called on Highland chiefs and the chiefs on clansmen,
the blood feuds of generations were laid aside and the clans
fought shoulder to shoulder, kinsmen in arms in a common
cause. The first instance of clan unity occasioned by a national
crisis, that appears in history, is found in the pages of Tacitus
where an inspiring picture is presented to us of all the tribes
north of the Grampians combining under a common leader,
Galgacus, to resist the Roman invaders.

Galgacus thus appears at the dawn of history as a great
national leader ready to sacrifice everything for the sake of
liberty and independence. The inspiring spirit which he symbol-
ises is found to run like a golden thread through the subsequent
history of Scotland. The ceilidh tale has it that the warriors,
before going to battle, used to go to the nunnery at Mealista
so that the holy women might put a 'sian' or charm upon them
against the dangers of battle. This was a living echo from the
religion of the pagan past.

When the clansmen were gathering round the standard, the war-pipe played the 'Cruinneachadh'. When marching away the 'Spaisdearachd' or pacing was played. When the army was drawn up in battle array the tune was the 'Brosnachadh-chatha', i.e., the incitation to battle. Then the bard or the harper would recite the battle song of long ago – telling them of the noble heroes from which they sprung, and reciting of their great deeds of valour and exhorting and inciting them to emulate them. Even among so many brave heroes, there would always be a redoubtable few. One would be the 'Ursainn-chatha' – the King Pin of the fight, and another would be 'fear bristeadh na bàrach' – the hewer through ranks, and the slogan for many clans was 'Buaidh no bàs'. The decay of living tradition is a deplorable loss to our knowledge of the past, and to the national character and culture.

> False wizard, avaunt! I have marshalled my clan,
> Their swords are a thousand, their bosoms are one.
> They are true to the last of their blood and their breath,
> And like reapers descend to the harvest of death.

Stories of national battles in which the clans undoubtedly took part are very meagre in living tradition, while those of local feuds, often earlier in time, cling tenaciously in the folk memory of the people. Tales are told around the ceilidh fire with a wealth of detail, of feuds, with their heroic exploits, as if they happened yesterday instead of hundreds of years ago; such as the story of Fionn and his heroes and Donald Cam and the Niseachs, also the fight between the Lewismen and Uisdean Gilleaspuig Chleirich with his Sleat Macdonalds, who were badly beaten, in spite of 140 of Clann 'ic Gilleadharain going over to his side.

78

Trial of the Mutineers of
the Ship Jane, 1821

Spanish Silver at Stornoway

THE SCHOONER-BRIG *Jane* of Gibraltar, 90 tons burden, belonging to a Jew, Moses Levy, of 'that port, left for Bahia in Brazil on 19th May, 1821, commanded by Thomas Johnson, an Englishman, with a crew of seven. Peter Heaman of England was mate, and Francois Gautiez, a Frenchman, served as cook. She carried, along with a mixed cargo, 38,180 Spanish silver dollars. These were packed in small canvas bags, and these bags were packed in sawdust in casks, six of eighteen gallons each, one of nine gallons, one of seven gallons; in all 124 gallons of Spanish silver dollars. There was no strong room in those days and the casked dollars were placed in the ship's hold.

From Gibraltar to Bahia was a distance of 4,000 miles. Gautiez, the French cook, started to covet the dollars, and Heaman was won over and tried to get the crew to fall in with their plans, but they refused their ideas. Paterson, the one responsible seaman, was openly antagonistic to any schemes for getting the dollars. Paterson was at the wheel one night while Heaman was officer of the watch. The cook crept into the cabin and shot the captain in his bunk with a loaded musket, while the mate attacked Paterson at the wheel and clubbed him to the deck with a musket. The bodies were thrown overboard, and aided by the Italian Dhura and the Maltese cabin boy they cleared away the signs of the struggle.

Smith and Strachan and two Scotsmen were locked in the forecastle. This murder took place 6.5 degrees north of the Equator and five days west of the Canary Isles. Then the ship's course was altered for the west coast of Scotland. They sighted Barra Head and the mate went ashore at Barra calling himself Captain Rodgers. He purchased fresh supplies and an open boat. They cut holes in the *Jane* and tried to sink her, and took to the boat with dollars aboard and tried to make for the mainland, but a gale drove them back and they put ashore at Swordale. The *Jane* did not sink but went ashore at Tolsta Head. Mr Maciver of the custom house questioned the men, and the cabin boy gave them away. They were arrested and cartloads of dollars taken to Stornoway and the revenue cutter took them to Leith. Gautiez and Heaman were tried, condemned and hanged on the sands of Leith. Odd Spanish dollars were floating around Stornoway for many years.

79

The Stornoway Sailing Packet,
Started in 1759

1797 THE FIRST STATISTICAL ACCOUNT says that the packet
from Poolewe to Stornoway was started in 1759 by the Government. It sailed once in a fortnight only – weather permitting.
In 1797 there was a new boat which crossed from Poolewe to
Stornoway once a week. There was a post office then at Stornoway, run by Murdo MacKenzie, father of Sir Colin MacKenzie,
and of Mary Carn. In 1791 fifty pounds was the total business
from Edinburgh to Stornoway.

1836 Lord Teignmouth tells us:

> The packet sails once in the week from Polewe to Stornoway. It is
> an ill-found vessel, its tackling ill-suited to bad weather, and its
> crew insufficient, being in summer only three, a fourth is added in
> the winter. The cabin was such that none of the passengers would
> venture into it, the hold affording far preferable accommodation.
> The government contributes £130 per annum to the support of the
> vessel. Warning should be taken from the fate of the predecessor,
> which foundered in the gale of November, 1824. The accident
> was owing to the unfortunate determination of the minister of
> Stornoway who insisted on the skipper sailing against his better
> judgment. The length of the passage to Stornoway is forty-two
> miles. A vessel leaving Polewe early may reach the Long Island
> before the wind changes at noon, but our passage was prolonged
> to 107 hours. We deviated from our course three points owing to
> the deficiency of compass. We landed in the harbour of Stornoway
> amid the ruins of an old castle. It is singular that notwithstanding

the importance of this harbour, and its being the resort of the vessels engaged in the Baltic trade, there is no lighthouse at its entrance. The Commissioners of Northern Lights properly decline to erect lighthouses in harbours till they have provided them for the principal headlands; but the expense of a lighthouse at Stornoway might be almost defrayed by the dues which are now uncalled for. There is a lighthouse at Scalpay (Glas) on the coast of Harris, and one is in progress at Cape Wrath; there is none on the Butt of Lewis. A lighthouse in the port of Stornoway would be rendered particularly useful by the liability to mistake the headlands to the northward of the harbour. There is a poor little inn at Stornoway, but I was rendered independent of its accommodation by the hospitality of Seaforth Lodge, the residence of Mrs Stewart MacKenzie, proprietrix of the island.'

The author goes on to tell that she is the daughter of the late Lord Seaforth, and that all her brothers died before their father, thus fulfilling a part of the mournful prophecy which was current in Scotland, respecting this family. Seaforth Lodge stands on an eminence, bare, except where a few trees appear in an adjacent glen (Shoeburn), and commands a fine view of the town and harbour of Stornoway, which is frequently crowded with vessels.

Stornoway is the principal town of the Hebrides, the only one possessing the advantage of trade. It contains, together with the parish, a population of 4,000 persons. It is partly of old and partly of modern date, spread over a peninsula formed by the two branches of the harbour, on which the best houses occupied by the merchants and other respectable inhabitants are distributed in streets, while the huts of the poorer classes have been gradually removed to the suburbs. One of the best houses in the town is the Freemason's Lodge in which the members of this body hold their meetings.

80

Evolution of Transport to Lewis and the North-West Hebrides

FIRST, SINCE THE 1790s there was a sailing packet once a week and then twice a week from Poolewe. Sir James Matheson had set up brickworks and paraffin works, and the exports from the island increased, so he had to get a quick means of getting these to market. Prior to 1846 the Southern Isles were served by steamers owned by G.&I. Burns, and in that year the proprietor of Lewis purchased an iron paddle steamer from Tod & McGregor of Glasgow which was christened the *Mary Jane* in honour of his wife. For eleven years she carried dry salt, fish, whisky, paraffin, black cattle, hides, tallow, salmon, whelks, lobsters, eggs, a wonderful export – see the list for 1855 as per *Encyclopaedia Brittanica* – direct to Glasgow, and she took back passengers and general cargo for the use of the island and this put Stornoway in the lead as the best harbour on the west coast.

Till the quay was built there used to be an old iron hulk called the *Amity* along the rock near the old castle of the Macleods and the *Mary Jane* came alongside her and the passengers used her as a gangway to get on to the landing place. The Stornoway man of this period boasted he had gaslight before Greenock had. In 1857 Hutcheson and MacBrayne took over the *Mary Jane* and put their pioneer boat the *Clansman* (another paddle boat) to open up the north-west trade. In 1879 when the Hutcheson Brothers died, David MacBrayne became sole owner of the fleet, which he augmented by buying up old ships. A government grant was given and service to isolated districts was increased, and social contacts and trade improved. The *Mary Jane* in 1875 was altered and a long deck saloon put on her, and she did service on the west coast under the name of *Glencoe* till 1931, a period of eighty-five years, when she was sent to Ardrossan to be broken up. She had still the original engines put in by Tod & McGregor nearly ninety years previously. They are on exhibition in the Kelvingrove Galleries, a tribute to Clyde workmanship. Sir James started a mail steamer service from Stornoway to Ullapool. The names of the steamers were SS *Stornoway*, the SS *Undine*, and the SS *Tusker*; the last had a breakdown near Arnish lighthouse and began to drift with a south west wind towards the 'Chicken Rock'. The late Rev. James Grenfield was aboard and mothers remarked about James, who was the best swimmer in Lewis at the time, 'If James can see land I am quite sure he will make it.' The *Tusker* was saved, and MacBrayne put on the *Lochiel*, a small slim steamer with a razor edge bow. *Lochiel* was wrecked near Portree in 1907 and she was broken up for scrap. She was seventy years old. The successor on the Stornoway–Stromferry route was the *Clydesdale*, 447 tons, two tall masts, two funnels, a fiddle bow with short bowsprit and whaleback forecastle head – a beautiful picture entering Stornoway harbour but an awkward boat to bring alongside a pier. There was no mechanical power to operate the rudder but she was manhandled by a wheel and two men to operate the rudder. In 1904 the *Clydesdale* was replaced by a new steel steamer called the *Sheila*, which was a good seaboat and carried on for twenty-two years, when, crossing to Kyle one dark morning in January, 1927, she was wrecked in fog on the Applecross coast. Her accommodation had become inadequate and Mac-Brayne's had a notice up 'This deck is available for passengers when not occupied by cattle'. Pressure from parliament was brought to bear on conditions and a 'Public Utility Company' was formed, the Government holding a financial interest in the concern. A new boat called the *Loch Ness* was built for the Stornoway–Mallaig run. It resembled a miniature liner with a cruiser stern, triple expansion engines, oil fired boilers, and could do fourteen knots if she went all out. She also had better accommodation.

In 1947 we got the faster and more luxurious boat *Loch Seaforth* – a real small liner with its high observation lounge. Some said she would be top heavy for the Minch, but up till now she has proved a very worthy seaboat, and very comfortable.

81

Smuggling in Lewis (1829–36)

Lord Teignmouth – Vol. I

The importation of smuggled foreign spirits into Lewis is much counteracted by the vessels belonging to the Revenue Service, which cruise constantly along the coast, and are very active in procuring information. These vessels are dreaded by the traders who are obliged to come to and to submit to be searched, etc . . . The importation of foreign spirits into Lewis is almost entirely carried on by vessels of other nations, particularly the Norwegian, which procure them in France, and being permitted to land them under bond for exportation, contrive to sell them to the inhabitants. The foreign spirit chiefly imported is gin, but whisky is the favourite beverage; and as there has been hitherto no legal distillery, it is principally the produce of illicit distillation. The Excise is utterly inefficient. The officers, now and then, set out upon an excursion, and do by chance stumble upon a still, when they meet with no opposition; as the islanders imagine that the ill-treatment of an Excise officer would probably lead to the quartering amongst them of a detachment of troops. So openly do the people admit the practice of illicit distillation in their festal hours that they ask their guests (and my informer was an officer of the Revenue) whether they prefer 'Coll or Gress'; whisky of these farms having a celebrated name. A more numerous and vigorous excise service is indispensable, and a cheap legal supply of spirits a needful preliminary to coercive measures. For this purpose Mr Stewart MacKenzie has adopted a plan which has been successfully pursued by the Duke of Sutherland and others of erecting a distillery. Its efficacy, notwithstanding the preference of the people to the illegal whisky, which being made in smaller worms is of finer quality, has been proved by experience. The confirmed habits of smuggling, which the people of Lewis have acquired, inclined them to predict the failure of the distillery at Stornoway; yet it has been so successful that another has been erected on the opposite coast of the island.

The distillery in the Shoeburn glen went on for many years, manufacturing whisky, but not very profitably, for Sir James Matheson's secretary records in 1857 – 'a large building used as a distillery was built by the late Mr Stewart MacKenzie at a cost of £14,000 or thereabouts, as I was told. It was a failure. The island of Lewis does not grow sufficient grain for the inhabitants.' The Shoeburn distillery was turned into stables and coach-house for Sir James' use. A bottle of the real old Shoeburn whisky was displayed in a window of the Royal Hotel for many years and was looked upon as a great curio and an interesting link with the past.

82

Mary Mackenzie's (Mary Carn's) Funeral

From Lord Teignmouth's Memoirs, Vol. 1 (1829)

During my stay at Stornoway I received an invitation to attend the funeral of a wealthy old lady, who had made numerous and liberal benefactions. She was a sister of Col Colin Mackenzie who long held with considerable reputation the post of Surveyor General for India.

Immediately after the decease of this lady, a cask of Madeira was opened in her house, a wake had been kept up, and the house nightly illuminated according to the custom of the country. The chief mourner, who arrived in an open boat from the mainland, was a minister, and the funeral was attended by all the principal inhabitants of Stornoway. Our party from the Lodge arrived too late at the house of the deceased to partake of the preliminary refreshments, but we overtook the procession on the road to the ancient cemetery of Eye, which is situated on the beach of Broad Bay, about four miles from the town. Another burial place, near the Town, has been so encroached upon by the ravages of the sea that the bodies will probably soon be consigned to a watery grave. An old chapel (St Colm's), the larger half of which is unroofed, stands in the cemetery. Beneath a flagstone on the pavement, undistinguished by any inscription, lies the body of the last Earl of Seaforth, who forfeited his title in consequence of his participation in the rebellions of 1715 and 1719, and lived and died afterwards in a species of exile in Stornoway. There are other monuments of the Mackenzies of Seaforth, some of which bear the family crest, the stag's horns assumed by an ancestor who saved the life of King Malcolm IV from the attack of a stag. The unroofed part of the chapel contains the tombs of nineteen of the Macleods, the ancient proprietors of the island. A warrior in armour is represented in basso-relievo. The graves of the principal families are enclosed by four walls forming a sort of mausoleum in the churchyard. That of the lady whose obsequies we were celebrating, contains a marble monument to the memory of Col Colin Mackenzie, bearing a highly panegyrical inscription. Stornoway is proud of his fame.

On the present occasion, as soon as we reached the cemetery, the coffin was deposited in the grave with all possible decency, and the whole body of mourners instantly adjourned to a tent pitched in the cemetery, within a few yards of the mausoleum, where we found tables groaning beneath a plentiful repast. As soon as we were arranged, one hundred and twenty in number, the minister, who presided as chief mourner, delivered a grace in the form of a prayer. The bottle was then circulated and many loyal, patriotic, and complimentary toasts, including the 'Church of England' and the 'Kirk of Scotland' followed; nor was the 'memory of the deceased' forgotten, while the toasts were as usual accompanied by appropriate speeches. The bottle was passed round many times and the party became more hilarious and the toast 'The Chief of the Macivers' was drunk with loud applause. Then the chairman and some of the party left, but the rest carried on the carousel. A man with a whip walked round the tent to keep the crowd away, using his whip to deal out chastisement on those that came too near to the tent. The carousel went on, and one member got so drunk that he had to be carried back to Stornoway on the bier which had carried the body of the old lady to the cemetery.

Lord Teignmouth says: 'A Highland laird, to whom I afterwards told these circumstances, observed that – "he was a very lucky fellow to get so good a berth." ' The festivities were, however, attended with much less excess and confusion than occur frequently on such occasions, There was a great multitude of young and old, attracted to the spot with the expectation of the gleanings of so plenteous a repast, and who thronged around and closed in upon the tent, eager for the signal for rushing in upon the remains of the feast. I am informed from another source, that when the signal was at last given they rushed in and set to upon the good things, that there was plenty of drink left for them and that they carried on the festivities till well into the next day.

83

Baile-Na-Cille – Dun Kenneth

O NE IMPRESSIVE PIECE OF EVIDENCE of the spirituality of human nature is the continuity of sacred places in the evolution of thought and culture. Once a place becomes invested with the aura of the sacred and the mysterious, it persists through all the changing phases of thought, culture and religions, and continues to inspire the minds of man 'with the joy of elevated thoughts, a sense sublime of something far more deeply interfused.'

A pagan temple becomes a Christian chapel, a Christian chapel a Mohammedan mosque – always a change of thought and culture, never a change in the fundamental nature of man, and seldom a change of place. Such a centre of reverential emotion is the old burying ground (St Christopher's) of Baile-na-Cille (Balnacille).

The conical mound wherein are buried the bodies of many Uig people holds a mysterious and sacred association still for those who come near it. For at least a thousand years they have gazed with reverential awe at this sight, and before that there was a pagan temple. There is a legend that the mound was first built up by one called Elidhean, who carried the soil (with panniers) on two white horses, from a hill in the vicinity which still bears his name, 'Cnoc Elidhean'. The mound is artificial, for the soil was heaped on a basis of rock. Some people say that the builders were the same Mediterranean incomers who built another conical mound like it on Silbury Hill in Wiltshire, and set up the standing stones which rouse in us a feeling of awe and wonder. We can believe that the ideas and beliefs of ages have persisted and mingled in strange confusion round the old sacred mound, and that the exceptional personality of Dun Kenneth in the seventeenth century gathered much of it round himself.

Was the mound ever called Dùn Choinnich?

The late J.N. Macleod thinks that Martin went wrong in calling the temple St Christopher, but that it was 'Cille Chriosd'. People persisted even till the end of the nineteenth century and beginning of the twentieth to say when a church had 'skailed' Sgaoil a' Chealla!

Donald Cam Macaulay (MacDhùghail) is said to be buried in the ancient St Christopher's chapel.

84

Tigh A'Bheannaich – Gallan Head

At Uig there is a well called 'Tobair na Circe', but no remains of the ancient church which was dedicated to St Christopher (Balnacille). Directly north of this site a long rise of grassy ground, spotted with small lakes, leads to the highly elevated peninsula of Gob a' Chalain, the grandest sea cliff in Lewis. Very sweetly and picturesquely situated in a small hollow, a mile or so short of its summit, is Tigh Beannachaidh, Blessing House; a not greatly dilapidated chapel, internally 18 feet 2 inches in length with a broken east window, altar, and a doorway, and a niche in each of the side walls, the south doorway entire and flat headed, the masonry very rude and without lime.

This is a quotation from *Ecclesiological Notes of some of the Islands of Scotland*, by T.S. Muir, 1885.

There is a picture of the ruins in Pochin Mould's book *West over Sea* showing the drystone overlapping type of building. The Office of Works say they are going to protect the remains of the chapel and I have a letter from Mr David Macintyre, V.C., to that effect. There is a Loch a' Bheannaich, Geò a' Bheannaich and Faing a' Bheannaich to the west of Aird Uig village.

Notes by Fear-gun-Dachaidh, who examined religious ruins in the Isles, 1861. Characteristics of Old Church Architecture

On Gallan Head, the chapel Tigh Beannachaidh 'Blessing House' or Tigh a' Bheannaich is, except that the roof is wanting, nearly entire. The internal dimensions are 18 feet 2 inches by 10 feet 4 inches. From the appearance of the masonry which is without lime and other peculiar features, it would seem to be a very old building. It is situated on a soft grassy spot near to the shore about a mile westward of the rude and very secluded homestead of Aird Uig, and close by, a small sheet of fresh water marked Loch a' Bheannaich is altogether singular and deserving a visit from Miabhaig or wherever the traveller may happen to have his location. [There is a diagram of Tigh a' Bheannaich.]

They say that when Donald Cam was buried:

Gun do mharbhadh seachd mart agus gun do thràigheadhh Tobar nic Fhearghuis.

This was a well near the old cemetery at Baile na Cille.

85

The Beehive Huts on the Uig and Harris Hills

Na Bothan – Proceedings Society of Antiquaries Scotland,
1904, p. 173, by Wm MacKenzie

'BOTHS' EXTEND FROM THE SHORES of Loch Resort and along the glen to the end of Loch Langavat. Capt. W.F. Thomas, *Proceedings Society of Antiquaries Scotland*, p. 127, Vol. III, and p. 153, Vol. VII – 'Primitive dwellings known as Beehive Houses' – (Bothain) – first reported 1858. Some of them were underground, as at Loch Thealsaidh, with radiating chambers for sleeping and others for keeping milk and cheese. Some of the underground houses were built of overlapping slabs, e.g., at Gress and on Ness machair. There were 'bothan' built at Ceann Thulavig (Cnoc Dubh), Loch an Sguir, Gleann Marstaig, Loch Coirgirod. There was one complete, on an island near little Bernera – Both Eilean Fear Chrothair. This overlapping roof was pre-Christian, and is found from Greece to Greenland. The Glen Marstaig 'boths' were used as summer shielings in 1832, and were so used until 1872, when the outer moor was taken from the Bernera people and the grazings made into a deer forest as far as Loch Langavat (Gleann Marstaig) and Scaliscro. The parts around Loch an Sguir and Loch Coirgirod were included in frith Mhorsgail. Previous to this Scaliscro and Morsgail had both been sheep farms. My granny from Tobson, when a young girl, used to live in these boths (as airighs), and fished Lochs Coirgirod and Langavat, which were teeming with trout. These pre-Celtic dwellings with the overlapping stone roofs coming to a point at centre, are found along the Italian and French Alps and used as houses by the shepherds. There are stories at Uig of women being killed by the roof of the both falling on top of them while asleep. This within living memory. These boths were used by the early hunting inhabitants, and then by a semi-pastoral people, who lived for months in them, making butter and cheese, 'salted' for winter use, from the milk of the black Highland cows. At Beannagil beyond Loch Morsgail, on the track, is a completed both intercommunicating with two other boths, both partly destroyed. No ashes of a fire are ever found in or near them. On the side of Ascleit are a group of boths still with the roofs on and one on Beinn a' Bhoth.

86

The Teampull – Flannan Isles

APPROXIMATE SIZE: Low quadrilateral building of dry stones in long flat slabs (running east to west).

External measurements:
   North and south sides 12 feet
   East end 10 feet
   West end 9 feet
   Height 9 feet

A vaulted roof higher than the supporting walls.

Internal measurements:
   Length 7 feet
   Width 4 feet 6 inches
   Height 6 feet

A door in the west end 3 feet by 2 feet

Bothan Chlann 'ic Phàil are on the headland called Maol nam Both. When excavations were carried out at these boths the following details were found. Two apartments (separate buildings) consisting of a large long narrow building approximately thirty feet long (internal measurements); two apartments, the east one eight feet square and the west one five feet square. A very low passage five feet long connects the two apartments. Another passage eight feet long leads into the larger compartment on its east side. There are the remains of a retaining wall running across the island separating the headland on which the boths are built from the rest of the island. These boths were built in the same fashion as the Teampull, and are supposed to be the ruins of two monk cells and probably a primitive monastery on consecrated ground. St Flannan was an Irish saint, son of Theodoric, King of Thomond. He is supposed to have built the temple and lived in seclusion on the island for years.

Eilean Mor 39 acres
Soray 8 acres
Starr is a stack
Eilean Tigh doubtful
Sgeir Toman 5 acres
Sgeir Ribhinn 3 ares
Roareim 7 acres
Eilean Gobhainn 12 acres
Bronacleit is a stack

87

Gealachos, Daughter of the Young Priest

MANY STORIES WERE HANDED down by word of mouth from father to son and here is one from the time of the Norse invasions.

Sweyn, King of Lochlann, came with a great fleet of warships and invaded Ireland. He was worsted in all the battles and raids he made, and had to retreat northwards along the west of Scotland and finally he put into Loch Roag on the west coast of Lewis for shelter. This large arm of the sea runs inland in many directions and ships can find anchorages and shelter from every wind that blows. It is studded with many islands, but the greatest of them all is Bernera major, which divides the fiord into two channels, east and west Loch Roag. This island is about six miles in length, and at its northern end, separated by a narrow channel, lies the low-lying fertile island of Bernera Minor, about a mile in length. At the time of Sweyn's invasion very many people lived there for it produced much corn and many cattle. There were from early times two religious edifices, with a great name for sanctity in this island, and looking after the people's spiritual and material welfare was a cleric called the 'Sagart Og' who was very well liked by them. People in those days had a much greater regard for their priests than they have for their parsons at the present day. This young priest had a young daughter, whose fame for beauty had gone far and wide, and her name was Gealachos (Fairfoot). You can imagine that the young men of the island fell very much in love with her, but none dared go a-courting the beautiful daughter of the island priest. It was her custom to take a walk round the island night and morning, and, free as a young roe, no one interfered with her. Many a time she sat on the knoll above the temple beach gazing across the sea to either coast, and though she had no book learning, she was well versed in the works of nature, the birds, the beasts, the fishes and the flowers; in fact the people of Little Bernera looked upon her as their own little princess.

One calm misty day, Gealachos was taking her usual morning walk, communing with nature and speaking to the creatures and the pretty flowers that were so numerous along the edge of the temple beach, when she heard the noise of oars and the voices of human beings. She stood listening with her ears intent towards the sea, and presently she saw a dinghy coming out of the mist and heard men speaking in a strange language, and she made off in alarm towards her home. These were the Norsemen, and Sweyn himself was struck by her beauty and her magnificent figure as soon as his eyes alighted on her, and he made up his mind to carry her away with him to Lochlann. He ordered his swift young warriors to jump ashore and capture her, and this they soon did while she struggled up the steep 'Baca-Mór'. She pleaded with them to let her go, but they paid no heed to her cries for they dared not disobey their king. Her cries grew louder and louder, but there was no one near to succour her, and the strong young warriors carried her aboard the dinghy where Sweyn sat in the stern. He tried to soothe her with honeyed words and gentle touches, but she refused to be comforted and cried all the more. By order of King Sweyn she was taken on board his vessel, and there she found herself miserable and alone, snatched away from her dear father and mother, a prisoner among men whom she had never seen before, and who were speaking a language she could not understand and whose ways were all foreign to her.

When she thought how her parents and fellow islanders would be seeking for her dead or alive in her favourite haunts and at each crag, cranny and bay on the island, it is no wonder she wept as if her heart would break, and this feeling grew worse as the Norse galleys gradually sailed further and further away from Little Bernera, her beloved island (and no hope of ever getting back). The musicians were ordered to play lively and pleasant tunes to cheer her up and make her forget, but she refused to be comforted, and kept staring into the west where her heart was. The dragon-headed ships of Sweyn tore on through the northern sea, and the men remembered and toasted the memory of their dead companions killed in the wars in Ireland, but now happy with Odin in Valhalla. The musicians played on. Again and again Sweyn made love to the beautiful Gealachos, and tried to show her what a great love he had taken for her and did all in his power to please her, but he could not shift the heavy black sorrow that was upon her. The ship came in sight of Norway and the musicians struck up lively airs of their country, and when she came to anchor in the bay the people on shore set up a great shout of rejoicing at the return of the fleet and their great warrior king. When Gealachos was rowed ashore in company with Sweyn, and all eyes saw the excessive beauty of her who was a stranger to them, they set up a great warm-hearted welcoming noise for her, but this did not lift the black depression from her mind. What she wished was to be free to roam once again the shores and hillocks of her beloved Bernera. Now and again Sweyn took her out to hunt the wild boar along with his companions in order to divert her and try to make her forget, but all to no avail. One day as they were sitting together in his great hall he tried to reason with her, and to prove that she was much better off than she would be in poor Lewis. He said:

> Na'm biodh tusa am Bearnaraigh Bheag
> Cha bhiodh aca fleadh no fonn,
> Ach Mactalla chreagan àrda
> Toirt fianuis air barcadh thonn.
> Fhreagair i gu socair ciùin,
> 'S deoir bho sùil a', ruith gu luath,
> 'Chaoidh cha toir mi 'Lochlann rùn,
> Le chuid shléibhtean mùgach fuar.'

> Wert thou in Little Bernera
> No feasting or fun would be there,
> But empty echo from craggy rocks

Proof of fierce dashing waves.
She replied soft and gentle,
And the tears running fast from her eyes,
'Never will I give Lochlann my love
With its cold snuffling heaths.'

'Never will Lochlann be to me like Little Bernera, where are the people that speak my mother's tongue, and where are all the people I love dearly! Never will come the day when I can be happy here, but I have to admit that during the long seven years you have kept me here, I have received nothing but kindness from you and your people, and with all my heart I forgive you though you snatched me away, and you cannot enter into all the misery I have gone through since then.'

The King then spoke gently and with much feeling:

'What caused me to take you away by force was that I fell deeply in love with you the moment my eyes alighted on you and I could not help myself. Little did I think when I rose that calm misty morn on Loch Roag seven years ago, that there was a woman on the face of this earth that could have got such a firm hold on my heart, my mind and my imagination, as you have done . Your beauty of face and form intrigued me so much that I cannot live without you. Many a cold day with slashing sleet did I sail across the cruel seas, and many a fierce battle did I wage and overcome my enemies, but I would go through fire and water and wage more fierce strife if I could get you for my very own alone. I was hoping when I took you, that through time you would turn to me and return my great love. Thou art my woman, darling, of all the women in the world, and I would give it in its entirety to you if I could only make you happy and win your love in return.' 'I realise', said Gealachos, 'that it was not for my undoing you snatched me from my people, and I am truly sorry that it is not in my power to give you my heart's love, for as a young girl I gave it to another, and I cannot pluck it from its roots to give it to you now, for the love of a woman is not such a light matter as you think. You have tried with your musicians and the company of your young warriors while out hunting the wild boar with you, to lift this black depression from my mind, but all to no avail – merriment, feasting, jewels and all your sumptuous palaces will not cheer my heart and make up for the loss of my people and Little Bernera. You have seen me on many an occasion weeping profusely and gazing towards the west where live my dear ones, whereon the sun shines early, and where late she is loath to say farewell below the ocean, and I constantly dream that I am back

215

there on my dear white strand about the temple, and talking to the beloved flowers and beasts and folk of the dear island, and in the morning when I awake, this verse in Gaelic comes to me:

"Ged nach 'eil mi am Bearnaraigh Bheag
Na creid nach 'eil e air m'ùidh,
B'àill leam na àgh do theach
Bhi a' coimhead nan clach 'san Stuigh."

'Oh, King, if there is a heart in thy bosom, and if you have any pity for me, do not keep me here a prisoner any longer, and the blessings of the power above, who rules us all, will bless thee and prosper thee more than thou canst even imagine. Oh, Little Bernera, you and all that dwell on its meadows are often in my mind and affection!'

Now when the King heard the pathetic, sincere way she spoke, and noticed that her good looks were beginning to fade with this constant homesickness and weeping, he came to the unhappy conclusion that it was no use his trying to win her love any longer, and he reluctantly decided to deliver the beautiful maiden he had snatched from her parents in the far Western Isles, back on to the strand at Little Bernera.

This plan was put into action, and he equipped his best galley with the most experienced sailors and with plenty of food and comforts for his dear Gealachos, and in the course of time he put her ashore on the exact spot at Tràigh an Tempuill from which he had snatched her. We can understand that it was with a heavy heart that Sweyn paid his last farewell to the island maiden who had thus melted his heart. There was great rejoicing on the Little Bernera, for the parents had long given up hope of ever seeing her again and all the islands looked upon her as one who had returned from the dead, and oh! what a welcome they gave her. She took up again her wandering about the island, and her beautiful form was often to be seen on the temple beach. She never married, though many handsome young men hankered for her hand, but after the experiences of the seven long winters in Lochlann and of the high cold mountains, she resolved to remain a maiden, and her early lover resolved to remain unmarried also. She did not spend her days in vain, for she made merry with those that made merry, and visited the bereaved and mourned with those that mourned; and where there was illness there she was to lend a hand and help with the nursing, for she was a born nurse. She lived to a great age, and when she died she was taken and buried on the edge of the temple strand, where she sleeps so peacefully within sound of the waves which gave her such great pleasure in the happy days of her youth.

88

Dr Macdonald's Speech on Opening the Lewis Film Society's Sale of Work

Ladies and Gentlemen,

I wish to thank you for asking me to come here to-day to talk to you and to open this sale of work which you have set on foot in order to get funds for your society, the Film Society of Lewis, for it shows me you have confidence that I am able to say something to further your project. I don't know why you should have picked on me except that you got to know that about forty years ago I used to go about the island taking pictures with a camera, and from these I have made slides on which I lecture about the ancient history of Lewis, describing customs and a way of life which is no longer with us. For these lectures, I have had to read deeply in archaeology and go far back into the early history of our island, and there is one thing I have gathered, that there was always some individual, or some group of individuals, wishing to teach us their ways to improve us, and make us what they called progressive civilised human beings, or take the consequences of refusing to be so civilised. From these many experiences we have become suspicious of the stranger even when he brings us gifts and promises us good things, and you will find that this spirit has persisted even unto our own day.

The earliest mention of us is from the Irish annals, when their learned saints and anchorites came in their light skin coracles and set up their small drystone bothies attached to which were their oratories or praying cells, and these can be found in many places over the Western Isles. These people spoke our language, so we allowed them to build upon the sites of old pagan temples, and graft their Christian ideals and stories on to our own old religion, and so life flowed along. Then fierce Vikings came from the north-east, they knew not our ways nor our language and they taught us a bitter lesson, killing most of our menfolk and taking away the women and children for their own uses and comfort. They were here from 800 to about 1266, when most of them went back to Norway leaving little behind but their colouring, physique and some queer place names. Then came the Macdonalds in their galleys led by the Lord of the Isles, and we promised to obey, join him in his wars, and pay tribute to his purse-bearer for our lands. We understood his ways and his language, and got a certain prestige from being under his banner; and though we grumbled at the tribute, and were annoyed when he left many mementoes of his visit without taking the trouble to give their mothers the benefit of clergy, we were too few to make any open resistance. This went on till 1493 when James IV broke up the Lordship of the Isles. We had a bad lesson from the east when the Earl of Huntly came with an army of the Crown to drive out Donald Dubh, last Lord of the Isles, who had escaped from a castle on Loch Awe side, and had taken refuge in the Lews. Huntly stormed the castle of the Macleods, which used to stand on a rock where No. 1 pier is now, and overran the whole of Lewis. Torquil Macleod, VIIIth of Lewis, disappeared from history, and Donald Dubh had to go back to captivity again.

In 1597 James VI, exasperated by the lawlessness of Old Rorie Macleod and his numerous offspring, legal and otherwise, tried to teach us a severe lesson; so severe that he signed a document for the complete clearance of the Leodhasachs, and the planting of God-fearing, civilised Fifers in their place. Three attempts were made to establish a colony, but that fearless warrior Neil Macleod and his band wiped most of them out, and sent the survivors back to where they came from. Then the Clan Kenneth, backed by guile and the government forces, came and overran the island, and made the bold Neil and his followers surrender on Beireasaidh (Berisay); and the Tutor of Kintail taught us Macleods, Macdonalds and Macaulays a drastic lesson; while his helpers, the Morrisons, and his kinsmen the Macraes, Macivers, Maclennans, Munros and Rosses, were put in the best tacks from Arnish to Baile na Cille (Balnacille). The Morrisons had quarrelled with Neil Macleod, and he had driven them over to Sutherland to their kinsfolk of that name. Then Dutch fishermen came and taught us new methods of catching fish and we seem to have got on all right with them for a few years.

Charles I and Charles II thought that Lewis was an 'El Dorado', and so established fishing stations in Stornoway and on several islands, but the Lewismen did not trust them and soon found ways of making the stations close down.

Cromwell had sent a garrison and built a strong fort where the custom house now stands. We behaved well under his stern Puritans, and must have picked up some good habits from them. We still retain a grim Calvinism, and a main shopping boulevard, called after the stern Protector. The English soldiers before they left did not forget to blow the old castle of Stornoway to bits, leaving only part of a tower the stones of which were used for building into No. 1 Pier in 1882. The Seaforths tried to bring the philosophy and culture of the south to change us, but the Lewisman remained suspicious of any innovations, even of the religion that was sent up from Edinburgh, and he soon mixed his pagan-cum-Catholic form along with what the ministers taught him. The Seaforths lived mostly at Brahan Castle, and we only saw them when they and their kinsfolk came to hunt in the famous deer forest of Park, yet their factors did not let us forget who were at the head of affairs, and duly lifted their rents in kind and the little money (Scots) that could be got, but nothing was ever done to improve the condition of the homes and lands of the common people. No wonder they were suspicious of improvers from far away. When the Education Act came into force after 1872 the Lewis parents would have none of it, for they said learning would make the children uppish, despise their parents, and become discontented with their station in life. In fact it would provide wings for them to fly away from the parental home. Who will now say that they were not right? We have had education now in the island for many years, and people have begun to think and reason for themselves. They question themselves and the world around them, and this causes a restlessness of mind, a discontent of many with their station in life, a desire to better themselves, and perhaps an envy of others; a doubting about religion and politics; one wonders if they are as happy as the generations which had not so much of this type of information pumped into them!

Now you may ask what has all this to do with the Lewis Film Society? I will try and make it clear. We have now further education for the adult; men do not work so long, and so have more free time at their disposal, and the modern inventions, the radio and the movie van, are reaching out to every village in Lewis. Most of our natives are suspicious of what these two may bring. Will they upset their ways, and interfere with their religious beliefs, which many believe are the only real and true beliefs? I fear them more in case they are hastening the departure of our dear Gaelic language, for the searchings and probings into the wonders of the Creator will refuse to be stilled or thwarted; and I fear that in the future this go-getting Anglo-Saxon language will be the one in which these mysteries will be unfolded to the bodachs in Bragar, Brue and Brenish. Now if we have picture houses and travelling picture vans, why are film societies set up? There must be a desire or a demand to provide something which the ordinary picture house does not supply. Surely it is not merely that a few overgrown boys, like Dr Ferrier and myself, want to play with an intricate toy like a film projector, and show off how clever we are. No! The society is a social club where one can discuss the merits and demerits of the last exciting film, a few of us at least have seen on the movies here or in the south, and also to show good films, educative and amusing, beyond and above those that are to be seen at the ordinary picture house.

In order to do this a body like the Lewis Film Society must have sufficient funds to be able to procure these special films, and also keep their projectors in repair, and sometimes to replace one with a more modern and efficient type of machine.

Now, ladies and gentlemen, you are gathered here to help this cause, which is part of our further adult education, and I need not point out to you, for you can see displayed, the articles that have been made by much labour, or procured in various ways; and I have no doubt that you are all itching to get to the stalls and buy whatever goods take your fancy, not forgetting the scrumptious tea which has been provided. The helpers and organisers are all to be congratulated upon the result. I have now, ladies and gentlemen, much pleasure in declaring this sale of work open. God bless you all!

89

Investigations and Commissions in Relation to the Island of Lewis and Harris Up to Our Own Day

THE ISLAND OF LEWIS AND HARRIS has for many years been the subject of investigations and commissions, which were set on foot by those in authority, very often not to its benefit and progress. Someone has always been trying to civilise the inhabitants and bring them round to the ways of the south – mostly from the Edinburgh and London directions.

The oldest written record is that of Donald Munro, who, as High Dean of the Isles, was sent up from Iona in 1549 to investigate and report on the condition of the people, and with a special eye to the religious houses, their glebes, and other agricultural possessions. His report remained in manuscript until it was printed in 1774 and it had no effect in improving the condition of the common working people.

After the troubles with the various sons (legal and otherwise) of old Rory Macleod, the island of Lewis fell into the hands of King James VI c. 1597. He had an investigation made and his commissioners reported that it was a land fruitful in corn and with abundance of fishings, in fact a veritable 'El Dorado'. King James, who was always hard up, resolved to benefit by this land of milk and honey, and you all know how three times colonies of Fifers were set up in Stornoway and how the resolute Neil Macleod and his band wiped them out and sent the residue of the last colony back to where they came from. Charles I and Charles II each had a report made on the islands as to the richness of the soil and the myriads of fish in the sea. To one of these reports, that of Captain Dymes, c. 1630, we owe a good deal of the information we have about the ways of the islanders, their agriculture, their fishing methods, their social pursuits, and their religious observances. English fishing stations were set up in Stornoway, and on various islets and harbours along the east side of North Uist, but they faded out due to the Civil War, the lack of financial support, and the sullen antipathy of the chiefs and their clansmen.

Lewis carried on under the Seaforths who used it as a summer pleasure ground, on holiday from Brahan Castle, and to raise what revenue they could by means of their chamberlain from the people who were ruled and overworked by the mainland tacksmen, until Seaforth caused the rentals to be paid directly to himself. In 1800 Lord Seaforth had a report made to him by the Rev. Mr Headrick, an expert on geology and botany, with a view to improving the revenues of the Lews, and it is interesting to note that the same advice was given by experts many years afterwards to the wealthy proprietors who wished to improve the natural resources of their vast property.

The Seaforths lost their money in various ventures and when Mr Stewart Mackenzie died in 1843, his widow sold the island to Mr James Matheson – a Sutherland man who had come home from China after making his fortune, and was looking for an estate at this time. He was one of the partners of the famous tea firm known as Jardine Matheson and Co. of Hong Kong, China. He paid £190,000 for the island; and he drew up a code of rules applicable to the management of the estate, and the human beings who lived upon it. He had many visions, and set out improving conditions in his island home, where there were no main roads, and no bridges spanned the rivers; where the people of one parish were strangers to those in another, for distance, moor, bog and mountain separated them, as we find at Ness, Lochs and Uig. An imposing castle with policies was built, which took seven years to complete; works to distil paraffin and its by-products, from the vast beds of peat, were set up and also brickworks to make bricks and tiles from the native clay were laid out at Garrabost in the Point area. The harbour was improved and a steamboat, called the *Mary Jane*, plied between Stornoway and Glasgow.

Though all these created work and brought money to the town of Stornoway and its environs, they did not seem to alter the way of life of the poor crofter – and Mr Matheson left the fisheries to the curers, the big merchants, and those who had previously been dealing with them, the fishermen. Mr Matheson left the management of the country people to his chamberlain and the ground officers – all wanting to please him and increase the revenue from his new estate. A dejecting fatalism had taken hold of the country villages for they had no fixity of tenure and could be shifted with their driftwood spars and rafters, plus some straw for thatching, at the will of the factor, to some other place, usually less desirable. Their lands were tilled in common so there was no incentive to improve on the old methods, and when the potato famines came in 1846 and 1851 these people were in a sorry plight and Mr Matheson had to spend over £30,000 on oatmeal and other necessaries to keep them alive. Some of this expenditure was paid back in labour by the crofters. Lord John Russell sent Sir John Macneil to investigate and report on the condition of the people, but he is said to have stayed mostly near the town of Stornoway and got his information from people who were biased and did not really know the terrible conditions prevailing in the far away parts of the island. He sent back word that the Lewisman was a lazy type, his house was a dirty hovel, and that he was an ungrateful wretch who did not appreciate the amount of money that Sir James, as he now was, had expended on his island and that, in any case, the produce of his holding, even in good times, did not support him for more than six months in the year.

Factor succeeded factor, but the discontent in the land grew worse; many emigrated to the colonies, aided by help from the proprietors, until in the year 1874 Donald Munro, the chamberlain of the Lews, brought matters to a head by breaking his written word to the people of Bernera, and when they would not obey his wishes, issued summonses of eviction against fifty-four crofters and their families and admitted in court that he considered it a small matter and not worth telling Sir James about it. The Bernera people marched in a body to Stornoway and informed Sir James of the illegal way they had been treated, though they had paid their rents and were sticking to their side of the bargain.

Munro was dismissed but these crofters' descendants are still in their holdings. The press made the most of the Bernera Riot and the sympathy of the nation was awakened. All this drew the attention of the government to the state of the crofters in the Lews and a commission was appointed, under the chairmanship of Lord Napier, which went to various villages and questioned many people so as to get at the facts and arrive at a means of improving the conditions and restore order, and create a sense that justice had been done to all. Their report was issued in 1884, but the Act was not passed until 1886. This gave the crofter fixity of tenure, compensation for improvements made by his forebears if he vacated the croft and the power to will his croft to a blood relation, but the Act does not seem to have had much effect on the conduct of the Lewisman, for in 1887 we had the famous Park Deer Raid, and that dangerous and very near bloodshed defiance of the law known as the Aignish Riot in 1888.

A series of good harvests, with bountiful catches of herrings and white fish, and the building of harbours at Ness, Carloway and Uig, accompanied by an increase in the population to near 30,000, spread a wave of contentment and prosperity to all parts of the island.

Another investigation was carried out and a report was issued by the government in 1902, which was meant to show the progress that had been made by the Lewis crofter. It proved that the Lewisman was not lazy and that with the help of grants and loans from the Board of Agriculture he could build a nice, clean and serviceable house, drain and plough his holding (now it was his own as long as he paid his rent), improve his flock of cattle and sheep, educate his children to a high standard at a moderate cost, and so the future loomed rosy for him compared with his ancestors.

However, clouds began to appear on the horizon. The population had increased enormously and the Lewisman did not want his children to go away from home, so he gave his son permission to build a house, share his potato patches and keep a cow. These squatters had no standing at law, and they looked with envious eyes at the green and gold well-tilled fields of the few remaining farms in the island. There was not enough arable land for all, even if these farms were broken up into smaller holdings, and so the restlessness and discontent started all over again and many emigrated or came to live in Stornoway. The First World War came – over 5,000 males left the island to take part in it – they were told that the land would be broken up for the servicemen when they returned and that they would have nice homes for heroes to come and settle down in happily.

Matheson* fell on evil days financially and in 1917 the island was bought by Viscount Leverhulme, the founder of Port Sunlight, and he started off with great visions of what he might make of Lewis, concentrating on the sea rather than on the development of the land – in fact, he did not wish the farms in the parish of Stornoway to be broken up as he wanted them to produce milk for the big important fishing town which he wished Stornoway to become. Plans were set on foot for the development of the burgh; many new houses were built, many roads were made and others improved – money was poured out to develop the fisheries – a canning factory was built and a new fishing company was formed. Leverhulme could not agree with the Government of the day over the farms – the slump came so he had to curtail his works and expenditure. The crofters raided the farms – wages then stopped and Leverhulme transferred his plans to Harris where he had been promised a free hand – but death put a stop to all his schemes in 1925.

Again there was mass emigration of the young people from the island. The Harris tweed industry had been gaining strength in the Lews, and many of the crofters had done well by it, and many had improved their crofts and houses before the Second World War took away the young men and women

---

* Sir James Matheson, Bart, entailed the estate of the Lews. He had no issue, and after the death of his widow the estate passed to his nephew, the Rev. Donald Matheson, who propelled it to his cousin, Major Duncan Matheson (afterwards Lieut-Colonel Matheson) who in turn with the consent of the next heir of entail, his elder son, Major James S. Matheson, sold the estate to Viscount Leverhulme.

once more from the island. On their return the ways of Lewis had changed. The fishing was no longer prosecuted, the motor car brought them in and back from town, wages had gone up, the people were older and many of the crofts wore neglected. It was easier and less back-breaking work and more money could be earned by working at tweeds with a loom. Many people crowded into Stornoway to work in the tweed mills and much building of new houses went on. In spite of all the squabbling about land and new crofts in the past, the young people did not wish to stay in the country. There was a spirit of unrest, the young women kept drifting to posts in the south, and the young men then to follow, leaving the croft drains to get clogged and the bulrush to cover the riggs once growing rich barley for their forebears.

Now another investigation and report, the Taylor Report, was made for the Government and a new Crofters' Commission has been set up of which the chairman of this gathering is the head, and I have much pleasure in handing over to him, as my friend, the finishing of this recital of past events, so that he will tell you from his chair what he and his colleagues intend and hope to do for this island of Lewis and Harris, which we all love, and I know he will do his utmost.

90

Names of Pre-Reformation Churches in Lewis

St Columkil in Lochs
St Phaerer in Kaerness
St Lennan in Stornoway
St Colum in Eye
St Cutchon (Constan) in Garrabost
St Aula in Gress
St Michael in Tolsta
St Collum in Garien (Garry beyond Tolsta)
St Ronan in Earobie
St Thomas in Habost
St Peter in Suainabost
St Clement in Dell
Holycross Church in Galan (Galson)
St Brigit in Borve
St Peter in Shader (Barvas)
St John the Baptist in Bragar
St Mary in Barvas
St Kiaran in Liamishader (Carloway)
St Michael in Kirivig
St Macrel in Kirkibost
St Dondan and St Michael, Little Bernera
St Peter's in Pabbay
St Christopher's Chapel in Uig
Stornoway Church
St Maelrubha (Mahonuy) may have been built on St Ronan, Eoropie

91

Early Medicine in the Lews

*The full text of an article written for the 1961 Lewis
and Harris Annual Gathering programme to introduce
Dr R. Stevenson Doig, M.O.H. for the islands*

A S THE HORDES OF THE GAELS passed across Europe to the
shores of the Atlantic and the North Sea many mishaps and
sicknesses must have attacked them. In each tribe the care of
the sick warrior or of his children must have devolved upon his
woman and it was her duty to look around and find herbs, roots
and plants, to make salves and extractives to soothe the fevered
brow or make the painful area less painful. In this process of
finding out the healing properties of roots, stems and flowers
of certain plants, they discovered that dyes of various shades
could be got which coloured their own skins and those of the
wild animals which they used to make clothes and other warm
coverings. These combinations of colours allowed the tribes
to distinguish one tribe from another even at a good distance,
and so we had the beginning of district and clan tartans.

The great magicians of antiquity among the Celts were the
Druids, who claimed that they garnered their knowledge of
healing and the heavenly bodies from knowing medicine-men
of the Babylonian and Egyptian priesthoods.

Each chief had a man skilled in letting blood, both from
animals as well as humans, and this man, in the isles, was not
the barber but the blacksmith! The son learned the art from his
father and the knowledge was usually confined to one family
in that clan area. During war he was close to the person of his

chief, to extract arrows, staunch bleeding, and often employed his implements for crude surgery, even amputations. The Lords of the Isles had a famous family of hereditary physicians and surgeons called in the Gaelic lighichean or leigh, whose surname was Beaton. The original one came from Ireland, but his ancestors were supposed to come from Egypt with the Princess Scotia in the dim past. When the Lord of the Isles came north with his galleys to visit the chiefs of the clans in fealty to him, he would no doubt have his medical advisers with him, and, no doubt, any Lewisman or Harrisman of that day badly needing his advice and attention would get some help from his superior skill. We have no knowledge that there was ever a member of these skilled Beatons practising in the Lews or in Harris, but we do know that some of them and their famous offspring practised for many generations in Mull, Skye and on parts of the mainland north of Islay. We also know that during Roman Catholic times the nuns, then as now, had a knowledge of nursing and the healing power of some herbs and their extractives. Colonies of these nuns, usually of the Benedictine Order, were found at certain points in the Hebrides, e.g. Tigh non Cailleachan Dubha at Mealasta in Lewis, and at Nunton or Baile nan Caillich in Benbecula. They spread the ideas of cleanliness and personal hygiene among the women, as well as imploring them to be of good spiritual behaviour.

We also read that Neil Macleod allowed his own special lighich to jump across the chasm at Dùn Eystin to extract an arrow from one of the wounded Morrisons who were cornered in the Dùn, after they had requested him for this favour under a flag of temporary truce, but the man did not recover in spite of the skilled surgery. Martin Martin tells us in his book, written in 1695, that many weird and wonderful powders and decoctions were made from dry earths, roots, leaves and from desiccated animals, and that each was used for a specific purpose and for definite symptoms. Oatmeal brochan laced with butter and a good measure of strongly distilled uisgebeatha was the favourite for most fevers when sweating was required. This is still a favourite diaphoretic in many parts of the Hebrides, agus co ris nach cordadh e? It is difficult to find the names of any qualified practitioners belonging to Lewis and Harris, for few, even of the tacksmen, could afford the expense of the long medical training for their sons, until we come to 'Dotair Ruadh' who was the son of the Macaulay who was tacksman of Linshader about 1830. This man had been instructed in the medical knowledge of his day, but he also seems to have had some training in legal knowledge and he had a sharp intellect naturally.

He goes down in island tradition as a red-haired haughty Macaulay with a very bad temper, who made a speciality of taking up the leases of farms from the Seaforth Trustees, finding legal loop-holes in these leases and going to law with them. In nearly every case he won and got a good compensation from the estate. His medical service was a sideline, yet he kept Iain Gobha,* who was his gille-na-coise-fliuich, busy going long distances with pills and bottles of medicine. In 1843 he got the lease of Ardroil and stocked it; and also a promise that the people of the Fourteenpenny Lands (Valtos, Kneep and Reef) were to be put away to other villages and their grazings added to the Tack of Ardroil. Sir James bought the island of Lewis in 1844, was very sorry for these people and paid off their arrears of rent and gave good compensation to Dr Macaulay, and further, bought back the lease of Ardroil, paying a high figure for each beast of stock on the Tack. Ardroil became the biggest sheep farm in the Lewis and continued so for many a year, but the name of the 'Dr Ruadh' still stinks in the nostrils of the West Uigeachs.

We next read of a Dr Miller being fixed up in Stornoway, and his practice was the whole island. He lived in a big house in Keith Street, which is still Dr Miller's House. Fancy having a call to the Port of Ness or to Breanish on a wild wintry night with the snowflakes coming from the north-west, blinding one, and duty and conscience prompting you from behind. In these days (1860s–1880s) people wore tough for the weaklings were weeded out in childhood. Lack of cleanliness caused most of the diseases, for the drinking wells got contaminated from the precious 'ocrachs' piled up near the houses and the ooze from the manure at the down-tilted end of the 'black house', usually built on a hard dry slope. Smallpox, typhoid, typhus, enteric

---

*John Ferguson from Crulavaig.

and skin diseases were endemic. It was not till about the 1890s that tuberculosis of the lungs became so prevalent: first called the stranger's disease, the tinneas caitheamh or the dreaded 'wasting'. Young girls started to go to service in Glasgow, and living in basements with lack of fresh air, sunlight and the food often poor and scanty, they goon picked up the pulmonary bacillus, got worse and worse and came back to their family to be nursed and fed on cream and cod-liver oil – but alas, too late! It was not believed, for many a day, that spitting out the slongaid on to the floor after a paroxysm of coughing, and that the purulent material which dried and floated in the air to be inhaled by everyone in the room, had any connection with the spread of the disease; but that one got it from wearing the old clothes and sleeping with the infected victim. Soon the other fine-looking members of the family became infected and it spread through that village like a plague. I have seen rows of houses in certain villages set alight, for often, all finally died except the old man and woman of the house. Measles also sometimes acted like a plague when it struck an isolated village where no case had occurred for years.

Then, two more qualified men were fixed up in partnership in the town of Stornoway, Dr Macrae, a son of the Rev. Wm Macrae of Barvas, whose father had done so much to enlighten the people of Barvas and the Cladach generally; and Dr Donald Macdonald (Domhnull Sheorais) from Garrabost, who in his early days was a joiner to trade and then got himself educated and qualified as a doctor. This pair did wonderful work among the burghers of Stornoway and also in the country villages of the parish. Their names are still revered in Stornoway for their skill and the human warmth they used in their practices.

Then came a Dr Sinclair who laboured for a few years at Lochs, and after him, a native of that parish, who made his headquarters at the farmhouse of Valtos. Dr Roderick Ross served his native Lochsmen with much skill and benefit to their minds and bodies. Dr Ross then went to Borve, and though he had passed highly in his medical classes and was offered much better-paid posts, preferred to help his backward country-men both spiritually as well as medically, and his name was a household word from Butt of Lewis to Shawbost.

After him came to Lochs Dr Cameron, uncle of Councillor Allan Cameron, who for many years carried on the practice of North and South Lochs mostly by sailing boat, getting as near to the villages as he could and using 'shanks' mare' to reach the outlying ones. His memory is held in great respect at Lochs.

Then there was Dr McLean who had to attend both East and West Uigs, and whose headquarters were in a new house built at Garynahine, still called 'Tigh an Dotair' though now occupied by a crofter. This practice could only be worked by sailing or rowing boat going along Loch Roag and up the many creeks that lead off this long sea loch. Is e beatha na bas a bh'ann on many occasions, when the weather was so fierce that no one could face the tempest, and it is astonishing to us what these dedicated early doctors put up with, yet they got great love and respect for their efforts and exertions from the poor people among whom they worked. Later a slightly younger generation of doctors who were more up-to-date came on the scene. They were slick and better dressed, and they had more modern instruments and more scientific methods of investigation.

Dr Murdo Mackenzie, a young man from Stornoway, when he qualified went into the army and became a surgeon. He lived on the corner of Keith Street and Francis Street, and set up in practice with Dr Donald Murray. They both shared a surgery on Kenneth Street nearly opposite the Free Church. Dr Mackenzie was for many years reputed as the only doctor in Lewis who was any good with the knife, and he dearly loved his little Cottage Hospital at the summit of Goathill looking out across the Minch.

Dr Murray, who retired to take a PhD at Aberdeen, later became M.O.H. for the whole island, and this allowed Dr Jack Tolmie to take his place as assistant and finally successor to Dr Mackenzie, our dapper surgeon. Dr Murray was worried about the lack of hygienic conditions in the Lews and the decimation caused by the TB germ, so he started a crusade against spitting anywhere, the importance of body washing, good food, windows wide open, pleaded for piped water, drainage in country villages and avoidance of contamination of wells and cows' milk: in fact, plumbing and more plumbing, and less of the crowding of infected people into confined sleeping quarters at am na h-orduighean, thus preparing the way for your speaker tonight, my friend Dr Doig.

When Dr Murray became MP for the Western Isles he was succeeded by a lady M.O.H., Dr Porter, and right well did she continue Dr Murray's crusade against ignorance, and was all for the open window and the clean hands before milking or touching food.

At Uig we had Dr Victor Ross who continued to battle with the elements and lived for a period at Miavaig Farm House before he was appointed the doctor for North Harris and lived and died at Tarbert. After him, to Uig, came Dr John Grant, brother-in-law of Lord Strathcarron (Iain McPherson), and a patient, persevering and dedicated soul if ever there was one. He continued to work among the Uigeachs, with no bridge to Bernera, till his once handsome and strong body was badly worn down by chronic malady which put finish to his work among people who revered him for his saintliness. We now get the Government after the First World War taking interest in the ways of life of the Western Isles and the western mainland of Scotland, and we have a vintage of youngish doctors who had been fighting somewhere settling down in Stornoway, such as Dr Angus Macrae, Dr C.M. Macleod, the late Dr P.J. Macleod, the late Dr Roddy Fraser, Dr Angus Macphail, Dr Angus Macleod and Dr Donnie Macdonald; all ministering to the needs of 'Stornoway of the Big Castle', and the many people in the country villages of the parish. Dr Donald Campbell, a Niseach, succeeded the worn-out Dr Cameron, and after a short time attending to both sides of Loch Erisort, a second doctor was fixed up at Gravir and new houses built for each of them, Dr Campbell's at Outer Leurbost. Dr Kenneth MacKinnon, a Balallan man, succeeded Dr Ross at Borve and made a great name for himself over a long period of years as the best diagnostician in the island, and many discontented ailing persons from other parishes made the long trek to Borve.

East Uig was separated from the western portion, and Dr Peter Aulay Macleod has laboured and helped them over many years from his big house at Carloway. This then, from my angle, was the medical position in Lewis when your chairman, Dr

Doig, took on the battle for the improvement of the health of the Lewisman and the betterment of their social and hygienic conditions, and I leave him to tell you the later part of the story up to our own time.

92

Leodhasach! Do Not Grumble!

Compare 1851 with 1956

HOW MANY READERS HAVE any idea of the conditions of rural Lewis before and shortly after Sir James Matheson bought the island in the year 1844?

There were two severe failures of the potato crop, one in 1846 and the other in 1851, and conditions were so overwhelming in the latter year that the four parish councils of the island sent a combined petition to the Government of the day, backed up by a personal letter from Sir James.

In it they asked (a) that financial aid should be sent to help the families of those who were willing to emigrate to the open spaces of America, (b) that financial aid be sent to keep alive the families of those left until the next harvest was gathered in.

Sir James's letter stated that over-population was the cause of the failure of all his schemes for the Lews. They had stopped in 1850.

Lord John Russell sent up Sir John McNeill to investigate, take evidence from various people, and report on the conditions in the island, in answer to this petition, and it is from his findings in 1851 that we know so much about the conditions then obtaining in the Lews.

Here is a portion of what the Rev. Mr Macrae of Barvas told him about his own parish:

In 1813 when I first went to the island the people were more prosperous than they are now; they had abundance of food, cattle, sheep and horses, and the prices being then high, money was much more abundant. Kelp was then manufactured, and the crofters got £3 to £4 per ton. Illicit distillation was much resorted to, and the small oats generally cultivated were made profitable by converting them into whisky; and this, though no doubt it tended to demoralise the people, increased nevertheless their pecuniary resources, and many paid their rents from this occupation. With the reduction of the duty on Barilla, kelp ceased to be manufactured, the illicit distillation of whisky was put an end to, and the fall in the price of cattle had the effect of depreciating their circumstances generally even before the failure of the potatoes in 1846; that failure, therefore, came upon them when they were depressed in circumstances.

When Mr James Matheson bought the island he appointed a Mr Scobie from Sutherland to be his factor, and this man immediately proceeded to carry out the improvements on the estate which the proprietor wanted, such as the building of Stornoway Castle, the Brickworks, the patent slip and the paraffin works, all to bring in revenue for the estate, but at the same time to give work and wages to people all over the island.

All these improvements did not affect the housing of the people or their method of tillage; they grew less barley and oats than their forebears, and came to rely too much on the easily prepared potato, and did not know that a blight could completely destroy their favourite diet. The years 1847 and 1848 were also poor years for the potato crop in the Lews, and two years after the proprietor bought the island he had to take upon himself the burden of relieving the starving poor upon his estate, and imported large quantities of meal for that purpose.

Sir John McNeill estimated the Lewis crofters and their families in 1857 at 14,000 individuals, and said that a croft did not provide food for an average family for more than six months of the year. Till the autumn of 1846, the produce of their crofts and of the fishings at home and in Caithness (where they went as hired hands) generally sufficed to maintain them; but on the failure of the crop of that year, they were in distress as already stated, and there, as elsewhere, the circumstances and condition of the working classes had declined from year to year, for, 'exclusive of paupers on the roll, there were at one time in 1850, in the Lews, 11,000 inhabitants receiving relief from the Destitution Fund.'

He further states that for the six years from 1844 to 1850 the proprietor of the Lews had expended on improvements £67,980 more than the whole revenue derived from the property.

Now Leodhasach! Own up, and say you would not like to change this period of the welfare state you live in! I hear many a one grumbling and talking of the good old days that were – but did you know of '46 and '51?

93

Antiquaries, etc.

Underground House at Gress

Reported to the Society of Antiquaries, Scotland, 1874, by Mr Liddle, Farmer

THIS UNDERGROUND HOUSE was found when some earth above it on the lawn near the Lodge at Gress collapsed. Digging took place, and fifteen feet under the earth's surface a house of overlapping stones was discovered built on the same principle as the Uig *boths*. There was a lintel-covered passageway from an entrance at the shore. A longish way. I have a picture of a collection of implements, etc., which were said to be found there:

(1) A wooden or bone spoon

(2) A series of soapstone whorls for balancing spindle (clach Narach)

(3) A small narrow stone perforated at one end – may be stone fishing line sinker

(4) A large pointed conical shell or eyetooth of an animal, for boring

(5) Pieces of pottery decorated with lines and markings

(6) Two stone axes, polished

(7) Two stone hammer heads, perforated

(8) Two large animal claws – (?) seal (?) bear

(9) A piece of a large deer horn used as a pick-axe

There was also a quern and a stone trough used for pounding barley for the pot found further in, in another eirde house connected by a passage with this one. Mr R. Stevenson says these objects never reached the museum – only the bits of pottery and the horn pick.

Dùn Othail – North Tolsta

Dùn Othail is a natural fortress, being an irregular peaked rock upon the sea coast, nearly 200 feet high and disjoined from the main by a perpendicular ravine, which, however, does not reach to the water. The sides of the ravine appear to have been the walls of a trap dyke, which has been denuded. The dùn is accessible only from the land on the south-east side, and there it is defended by a wall. The Rev. M. Macphail says there is no defensive masonry upon the rock. It is so difficult of access that the path which leads upwards could be defended by a single individual.

An oblong ruin upon its extreme point is supposed by Mr T.S. Muir from its architecture to have been an early church chapel.

Dùn Othail is famous in the Lewis legends, especially those of the Macleods and Morrisons. Coinneach Odhar has prophesied that there will be a great destruction of Lewis people by the sword, but

> Abhainn Lacasdail fo thuath,
> Aig an cruinnich am mór shluagh,
> . . .
> . . .
> Ach hig a mach, a Dùn Othail
> Na bheir cobhair dhoibh 's fuasgladh.

The deep ravine dividing Dùn Othail from the mainland is called Leum MhisNiceall and it is the scene of this legend. MacNicol, for some misconduct, was sentenced by the Chief of Lewis to be mutilated. In revenge he ran away with the only child of the Chief. Being pursued, he leapt over the chasm to Dùn Othail with the child in his arms. Persuasion was used to get him to deliver the child, but he refused unless the chief would undergo the same operation as he had gone through. Several subterfuges were tried, but in vain, and to save the child the father consented to be mutilated. When MacNicol was sure that this had been done, he sprang with the child in his arms over the cliff into the sea, saying in Gaelic – 'Chan 'eil oighre agamsa, 's cha bhi oighre aigesan.'

Dùn Eysteinn

Dùn Eisdein (Eysteinn) is a natural stronghold at the north end of Ness in the township of Cnoc, to which the Morrisons were wont to retire when hard pressed or in times of war. It is a flat, cliffy island, of a somewhat oval shape about seventy-five yards long by fifty yards broad, and is separated from the mainland by a narrow perpendicular ravine through which the sea flows at high water. The ravine is between thirty and forty feet broad and about the same in height. The remains of a strong wall follow the edge of the cliff on the landward side of the island, and through the wall there are said to have been squints or loopholes for observation and defence. Towards the northeast corner of the island is a dùn or stronghold called 'Tigh nan Arm' – the house of arms, but now reduced to four and a half feet in height. The outside of the dùn is oblong in shape, twenty-three feet by eighteen feet, and the basement is solid in the central area, which is oval in shape, measuring only six and a half feet by four and a half feet, and there is no appearance of any doorway. The entrance or doorway was no doubt at the height of the first floor, similar to a dùn in the Isle of Taransay. The walls are of drystone masonry, but that is no proof of age in this part of the country.

When exploring the ruins, the Rev. M. Macphail, who took the above measurements, found a small piece of flint, fragments of charcoal, and a strip of leather such as was used for making brogues. There are remains of huts upon the island, and on the south side there is a flat ledge called 'Palla na Birlinn' – i.e. ledge for the galley, whereon tradition tells us that the Morrisons used to haul up their long boat.

There is no record who this Eisdein was, but the name was common among the Norse. The Macleod and Macaulay union forced the Morrisons, who had sided with Kintail enemies, to leave Lewis for a time and stay with their kinsfolk in Durness and Edderachyllis in Sutherland, but they came back when Neil and the Macleods were beaten by the Government and the Saileachs in 1610.

St Columba's – Eye

1506	Sir John Polson presented by James IV.
1534–36	Sir Magnus Vaus appt. to Eye.
1552	Sir Donald Munro Rector.
1559	Sir John Finlay dies and Queen Mary presents Mr Lachlan Maclane Rector.
1561	Parsonage of Eye (Eie) in hands of Bishop of the Isles.

> . . . a chapel near a field.
> A broken chancel with a broken cross,
> That stood on a dark strait of barren land.
> On one side lay the ocean and on one lay a great water.

These words might well be taken as a description of the old church and graveyard at the Eye peninsula (Aignish) in the Lews. The building is supposed to be one of the oldest churches in the island, the oldest part of it dating from about the twelfth century, and there was probably a place of worship on the site from pagan times. It is situated on the isthmus that joins the peninsula to the mainland at the end of a lovely curving bay with the whitest of white sand, and there is actually a loch near at hand to which one can imagine Sir Bedivere striding across the ridge and into which to throw 'Excalibur'. When one enters the roofless building with its narrow windows, one is almost overwhelmed with the sense of mystery and the secrets of history these old walls could reveal if they could only speak. Of actual history very little is known except that the churchyard was the principal burying ground in the Lews for many generations, and that here was the burying place of the Macleods (dedicated to St Catan). Nineteen of their chiefs are said to lie beneath the floor of the church. William Dubh, the fifth Earl of Seaforth, who was attainted after the '15 and the '19, died in Stornoway and was buried here in 1740. The Earldom was never restored to the Clan Kenneth again. Here also is the last resting place of Roderick Morrison, the Chlarsair Dall, harper and song writer to Macleod of Dunvegan for a time, and contemporary with Mairi Nighean Alasdair Ruadh, the bardess of Siol Tharmoid. There is a fine late fifteenth century effigy of one of the Macleod chiefs in kilt and bassinet, said to be Roderick, Seventh of Macleod (Siol Torcuil) standing against an inside wall, just similar to the effigies of chiefs to be seen in Iona, and of the same period. There is also a very fine tombstone with intricate interlace carving work of Celtic design, to the memory of Margaret, daughter of the same Roderick. The great number of Macleods laid to rest in this hallowed ground was in itself sufficient reason to give the church and burying ground additional sanctity in the eyes of the local people. There is in the burying ground an interesting open grave made by a strange character who is said to have made similar graves in various burying grounds all over Lewis, because he wanted to be sure of a last resting place, but unfortunately he was drowned, and his prepared mason-dressed graves are still unoccupied.

Tradition says that on one occasion at least the one in Eye churchyard was used to good purpose. It seems that even in Lewis, in the 'good old days', cattle lifting was carried on, and also it seems, people used to take cattle secretly to feed at night on the lush green herbage that grew in the churchyards. This custom went on in Eye as elsewhere, and one night in the long ago a local woman took her cattle to feed in the churchyard and she herself hid in the handy open grave.

She must have done this on many occasions having heard that cattle were often lifted at night, sometimes from this same place. She prepared herself this time by covering herself with a white cloth and waited for whatever might happen. The raiders came that night and she saw her cattle being collected and herded ready to be driven away, so up she rose from her open grave, yelling at the pitch of her voice, 'A Chlann 'is Leòid, Chlann 'ic Leòid, éiribh. Tha iad a' togil nam bó, éiribh.' Tradition says the ruse was successful, for the raiders fled, frightened of the spirits.

The Pigmies' Isle – Luchruban – Ness

In 1549 Dean Munro gives a description of the Isle and hermit's oratory, containing small bones. 1580, George Buchanan in his *History of Scotland* quotes the Dean's description 'Little Kirk and bones'. In 1630 Captain Dymes, too, dug there himself and says: 'My belief is, scarce big enough to think them to be human bones.' Circa 1680, Indweller scoffs at the pigmy theory and 'believes the bones to be those of small fowls'.

This gave rise to lusbirdan – Lugh spiorad – little spirit – lusparden – pigmy (compare luchag mouse). Blaeu's map gives 'Glen Dunibeg' – Luchrupain, opposite of Uamharan – Fomorians, Giants. The Irish Ecclesiastics used to dig up the tiny bones on floor of cell (chapel). In Collin's 'Ode on the popular Superstitions of the Highlands' 1749, the little islet is mentioned. MacCullough denies the existence of the Pigmies' Isle when doing his geological wanderings. W.C. MacKenzie wanted to prove that Dean Munro was right and MacCullough wrong and found the exact position north-west of the Butt of Lewis from an old map of Captain Dymes. The late Dr MacKenzie and Mr C.G. MacKenzie paid a visit and had the structure uncovered. Alexander McDonald, C.E., made a plan from measurements taken. Tiny bones and some lined pottery was the total find.

W.C. Mackenzie holds that there were traditions of little men in Ness from pagan times and the finding of the bones only enhanced the tradition. The bones found were those of birds and mammals upon which the holy man lived. There is a similar construction on Eilean Mor, Flannan Isles. Local traditions connect a St Frangus with the pigmies on the Luchruban. He lived on the sands at Lionel. Frangus was unkind to them and they hanged the saint at Bruich Frangus. The pigmies are supposed to be 'Spaniards' (Mediterranean) who came to Lewis 500 BC. Then big yellow men from Argyle came and drove the little men from Cunndal, a cave near the Luchruban, to that little islet, but when they got numerous they emigrated to Knockaird and Eoropie and lived on wild animals killed by throwing sharp pointed knives. Thus we have the corroboration of the wee Mediterranean man invaded by the golden-haired Celt. Some twenty-five stone hut (circular in form) ruins found at Cunndal are prehistoric dwellings. The pigmies of Ness and the dwarfs of the sagas are probably the same as the Lapps of Finland today, 'a short, thick-set, snub-nosed, dark-haired, dark-eyed race, who lived in caves and earth houses, came out at night and dodged the tall fair ones,' which gave rise to tales of fairies – 'na doine sìdhe'.

Hoard of Bronze Implements Found in Lewis – Joseph Anderson
Proc. S.A.S. 1910–1911, page 27

These were found by Donald Murray at Adabrock, Ness, under nine feet of peat. There was no bag, box or container seen, but thin decorated pieces of bronze vessel may have been used to contain them when they were deposited at this spot. This hoard was acquired for the museum of the society.

(1) Thin pieces of a bronze vessel (decorated) probably the container.
(2) Two socketed axes of different sizes.
(3) A socketed gouging instrument.
(4) A spearhead with rivet holes in socket.
(5) A tanged chisel with stop ridge and expanding cutting edge.
(6) A socketed hammer.
(7) Three thin oval tanged blades used as razors.
(8) One whetstone of hard sharp sandstone.
(9) One whetstone of hard dark-coloured micaceous clay-stone with planed and polished edges.
(10) A thin double conical bead of beaten gold.
(11) Two beads of amber.
(12) One bead of greenish glass with dull white spots on it.

Such bronze hoards have been found throughout the British Isles, and give one the impression that they were deposited for temporary concealment and for some reason never recovered. They are of three types:

(1) Hoards concealed by a private owner.
(2) Hoards of a trader. These have multiple items of same implements.
(3) The stock in trade of a bronze manufacturer, or a store of old ones.

The collection found at Ness looks as if it was a private collection and the gold and amber and glass beads would probably have belonged to the depositor's wife. This find of bronze articles was at the same depth under peat as the find of swords at South Dell.

Two Bronze Swords Found at Ness

Peat is said to grow an average of one inch in fifteen years. Therefore nine feet equals 1,700 years.

1891–1892 *Proceedings of Society of Antiquaries Scot.*, page 38. Bronze sword found by Murdo Maciver Aird, South Dell, Lewis, under nine feet of peat. The following February a portion of a second sword (bronze) was found within a few feet of the first one. Nothing else was found in the area. The sword is leaf shaped and well preserved, twenty-four inches long by two inches broad, handle had been struck and marked by the spade. The swords are in a museum in Edinburgh.

94

Chief Magistrates of Stornoway

1864–1867 Norman Maciver – Shipowner.
1867–1874 Donald Munro – Chamberlain of the Lewis.
1874–1877 Donald L. Mackenzie – Shipmaster.
1877–1882 William Mackay – Chamberlain of the Lewis.
1882–1885 Matthew Russell – Merchant.
1885–1891 Murdo Macleod – Bank Agent.
1891–1892 Donald Smith – Fishcurer.
1892–1897 Provost Donald Smith – made Provost.
1897–1909 Provost John Norrie Anderson – Solicitor.
1909–1916 Provost John Mackenzie – Fishcurer.
1916–1919 Provost Murdo Maclean – Fishcurer and Merchant.
1919–1922 Provost Roderick Smith – Chemist.
1922–1925 Provost Kenneth MacKenzie – Wool Manufacturer.
1925–1930 Provost Louis Bain – Fishcurer.
1930–   Provost Alexander Maclennan – Merchant.

95

Dr Macdonald's Speech on Opening a Sale of Work in Aid of St Peter's Church Funds

Ladies and Gentlemen,

It was my wife who was really asked to open this function, but, as she is very nervous of speaking in public, I have been pushed in to do it instead. All the same, I wish to thank you for the honour you have done in thinking me worthy to be able to do so, and further the cause of St Peter's Episcopal Church of Stornoway, of which my wife is a staunch supporter. I have been reading a lot about the history of this island, and any book that tells me something about my native town of Stornoway I read with avidity. From these I learn that there was a form of Episcopacy planted on the old mixture of paganism and Romanism that stood for religion in this island, and we know that the ministers of the time conformed, but in many cases we have no knowledge where they worshipped. The later Seaforths were Episcopalians, and part of St Columba's at Aignish was repaired and re-roofed for worship in their time, but we definitely know that the foundation stone of St Peter's was laid in 1839, during the proprietorship of Mr James Stewart MacKenzie and his Seaforth lady.

This was five years before Mr James Matheson bought the island of Lewis, and we know that his mother-in-law, Mrs Perceval, and her daughter, Lady Matheson to be, did a great deal to support the new church and encouraged greatly the priest who was put in charge. St Peter's had a stiff fight at first, and it was known, and is still to the present day, by the Gaelic speaking folk as the Sagairt's Kirk – a term of slight opprobrium and veering towards the Roman Catholic. In 1843, one year before Sir James bought the island, the disruption took place, and I read that nineteen 20ths of Lewis went over from the Church of Scotland to the Free Church, but they left poor little St Peter's alone. Latterly they broke into sects and factions, quarrelling among themselves, till later, in the Ness district, the Marines had to be called in to overawe them and keep law and order. St Peter's carried on bravely, having Sergeant Craig, Janet's grandfather, as a strong bulwark and church officer and he is buried in the churchyard in honour of his work. The same zealous duty was carried out in my time by his son, Janet's father, ably supported by his family. We all knew and loved Sergeant Craig, our music teacher at school. I can remember many priests coming and going, and St Peter's had its ups and downs, but it had a very flourishing period when the Naval Reserve Battery was stationed in Stornoway. The church was well filled with the officers, instructors and coastguards, with their families, who had come from the south to train the Lewismen, especially in the winter season; yet St Peter's was still a small, select congregation compared with the huge congregations that flocked to the Free and United Free Churches. Some of the priests in charge were very interesting men who added to the upliftment of our town in their day. A gloom was cast over Stornoway the day the Rev. Mr Catcheside's boat capsized at the Cuddypoint, and the tragedy was talked about for many a year afterwards. His is the grave of white marble that one saw as one went into the church, or when one gazed over the gateway in the wall. The Mathesons at the castle continued to attend, and gave St Peter's their backing and patronage, especially the Major himself, as he was then called. All that feeling of suspicion and enmity towards the church of the Priest gradually disappeared, and is now practically gone; people are beginning to see that *no one* sect can claim the sole right of approach to our Maker, the Architect of the Universe, hence the proof of this is that so many of you are here from various denominations, for you see that this church of St Peter's is doing a good work in its quiet way for the good of our town of Stornoway.

One day there came to Stornoway a young priest to take charge of St Peter's, a Mr Anderson Meaden, who soon became so enamoured of his work and this town, that he determined by body, soul and mind to uplift and make the church of St Peter's a power for good in the town of Stornoway, if not in the rural areas. To him we owe the Boys' Naval Corps and many a Stornoway boy has had reason to bless the time he spent there learning drill, navigation and manners. He himself was raised to the status of Canon for his services to humanity, and now lies alongside the Rev. Mr Catcheside near the door of the church, which he so often entered, and to which he devoted his whole lifework. We have now in Mr Downie a worthy successor, a man of the people, who goes quietly among us, and by his example and his zealousness to his duties is raising the attendance roll of his church to a goodly number. He has married one of our Lewis girls, a niece of a pal of mine, Captain MacKenzie, late of SS *Esperance Bay*, and we like him all the more for that. She is a good help to him, and has gathered round her a staunch and capable band of women helpers to further the cause of the Church, and here they are for you all to see. I would also have you look carefully how they and their friends have worked so hard, with needle and other implements, to bring such a grand display of good and pretty things before us on these stalls today. A church like St Peter's needs money to keep going and free from crippling debt, and I know you will soften your hearts and unloose your purse strings, and buy some of all these wonderful and tasty items that are so beautifully displayed before you. You will not regret it, for you are helping a worthy cause in this your own town.

Now, ladies and gentlemen, I have much pleasure in declaring this sale of work on behalf of St Peter's duly open, and may God bless all your efforts.

96

Lewis After 1851

IN MY LAST LETTER I painted a gloomy picture of the Lews taken from the report of Sir John Macneil, after he had investigated the effect of the potato famine in 1851 on the natives of this island.

In the succeeding years there were fair crops, and when Mr Munro Mackenzie, the factor, left Lewis in 1854 he considered the people were in comparatively comfortable circumstances, and this is borne out by the great variety of native products that were exported from the quay at Stornoway in 1855, as given in the *Encyclopaedia Britannica* for that year, and which I some time ago gave you to print in your paper.

How many of your young readers have any idea of the money that was expended in this island from 1844–1850 by Sir James? I will give you a list as taken from a government blue book of 1902, which is probably taken from the estate records.

Part of these huge sums must have got into the pockets of some of the Lewismen and may in part explain why the improvement set in after 1851. Here is the list:

Stornoway Castle buildings, grounds and policies	£100,495
Buildings and land reclamation	£99,720
Roads and bridges	£25,593
Brick works	£6,000
Patent slipway for shipbuilding and repair work	£6,000

Bulls for improving the crofters' stock	£1,200
Fishcuring houses, sheds, etc.	£1,000
Quay for steamers at Stornoway	£2,225
Chemical works to make paraffin from peat	£33,000
Cost and outlay on shooting lodges	£19,289
Gas company	£350
Meal and seed potatoes for crofters	£33,000
Industrial and other schools	£11,681
Loss on steamers to the mainland	£15,000
Loss on contract for carrying mails by steamer	£16,805
Helping 2,231 persons to emigrate to Canada	£11,855
Add original cost of the island of Lewis	£190,000
Total	£574,363

In spite of all this stir and expenditure by a benevolent proprietor, the people in the crofting villages were not really happy – for there were far too many of them for the number of holdings available, the population kept on increasing and subdivision of crofts was their answer though it was against the law of the estate. They could not improve their crofts nor build new modern houses, for they were very poor, and as they had no fixity of tenure they could not trust the factor that he would not shift them to another croft or even to another part of the island.

The new factor who came after Munro Mackenzie in 1853 was a lawyer, who was also the Procurator Fiscal. He was devoted to Sir James, and was determined that the new property should be squeezed of its wealth as much as possible to show a grand increase in the island revenue.

The crofting areas were suspicious of the burghers of Stornoway, for if one looks at their names in the rent rolls one can see Mackenzies, Munros, Lees, Crichtons, Maclennans, Macivers and Macraes – all the names that came over with Seaforth in 1610 or from the south, and these were their descendants doing themselves proudly with their slated houses and their own shipping in the harbour – while the crofters were crouching in their black bothies, and keeping life together on a diet of brochan and barley bread. Even in my own youth old women at Uig hissed in a venomous sort of tone when I mentioned any of these surnames, Na Tailich ghranda – showing that the old bitterness of the Macleods, Macaulays and Macdonalds had not quite disappeared.

The stern ruling of Donald Munro, coupled with the land unrest and the spirit that was abroad in the islands further south, came to a head in 1874 when the crofters of Bernera marched to Stornoway to put their petition into the hands of Sir James himself. As many of your young readers ask me about the so-called Bernera Riots and the trial of the three men who were said to have plastered the sheriff officer with plocks and torn his oilskins, I will let you know how that affair came about in another letter, when I can find time to write at such length as it will require.

97

Stornoway in 1803

A Tour in the Highlands in 1803,
by James Hogg, the Ettrick Shepherd

I AM SURE THAT MANY READERS do not know that James Hogg, the Ettrick Shepherd, paid a visit to Stornoway in 1803, and that he left a record of his visit in a series of letters he wrote to his friend, Sir Walter Scott, at Edinburgh.

He set out from the Ettrick valley early one morning, provided with many letters of introduction to people of consequence in the West Highlands. We find him walking from one county to another, describing the scenery, the people he met, the hospitality he received, but always with a special eye on the mountains as to whether they would be suitable to stock with the large border sheep. He often went long distances without food, and taking his chance of finding the people he sought at home.

He finally reached the Loch Broom area, and heard that there was a schooner from Stornoway loading up a mixed cargo, and taking back an important lady of that town as a passenger, so he arranged to take a passage in order to explore the mysterious island he had been seeing across the Minch.

They set sail and the vessel became becalmed and at the mercy of the tides and currents. At one time they were on the level of the Ness peninsula, and the next they were carried southwards and found themselves off the Shiant Isles, and to make matters worse a whale kept close to the ship, and from time to time rubbed himself violently against the sides of the vessel, which alarmed Hogg and the lady very much, though the crew did not seem to worry in the least, but said to Mr Hogg, 'He be wanting you to come down and have breakfast with him.' He says neither could get off to sleep for fear of the whale overturning the ship.

At last a breeze got up and they landed at Stornoway sixty hours after embarking at Loch Broom. He booked a room at the only hotel in the town, probably where the Star Inn is now. He calls it 'a wretched little inn on the south beach run by a Mr Creighton.' He has not a good word to say about the landlord, but he liked his wife very much, and praises her housekeeping and good baking.

The Ettrick Shepherd writes:

On the very night of my arrival a desperate affray took place in the room adjoining to that in which I slept. Several respectable men, the collector and one of the bailiffs were engaged in it. It was fought with great spirit and monstrous vociferation. Desperate wounds were given and received, the door was split in pieces and twice some of the party entered my chamber. I was overpowered with sleep, having got none at sea, and minded very little, but was informed of all by a Mr Marshall of Fochabers.

A ship's captain, in particular, wrought terrible devastation. He ran foul of the table, which he rendered a perfect wreck, sending all its precious cargo of crystal, china, etc., to the floor, and attacked his opponents with such fury and resolution that he soon laid most of them sprawling on the boards. Some of the combatants were next day confined to their beds, summonses were issued, and a prosecution commenced, but the parties being very nearly connected, a treaty was set on foot, and the preliminaries signed before I left Stornoway.

I had a letter for Mr Chapman of Seaforth Lodge, but he was absent in Uig, parting some land. I had a letter to Mr Donald Macdonald and another to Mr Robertson, both of Stornoway, and in whose company I spent some time. I wandered about the town and country for three days, sometimes in company with one, and sometimes with another. I was indeed greatly surprised at meeting with such a large and populous town in such a remote and distant country. It was but the preceding week that I heard of it, and yet it is quite unrivalled in all the west of Scotland north of the Clyde, either in population, trade or commerce. Mr Macdonald was certain that there were above a thousand inhabitants. There is one full half of the town composed of as elegant houses, with even more genteel inhabitants than are generally to be met with in the towns of north Britain which depend solely on the fishing and trade. The principal and modern part of the town stands on a small point of land stretching into the harbour in the form of a 'T', and as you advance back from the shore, the houses grow gradually worse. The poor people have a part by themselves, on a rising ground to the Northeast of the town, and though all composed of the meanest huts, it is laid out in streets and rows as regularly as a camp. The houses on the shore to the eastward, and those at the head of the bay, are of the medium sort. It hath an excellent harbour and is much ornamented by the vicinity of Seaforth Lodge, which stands on a rising ground overlooking the town and harbour. The town is much incommoded by the want of streets and pavements. Even the most elegant houses facing the harbour, saving a small road close by the wall, have only the rough sea shore to pass and re-pass on, which, being composed of rough stones which fly from the foot, grinding on one another, forms a most uncomfortable footpath. I shall only observe here, that the well-directed and attended schools, the enlightened heads and enlarged ideas of a great number of the people of Stornoway bid fair to sow the seeds of emulation, and consequently of improvement in that remote country. During the day-time, there were thousands of white fish spread on the shores to dry on the sand. When night came they were gathered and built in large heaps, and loosely covered with some coarse cloth, and when the sun grew warm the next day, were again spread. Now, my dear sir, I'll wager you durst not have exposed your fish in such a manner at Edinburgh, for as fine a place as it is.

The Ettrick Shepherd soon grew tired of wandering round Stornoway and its environs, and wished to go and see what the conditions on the other side of Lewis were like, so listen to a bit of Hogg's own story:

On the evening preceding my departure I hired a lad to accompany me round the island for eighteen pence per day. At Creighton's, the entertainment was as good as could be expected, for although they have neither brewer, baker, nor barber in the town professionally, yet every man privileged with a beard is a barber, and every woman unencumbered with a family is a baker, and I suppose Mrs Creighton is none of the most inferior practitioners, as we got very good wheaten loaves, though not exactly conformable in shape to those used in our own country.

Our breakfasts were thus rendered as comfortable as they are anywhere, and though at dinners and suppers we had seldom any beef or mutton, we had great abundance, as well as variety, of fish, fowls and eggs.

I expected my bill to run high, but how was I surprised on calling for it to see that I was charged not more than sixpence for each meal. I was agreeably deceived, and observed to my hostess that a man might eat himself rich here and fat at the same time.

Thus being furnished with several letters of introduction, some whisky, biscuit and a full half of a Lewis cheese, as hard as wood, the boy Malcolm and he set out in the morning taking the only road in the whole island, namely the one going north in the direction of Barvas. This road had been commenced in 1793 under the direction of Lord Seaforth, but owing to lack of funds, the work had to be discontinued on several occasions, and in 1803 Hogg tells us, 'our road, after carrying straight on for ten miles like several of the Highland roads, left us all at once in the midst of a trackless morass, through which it had been cut at the deepness of several yards.'

The boy, who was carrying the load, had fallen about a mile behind, so the poet carried on in the same direction, and in time came in sight of the Atlantic ocean, and soon could make out the manse of Barvas on the hill, to which he bent his course. He reached it just as the minister and his family were rising from breakfast. He produced his letter of introduction which the minister read, but it really was not necessary, for they gave him such a warm welcome that he knew that they were sincerely glad to see him, for they seldom saw strangers from the south in those days.

Hogg was greatly taken with the minister of Barvas, and wrote:

The Rev. Donald Macdonald seems to be a person in every way qualified for opening the eyes of an ignorant people to their real interests, both spiritual and temporal. His aspect and manner are firm and commanding, yet mixed with the greatest sweetness. He is well versed in agriculture, and the management of different soils, which is of great importance in such a place; yet the people are so much prejudiced in favour of their ancient and uncouth modes, that but few follow his example. He is a Justice of the Peace, and is continually employed in distributing justice, for although the people are not much given to quarrelling or litigation, their rights in their farms are so confused and interwoven, that it is almost impossible to determine what share belongs to each. Supposing ten tenants possessing a farm, which is common enough, and every 'shot' or division of their arable land to consist of ten or more beds or rigs, they do not take rig about and exchange yearly, nor yet part the produce, but every ridge is parted into as many subdivisions as there are tenants, into tenths, twentieths, fourths, fifths, etc., everyone managing and reaping his own share, so that it would take a man to be master of fractions to be a tenant in Lewis. The pasture is regulated by the number of cattle, sheep or horses each possesses, and as there is no market for these save once a year at the great tryste, some of the companies are often obliged to encroach on their neighbours' rights, or impose on their goodness. Thus it may well be supposed in what manner the ministers are harassed by continued applications for settling the most intricate differences. From his court there are no appeals.

The minister of Barvas took the Ettrick Shepherd for a walk along the shore of the northern ocean, and he proved a most interesting guide for he was well versed in the lore of the parish, and a keen observer of living creatures, especially the birds.

They were very much intrigued by a large, dark, sooty bird which kept chasing one special solan goose and so persistently did he do so, that the said solan goose discharged his half-digested meal of fish, and this sooty bird caught the food before it struck the surface of the water. The minister called it the 'Squeezer', in Gaelic the Faisgeadar, the same name as the St Kildans called him. We in Lewis now call him 'Dirty Allan', and the scientists, the Great Arctic Skua.

They came upon the ruins of the ancient temple of St Mary the Virgin – the walls and gables still standing and a baptismal font still in its own niche in the wall, but the shifting sand hills had hemmed it in and were as high as the gable, though the building itself was at that time standing clear in outline. It was not till after 1844 that the tussac grass was imported from the Shetland Islands, and planted to spread in all the machair land in Lewis and so the excessive burying of the crops by shifting sand dunes no longer takes place.

The minister could not tell him anything about the history of St Mary's, but said it was a temple from pagan times. He did not tell him it was at Barvas that Sir Patrick Macmaster Martin held sway, and that it was he who wrote on behalf of Old Rorie Macleod to John Bishop of the Isles, because 'Old Rorie could not writt himsel', and that it was this same parson who took down the deathbed confession of Hugh Morrison, the Brieve, at Habost, anent Torquil Conanach.

The minister took him further down the coast towards Ness and he was astonished at the size of their ploughed holdings and the industry they had put into the clearing of the ground from stones, compared with other places he had seen in the island.

He says:

> Mr Macdonald also showed me a hill of small size from which he had seen sixty ploughs all going at the same time. This will give you a very high idea of the fertility of the Lewis, at least this district of Ness, and if it were not overstocked with people and that it is under the most clumsy and untoward of all modes of cultivation, is certainly a fertile place.

He says that this area is freer from rain than any other part of the island as it has no mountains to break the clouds that blow in from the west or south-west and with winds from the eastern quarters the weather is usually mild and dry.

The ploughs he saw were very slender and shabby pieces of workmanship. They consisted of crooked tree selected for the purpose. Through each of these a square hole was cut at the most crooked end, and here the stick that served for the plough-head was fixed, and by wedging it above or below gave the plough more or less depth with great facility. I have only seen two of them at work. A greater curiosity can hardly be exhibited to one who is a stranger to their customs. I could venture a wager that Cain himself had a more favourable method of tilling the ground.

He says that one man kept the point of the plough in the ground while another man walked backwards pulling four little Highland horses that were attached by a pole to the plough. He says the ground must have been really good to produce such crops with such a superficial scratching and trampling treatment.

The people of the parish he says 'are industrious fishermen, and although their plans are the most simple they seemed always to gain most of the prizes held out by the Fishing Society for dog-fish, codling, and tusk. They have a terrible sea to fish on, and as terrible a shore to land upon. I could not avoid the old proverb, "Rather them as me." '

When they had explored down as far as the eye of the Butt, they returned to the hospitable manse at Barvas.

Next morning Mr Hogg, accompanied by Malcolm, set off to go to Loch Roag and they must have taken a route between the Barvas Hills and Bein Bhragair. He describes the bogs and the great number of lochs in their way, causing the deer to run and make for the shelter of the Barvas hills. They got hungry, but found that they had no knife to cut the hard kebbock of cheese they had, so at the first sheiling they found occupied they borrowed a knife which consisted of a piece of iron from a kelphook stuck into a piece of deerhorn. They tried to cut the cheese with this but could make no impression on it, then with the help of stones and the knife they managed to break off unsavoury looking chunks and with the biscuit, whisky, cheese and water, they partook of lunch. Then they set off in the direction of where they thought Loch Roag should lie. They would be making for Callernish, probably in order to get a ferry from there to Uig, but the letters finish, so I cannot tell you what happened to Mr Hogg and Malcolm, or if they ever got as far as Uig, but it would be very interesting to know what conditions were like in that remote area in 1803.

98

The Aignish Riot – 1888

THE DEER RAID AT PARK had caused excitement, accentuated the discontent, and troops were stationed at various parts on the island.

The cottars of the Point District, numbering several hundreds, intimated to the estate officials that on a certain date and at a certain hour they would drive off the farm of Aignish every cattle beast and sheep they could find upon it. The matter was not kept secret, and it was decided to resist these unlawful proceedings with both military and police.

In the early morning of the date stated, a detachment of the Royal Scots, stationed at the Manor Farm, were issued with ammunition, ten rounds to every man, provided with a local guide, and marched to the farm of Melbost. Here they were posted in case of emergency.

At about 6 a.m. a considerable number of marines were landed from a gunboat called the *Seahorse* in Sandwick Bay. They were guided by a local man past Melbost till they came to the farm of Aignish where they quietly took cover in the steading. These had been followed by two Glasgow pressmen, much to the annoyance of the officer in charge of the marines.

About seven-thirty, half-a-dozen policemen reached Aignish from Stornoway and they were soon joined at the farmhouse by Sheriff Fraser and the Depute Fiscal John Ross.

When daylight came, around a flag on top of Knock Hill

could be seen a motley gathering of about four to five hundred men and women. A considerable number were armed with sticks, but the majority had but their naked hands and the stones which they could pick up on the field.

The sheriff was a Gaelic-speaking Highlander and was no coward, and no one knew better than he that there was real danger in that tumultuous crowd. He knew that if the High-lander is slow to wrath, he is, when desperate with hunger and wincing under years of oppression, a dangerous man.

At last there was a movement on the hill, and a compact mass of men, numbering about a hundred, began to descend quickly making direct for the farm steading. The sheriff and the fiscal proceeded at a smart pace to meet them.

The sheriff warned them, in Gaelic, of the dangers they were incurring. While this parley was going on the rest of the raiders on the hill gave a mighty yell, rushed down on the fields and spread themselves out driving the animals in front of them in the direction of Stornoway.

The police and marines then charged the raiders and for half-an-hour a fierce battle raged – a milling mass of cottars, redcoats and policemen, and yelling women mixed up with stragglers of cattle and sheep. In the end thirteen raiders were captured.

The most exciting part of the fight took place when a deter-mined attempt was made to rescue the prisoners. The crowd, which now numbered over a thousand, blocked the road to Stornoway, knowing that the prisoners would be taken that way to jail.

A reporter writes: 'I stood beside the Sheriff on the Aignish dyke when he read the Riot Act, first in English and then in Gaelic. He was an old man with his life already touching the horizon, and his voice had in it the ring of fear, the fear that something appalling might happen that would be spoken of for generations.'

An incident occurred at this stage fraught with danger. Two policemen were struggling with an infuriated raider some dis-tance from where the sheriff stood, and the fiscal, who was armed with a revolver, went to their assistance. The mob saw the revolver brandished by the fiscal, and immediately he was assailed, and in fact was in danger of being seriously injured. A dozen marines sprung forward and held the crowd back from him at the point of the bayonet. The raiders still pressed forward, till the blue steel almost touched their breasts.

The wild tumult for a moment, and only for a moment, subsided, and the boldest held his breath, expectant that something dreadful was about to happen. Then the sheriff's voice was clearly heard above the din, and whatever was said the extreme tension gave way. The raiders drew back from the points of steel within an inch of their breasts.

Someone shouted in Gaelic, and the sheriff heard it, 'If there is a single shot fired we will not only disarm the soldiery but strip them of their uniform, and we mean it.'

When one of the prisoners saw the danger in which his friends were placed he called out to them in Gaelic, 'Falbhaibh dhachaidh agus marbhaibh na cearcan airson biadh.' At this advice given under such strained circumstances the crowd broke into loud laughter and the tension was released.

A second fierce attempt was made to liberate the prisoners, but now the Royal Scots, who had been summoned from Melbost farm, appeared, and after some difficulty they were handcuffed and marched to Stornoway where they were lodged in jail until put on board a gunboat that evening.

While this was going on the soldiers with their bayonets held back the wild mob. Some of the raiders succeeded in driving the Aignish farmer's cattle a distance of seven miles from their steading, and this part of their purpose was accomplished.

The prisoners were taken to Edinburgh for trial, and heavy sentences were passed upon them at the High Court. One woman at Aird said they got better food and living quarters than they could get at home.

An old Stornoway boy tells me that when in the classroom at the Francis Street school, they heard the tramp of the soldiers marching past with their prisoners towards the jail, they all rushed to the windows, and there they saw John Ross, the fiscal, riding in front on a horse, hatless and with a bleeding bandage round his forehead.

99

History of the Park Given in 1888 by Mr Wm Mackay, Chamberlain

THE PARISH OF LOCHS appears to be the most recently inhabited parish in the Lews. At the time of the first Earl of Seaforth (1623), the whole of what is now known as Park was a deer forest, and the tenants or crofters of Uig used to graze their cattle in summer and had their sheilings there. Where the Park deer-raiders encamped for the night is named Airidh Domhuill Chaim. It has been said there were crofters here, but Donald Cam resided in Uig, and merely had a sheiling in Park. Early in the present century a company of four gentlemen from Skye took what was then known as the farm of Park; one of the company was Lachlan MacKinnon of Corry. The manager of the farm was a Donald Stuart from Perthshire who afterwards became tenant, and after him his two brothers Alexander and Archibald Stuart, who held the farm till 1842, when it was let to Walter Scott, Hawick, at fifty-eight pounds rental. His lease terminated in 1857. Thereafter the farm was let to Mitchell Scobie, when the crofters of Stiomrabhaigh, being in the centre of the farm, were removed to Leumrabhaigh, which was then part of Park Farm. Mr M. Scobie made over his lease to Mr Peter Sellar, whose occupancy terminated at Whitsunday, 1883. The farm was then advertised, but a tenant could not be got for it. It was then advertised as a deer forest, and let as such to Mr Platt in 1886. Of the lands held by Mr Sellar, Seaforth Head and Shieldinish were let to six crofters at fifty-seven pounds, Stiomrabhaigh and Orinsay, containing about 3,000 acres, with the Shiant Isles, were let to Mr Roderick Martin, tenant of Crobeg. Island Ewhart in Loch Shell was given to the crofters of Leumrabaigh without any additional rent being charged. The whole area of the peninsula between Loch Erisort and Loch Seaforth is 68,000 acres, of which 42,000 acres form the deer forest of Park, and the remainder is under crofters, with the exception of one tenant, paying over thirty pounds of rent. The farthest back rental of the Park is that of 1828, though, no doubt, there were crofters along the coast in Park previous to that date. In 1828 there were eight crofters in Shieldinish, fifteen in Eishken. Orinsay was let to Miss Maciver, who is supposed to have had sub-tenants. Leumrabaigh and Stiomrabhaigh were let to a Roderick Nicolson who was also supposed to have had sub-tenants; and Park Farm proper was held by Alexander and Archibald Stuart at a rental of £326. The Stuarts had this farm for many years previous to 1828. In 1831 there were seven crofters in Shieldinish, sixteen in Eishken, seventeen in Orinsay, twenty in Leumrabhaigh and eight in Stiomrabhaigh, and the Stuarts held the farm of Park. The crofters in Eishken were removed in 1833, those in Orinsay and Shieldinish in 1838, and Leumrabaigh in 1841. In all sixty crofters were removed; but this took place previous to Sir James Matheson purchasing the estate. It is thus impossible to give the destination of the crofters removed from Park but a number of them emigrated. Others were sent to Crossbost – Lochs, twenty-seven were sent there, it had previously been a farm. Others were sent to Tong and Tolsta in the Parish of Stornoway.

(In the rent roll of 1718 no mention of any village in Oservaul (Park) except Habost.)

100

The Small Remnant

NINE LEWISMEN SIGNED A letter sent to the Bishop of the Isles in 1738. They were Episcopalians, and they asked for an annual visit from a pastor, being unable to support a full-time minister. Their letter has been found in the *Records of the Dioceses of Argyll and the Isles, 1560–1860*, by Dr D. Macdonald, Gisla, who wonders if any of the descendants of the men who signed the letter survive in Stornoway. He notes that it was a hundred years later, in 1839, that the foundation stone of St Peter's, the town's Episcopal church, was laid.

Right Revd Sir,

Your Commission to the Reverend Mr John Williamson was a testimony of your care of the small remnant remaining stedfast among us in this Island, to whom he did seasonably and most agreeably exerce himself in the ministeriall office by preaching and administering the Sacrament to the comfort and satisfaction of all of us who were hearers and partakers of these Divine ordinances, for which we bless God and entertain a grateful presentment of your care and regard for us, which is expected to continue in order to further the growth of grace and virtue 'monst us.

We regrate our straits and circumstances to be such as that we cannot propose to have one of the pastors of the orthodox Church settled with us to dispense the word and sacraments to well-inclined persons in all parts of this desolate Island, and, therefore desire your pastorall care towards us might in charity move you to send one of your presbyters, and especially the Revd Mr John Williamson, if consistent with his health, interest and yr conveniences, annually during the happiness we now enjoy under your Episcopal care. We pray for the prosperity of the Church and remain Right Revd Sir, your affectionate sons and humble servants,

Allexr MacKenzie,
Murdoch MacKenzie,
Allexr MacKenzie,
John MacKenzie,
Donald Morrison,
Aulay Macaulay,
John MacKenzie,
John MacKenzie,
Daniel MacKenzie.
Stornoway, 22nd August, 1738.

101

The Old Bell of St Lennan's

IN 1829 LORD TEIGNMOUTH was staying as a guest at Seaforth
Lodge, where the Lews Castle now stands. You already know
his story of the funeral of Mary Carn at Aignish Cemetery.

He tells us that the tide sometimes came up so high on the
North Beach that it exposed the bodies buried in the old churchyard of St Lennan, which with its ancient ruined church stood
on the area where the National Bank and the Sailors' Home
now stand.

The ruins were falling and becoming a danger, but among
the common people there was awe and reverence for the old
structure, and no one could be got to start pulling any of it
down.

At last one, Donald Ceard, was bribed into doing so by the
gift of a boll and a half of meal. This gave cause for a saying in
Gaelic which translated goes: 'Oh, Donald Ceard of the boll and
a half of meal! Had you been given the other half you would
have had even the Pope's own image on the ground!'

It would have been about this time in the first half of the
19th century that the bell of St Lennan's was taken down.

During the Matheson period it was hung in the Manor Farm,
and we know that it was rung to summon the Royal Scots on
parade, when they were quartered at the farm during the agrar-
ian disturbances of 1887–88.

The bell eventually found its way into the hands of the late

John Morrison of Galson Farm. He became very friendly with the late Canon Meaden of St Peter's Episcopal Church, a man who prized ancient relics and who, seeing the date and the name on the bell, had it fixed up at St Peter's where it once again summons some of the Stornoway burghers to their devotions.

Index